"FIRST, DO NO HARM"

(The Hippocratic Oath)

DEDICATION

To our three beautiful children,

Stephanie, Jonathan and Debbie;

and to our beloved grandson, Jake

and exceptional son-in-law Sam.

To Patsy, Audrey and Alex whose

goodness to us was life-saving.

To Maurice, Sarah and Gerry

To Mary Gill, a true friend.

To Marjorie Phillips

(Phillipians 1:3)

and

In Memory of

the late Kenneth Phillips.

a man of unshakeable faith,

unmatchable kindness and

unforgettable good humour.

ACKNOWLEDGEMENTS

As the idea for this book arose out of a course of lectures we gave at

The University of York UK, Centre For Life-Long Learning, we would

like to thank the following people: Leslie Booth MBE (Director),

whose commitment to life-long learning is inspirational, and who,

notwithstanding her title, never made us curtesy!

And the staff at The Centre for Life-Long Learning,

Iain Barr

Hannah Lyus

Helen Briggs

We would also like to acknowledge:

Noelle   Guillermo   Catherine

Eileen   Julia

Sue   Ann

Anne

Thanks also go to the helpful night porter whose name we don't know, who came to our assistance on a number of occasions when we and our ardent students got locked into the University because we were so engrossed in discussions of Montessori matters that we didn't notice the lateness of the hour.

Thanks To All

CONTENTS IN BRIEF

CONTENTS IN DETAIL

PART ONE
DID SHE DISCOVER THE "BLUEPRINT"?

PART TWO
HOW LONG DOES IT TAKE TO BUILD A HUMAN BEING?

PART THREE
HOW DOES THE CHILD CONSTRUCT HIMSELF?
(The Years 0 to 6) (The Age of Absorption)

PART FOUR
HOW DOES THE CHILD COMPLETE HIMSELF?
(The Years 6 to 12) (The Age of Imagination)

PART FIVE
HOW DOES THE ADOLESCENT CONSTRUCT HIMSELF?
(The Years 12 to 18) (The Age of Passion)

PART SIX
HOW DOES THE YOUNG ADULT COMPLETE HIMSELF?
(The Years 18 to 24) (The Age of Commitment)

PART SEVEN
CAN WE RE-CONSTRUCT A HUMAN BEING
(The Later Years)

PART EIGHT
PREVENTIVE MEDICINE
(Montessori for a New Generation)

PREFACE

This book is being launched at this particular time to celebrate the Centenary of "The Glass Classroom," a model environment set up before the eyes of the world in the Palace of Education during the Panama-Pacific International Exposition in California in 1915.

This extraordinary model environment showed the world "how to build a human being" during the early years. The model was so successful it ran away with both of the only two gold medals awarded in the field of education.

Our book wishes to expand on this and show the world "how to build a human being" from birth to old age, using the discoveries of the doctor, educator, reformer, humanitarian and three times nominee for the Nobel Peace Prize, Dr. Maria Montessori.

Some years ago, the philosopher, Mortimer Adler stated that at the end of the 21st century only two names would be celebrated in history, the names Einstein and Montessori.

Most of us have already heard of Einstein, regrettably many have not yet heard of Montessori.

If this book contributes to a better understanding of who Montessori was, what "Montessori" is and what "Montessori" could be, it will have been a very worthwhile project indeed.

PART ONE

DID SHE DISCOVER THE BLUEPRINT?

"THE GREATEST WOMAN EDUCATOR IN HISTORY"

(Carnegie Hall 1913)

The year is 1913. The venue is Carnegie Hall, New York. The auditorium is packed to capacity, yet more than one thousand people have to be turned away. The event is a lecture with moving pictures. The subject matter is "The Montessori Method in Education". The speaker is a forty-something Italian doctor and brain specialist, now turned educator. She is introduced to the audience as, "The Greatest Woman Educator in History".

What had this Italian woman done to deserve this extraordinary recognition and acclaim? To answer this, we must travel back to Italy, to the little province of Ancona, where in 1870, Maria Montessori was born.

She was the only child of middle class, conservative parents. Her father, Alessandro Montessori was initially a military man and then a successful government official. Her mother, Renilde Stoppani was the niece of a celebrated Italian academic.

Very little is notable about Maria Montessori's childhood, but in her teens she stood out among her peers because of her passion for mathematics. It was this passion for mathematics which prompted her to persuade her conservative parents to go against tradition and allow her to attend two, virtually all male technical schools, in order to pursue her mathematical studies, since, at that time, schools for girls did not teach mathematics or the sciences.

Attendance at these virtually all male technical schools led Maria towards a further unconventional plan. In 1890, when she had completed her scientific and mathematical studies, she announced, to the shock of her friends and family, that she wanted to enrol in University to become, of all things, a medical doctor!

Nowadays, this would be an excellent aspiration for any girl, but in 1890, such a suggestion, from a female of a genteel back-round, was unthinkable.

The suggestion brought her immediate opposition from three separate camps, namely, her father, the faculty of medicine and her peers.

At that time, medicine was traditionally an all male preserve and it was unacceptable for a young woman to want to enter it.

Despite huge opposition, Maria Montessori persisted and eventually at the age of twenty two, she gained admission to the faculty of medicine at the University of Rome.

There, she spent the next four years struggling to succeed in a man's world, fighting against the prejudice of her male peers, and winning scholarship after scholarship for her academic brilliance.

In 1896, she graduated from the University of Rome with a double honours degree in surgery and medicine.

Such was her reputation for hard work and excellence, that immediately upon graduation (and, in fact, even during the year prior to this) multiple doors began to open for her into general medicine, research and psychiatry.

Of all the posts Maria Montessori accepted, (and there were many), the most significant for her future work, was her appointment as assistant doctor at the psychiatric clinic attached to the University of Rome.

Part of her duty at this clinic, was to go out to the insane asylums in Rome to select suitable candidates to bring back to the clinic for study. It was through this work, that she came into contact with what were then called "idiot" children.

These were children who had, what we would now call "special needs". They were regarded as unteachable and were literally abandoned in asylums, often amongst the adult criminally insane.

Her first biographer, E.M. Standing recounts how, in one of these asylums she came across a number of these abandoned children who were, "herded together like prisoners in a prison-like room". The woman who looked after them was openly contemptuous of them. When Montessori asked her why she held them in such contempt, the woman replied, "because, as soon as their meals are finished they throw themselves on the floor to search for crumbs".

Standing describes how, "Montessori looked around the room and saw that the children had no toys or materials of any kind - that the room was, in fact, absolutely bare. There were literally no objects in the environment which the children could hold and manipulate in their fingers". He wrote:

> "Montessori saw in the children's behaviour a craving of
> a very different and higher kind than for mere food".

(E.M. Standing, Maria Montessori, Her Life and Work. p28)

What Montessori saw was this: she immediately recognised that these were not greedy children looking for more bread, they were intellectually starved human beings. They were starved of stimulation, starved of opportunities to handle, touch and manipulate objects. They were using the breadcrumbs as toys, as learning materials. From pondering on the behaviour of these children, Montessori made one of her first very important discoveries, the discovery that nothing enters the brain of the child that hasn't at first come through his hands, and that even in the most deprived of circumstances, nature compels children to look for something to manipulate, to roll, to squeeze, to touch, to handle, to investigate, in order to feed the brain with information.

This was to become one of the most fundamental Montessori Principles, i.e. that the brain of the young child is literally "hand-made". Who would have guessed that an incident with breadcrumbs in an insane asylum would lead to such an important discovery.

And so, from the outset, Montessori saw that the problem with these children was not so much a medical one but an educational one. She took some of these children back with her to the Psychiatric Clinic at the University of Rome and she began to work with them.

Initially, nothing dramatic happened. But, over the course of the next three years, Montessori began to campaign ceaselessly for special schools for mentally deficient children so that they could be taken out of the asylums.

In 1899 she got her wish. The Italian government, as a direct response to Montessori's campaigning, opened a State Orthophrenic School into which all of the mentally deficient children from the asylums in Rome were transferred.

Montessori was made co-director of this school and she was requested by the Minister for education to lecture and to train teachers in special needs education. It was at this Orthophrenic School that Montessori began her great educational work and started to make extraordinary discoveries about how children learn.

For two whole years, 1899-1901, Montessori worked tirelessly from morning till night at the Orthophrenic School with the mentally deficient children. There, she trained teachers and worked with the children.

She researched everything she could find on the treatment of mentally retarded children. Her research lead to the works of two long forgotten French doctors, Jean Itard and Edouard Seguin, who had devoted their whole lives to the education of defective children. Their work was to have a major influence on Montessori and would contribute to some of her most important discoveries. Itard, had developed a method which trained the child's senses and led the child from concrete to abstract thought. Seguin, had developed a physiological method which relied on movement to bring about learning in the child.

Montessori took these two principles - "education of the senses" and "education through movement" and she fused them into her own body of ideas. She adapted them and developed them into an approach which she now used with the children in the Orthophrenic School. She also adapted some of the materials Itard and Seguin had developed and she used them with the children.

Using these methods and materials, Montessori succeeded in teaching some of these deficient children to read and write so well that she was able to present them for the public examinations held in Rome for normal children.

Not only did many of Montessori's "idiot" children pass the exams but some of them surpassed the normal children in the exams.

Word quickly spread, not just around Italy, but in the press all around Europe, of this extraordinary achievement.

Montessori was hailed as a miracle worker. But rather than bask in her success, Montessori became obsessed with the question of how it could come about that normal children "could be equalled in tests of intelligence by my unfortunate pupils".

She came to the conclusion that there must be something very wrong with the methods used in normal schools if these poor unfortunates could reach the same standards as normal children, in such a short space of time with only makeshift materials and no firmly established educational method.

The more she pondered over this, the more Montessori became convinced that if the methods she had used with defective children could be advanced and used with normal children, wonderful results would ensue.

She longed to have an opportunity to work with normal children to try out some of the methods and materials she had used with the defective children. But the strict rules in Italy governing compulsory school attendance from six years on did not allow for this.

As fate would have it, it was going to be another five years before she would get the opportunity to work with normal children.

But now, in 1901, after two years of intensive work at the Orthophrenic School, and after achieving such astonishing results in the state exams with the children, Montessori suddenly resigned from her position at the Orthophrenic School.

She enrolled once again in the University of Rome, this time as a student of educational philosophy, experimental psychology and pedagogical anthropology.

Her aim was to find out why the educational methods being used to teach normal children were failing them. She also conducted pedagogical research by visiting the public schools and observing and recording the teaching methods that were being used there and the reactions of the children to them.

Needless to say, she was appalled at what she saw. Education was very much a matter of rote learning in very strict and austere environments. Schools were more like prisons than places designed to help development.

In 1904, Montessori was appointed Professor of Pedagogical Anthropology at the University of Rome. She used her lectures as Professor to inspire and motivate prospective teachers to be people with a mission, not just to "teach" but to "redeem humanity".

She captivated her students, telling them that the goal of education should be "the regeneration of mankind". She ignited a flame in her students and urged them to see themselves not as importers of dead and lifeless knowledge but as social engineers, people who had the ability to change things, to bring about a more just society.

She inspired her students to see themselves as innovators, reformers, people whose mission should be to bring about a better humanity.

She herself had not given up her ambition to work with normal children to see if a different approach to education could bring about better human beings and create a better society.

In 1907, her dream of working with normal children was about to become a reality, and the discoveries she was soon to make in a place called San Lorenzo in Italy, were to change her life forever and make her famous throughout the world as, "The Greatest Woman Educator in History."

2

"THE NEW CHILDREN"

(The San Lorenzo Experiment)

For many of us the name San Lorenzo evokes a picture of sun, sand and sea. However in 1907 San Lorenzo, in Italy, was sadly lacking in sun sand and sea. In fact, it was one of the most derelict, downtrodden places on the face of the earth. It was a haven for criminals, murderers, prostitutes and homeless beggars.

This situation had arisen as a result of the collapse of the Italian property market. San Lorenzo was filled with half built tenements that had been abandoned by bankrupt speculators and the buildings were mostly inhabited by squatters.

In the 1900s, an Italian building society, took an interest in these derelict tenements and saw a way they could make money out of them. They drew up a plan. They decided to:

> Clear out the criminals.
> Refurbish the buildings.
> Then rent them to poor but stable families.

Hundreds of such families were descending on Rome from the countryside to take up work in factories. The project started, but immediately a serious problem arose. The problem was this. While the parents worked all day in the factories,

> the children six years and over went to school,
> the babies were cared for by relatives,

but, the children between three and six were uncared for and were left running wild around the tenements all day, defacing and vandalising the buildings. This vandalism was costing a serious amount of money. A solution was needed. The solution the building society came up with was simple: set aside a room in each tenement to house the 3 to 6 year olds during the day and pay a woman to keep them out of mischief.

Since it was planned to have quite a number of these facilities, someone was needed to coordinate the project. Instantly, the name Maria Montessori came to mind, after all, she was famous in Rome for her work with difficult children. Montessori was approached and asked to direct the project. She agreed immediately, seeing this as an opportunity to further her research. The children were quite a bit younger than the age she had always hoped to study, but she believed she could make scientific comparisons between the capabilities of normal children in the younger age category and deficient children in the older age category.

She was given:

> An empty room in a refurbished tenement.
> Some funding for office furniture.
> Some funding to hire a woman to control the children.

And that was it. There was no funding for educational materials, no funding for desks or chairs or anything which we would now call school furniture. There wasn't even funding for a proper teacher, so the job went to the porter's daughter and later to a seamstress from a local factory. All this was to prove fortuitous because if funding for a teacher and school furniture had been available, the school would have taken a traditional course and the extraordinary happenings which were yet to occur in that tenement room would never have occurred.

The school opened officially on 6 January 1907. Within weeks, Montessori and hundreds of visitors witnessed the following changes in the children.

COGNITIVE CHANGES IN THE CHILDREN

Amazing Mental Concentration.

One of the first astonishing changes in the children which was witnessed and verified by many visitors, was their sudden ability to concentrate for long periods of time on an activity and to give it their whole attention.

When the children first entered the Casa in January 1907, they showed an inability to focus on anything, a lack of concentration. They couldn't even remember how to make the simple military salute which the porter's daughter had taught them for the opening ceremony.

Yet, in a short period of time, in the Casa, the children, slowly but surely began to find objects that attracted them. They then began to focus their attention on these objects and work with them. For each child it was something different that attracted them. For some it was a dressing frame that caught their attention. The challenge of the buttons or the hooks and eyes transfixed them. For others, it was cylinder blocks or the geometric trays that attracted them and they immersed themselves into the challenge of putting the pieces in and out of their sockets. But the result was the same for each of these children. They revealed that, young as they were, they were indeed capable of amazing mental concentration.

Note: This surely is a very significant discovery for teachers, in an age when Attention Deficit Disorder, is supposedly epidemic and doctors and teachers alike are looking for solutions to treat it.

Ability to Teach Themselves by Repetition.

One extraordinary characteristic that Montessori began to witness in the children was a tendency, one might even say a compulsion to repeat the same activity over and over again. All the children showed this tendency. It was something that Montessori had never witnessed before. For example, one little girl about three years old painstakingly put the 10 wooden cylinders in and out of the cylinder block more than 42 times!

And it wasn't just with educational materials that the children felt this compulsion for repetition, they did it with every activity, especially hand washing. Montessori became convinced that this tendency to repeat the same activity over and over again, even when he appears to have mastered it, is an important feature of the young child's manner of learning.

She concluded that since some inner directive seems to urge the child to do it, it must answer some deep psychological need in the child.

She also became convinced that this repetition is nature's way of helping a young child to teach himself, at a time in his life when he is not amenable to direct instruction from anyone else. By repeating activities over and over the children in the Casa developed their cognitive and physical abilities to an extraordinary degree. They were literally able to teach themselves.

Note: This is also a very significant discovery for parents and teachers alike. If children need to repeat activities over and over until they themselves feel that they have mastered them, then we need to facilitate that need. In recent years, research in neurology has shown that human beings "cement" things into their procedural memories by the act of repetition.

The Explosion into Writing.

Perhaps the phenomenon which attracted the greatest attention to the Case and which grasped the interest of the whole world was the fact that after only a few months in the Casa, many of the four and five year old children "burst" spontaneously into writing without having ever been taught.

Initially, Montessori had no intention of teaching writing or reading to the children because she shared the general belief that they were too young for this. However, when the children and their illiterate parents began to beg her to teach them to read and write she gave in. She introduced the sandpaper letters that she had used with the children in the Orthophrenic clinic to the children, and simply showed them how to feel the letters while pronouncing their sounds. The children loved this. Then the children started to spontaneously blend sounds together to make words. But the concept of writing hadn't occurred to them yet, they just placed the letters side-by-side to make words.

Then one December day, all of a sudden, a little boy sitting beside Montessori on the roof terrace, cried out "I can write, I can write." Using chalk he wrote on the pavement the word "mano" which means hand. Then, he wrote "tetto", which means roof, still crying out "I can write, I can write." Other children started to gather around him, saying to Montessori "Give me the chalk, I can write too". And so one after another the children began to write words on the roof terrace, in what Montessori called "frenzied joy".

There was such an "explosion" into writing that Montessori wrote: "In those first days we walked upon a carpet of written signs. Daily accounts showed us that the same thing was going on at home and some of the mothers, in order to save the floors of their houses, and even the crust of their loaves upon which they found words written, made their children presents of paper and pencil".
(The Montessori Method p 267)

Note: This is most definitely a discovery of great significance. It proves that writing comes about naturally through indirect preparation. It was because of the "muscular memory," developed unconsciously by feeling sandpaper letters, that these children were enabled to write spontaneously.

The Discovery of Reading.

When word got out about the explosion into writing in the Casa, people started sending beautiful books to the Casa assuming that if the children could write, they could also read.

But here, there was a surprising discovery in store for Montessori. The children were not interested in the books. They couldn't grasp what reading was all about. They were just absorbed in the joy of writing and were not ready for reading yet. Montessori wrote little messages on the blackboard, things like: "If you can read this, come up to me," and "If you love me, give me a kiss". For several days, nothing happened. It was as if the children thought Montessori was just writing for her own pleasure, just as they were.

However, on the fourth day, a little girl came up to Montessori and said "here I am." A short time after that, another child came up and gave her a kiss.

And so, the penny dropped, and there was great excitement. The children suddenly understood that reading simply means one person can communicate their ideas to another, without speaking. The children were thrilled with this discovery and they really took it to heart.

Now, when visitors came to the Casa, instead of saying 'good morning' or 'hello' some of the children would rush to a blackboard and write a greeting in chalk obviously enjoying the thrill of this new way of communicating.

And so Montessori learned a very important lesson and it was this: contrary to public opinion, writing comes before reading. Also, before children are ready to read books, they need time to practice puzzling out words, ordinary everyday words. These children started to puzzle out everything. They deciphered notices, street signs, calendars, shopping lists and so on. Only after they had puzzled out these things for some weeks did they finally turn to books, and then their love for reading books became truly amazing.

Note: This is surely another discovery of real significance. In education circles, we talk of reading and writing. Very few people know about Montessori's discovery that writing comes naturally before reading, and that children often need plenty of practice just writing for pure pleasure before they are ready for "reading."

PSYCHOLOGICAL CHANGES IN THE CHILDREN

A Compulsion for Order.

One of the most striking psychological changes that Montessori witnessed in the children was their feeling, one might even say their compulsion for order.

When the children first came to the Casa, they were disorderly, even chaotic in their behaviour. Yet, within a short time in the Casa, after they had started to focus on activities, they developed a love, one might even say, a passion, for order.

They relished putting things back on shelves in the right order. They loved routines. They showed an extraordinary and unsuspected need for order and structure, down to the last detail.

They became happy and calm when materials were kept in the same place and they became disturbed and anxious when things were out of place.

Note: This is surely a very significant discovery. We live in an age when young children are being diagnosed with Autistic Spectrum Disorders (ASD) at an alarming rate. Could it be that many young children are unable to build "sound" minds because they are deprived of the order they need in early childhood to construct a sound mind?

A Preference for Work rather than Play.

Another extraordinary characteristic that Montessori and many visitors witnessed in these small children was that, very quickly, they began to prefer work to play. Montessori found this very hard to believe, but the evidence was incontrovertible. The children constantly selected the challenging activities that the Casa offered rather than the toys that Montessori's wealthy society friends had donated.

Initially, the children played with the toys, but after a few days, they abandoned them, and returned to the learning materials, which seemed to captivate them much more than the toys.

This fact that the children preferred work to play was independently witnessed and commented on by visitors to the Casa over and over again.

Note: This is surely a very significant discovery for us in a day and age when children have homes full of toys yet often display huge behavioural problems and signs of unhappiness. Could it simply be that children are crying out for meaningful activities i.e. "work," rather than just "play"?

The Children Refused Sweets.

Here we have a phenomenon in the children which was so incredible that Montessori just couldn't believe it herself. The children constantly refused sweets! Now, these were poor children, street urchins, not used to treats of any kind. Yet it was an undeniable fact, witnessed by hundreds of visitors, that the children refused sweets.

Note: This is surely a discovery of huge significance to us in an age marred by childhood obesity problems. The phenomenon raises serious questions such as:

- Why did these impoverished children refuse to eat the sweets? Were they now so psychologically well adjusted that they just didn't feel the need for "comfort" food?

- Are today's children becoming obese simply because they are being driven to "comfort" eating as their fundamental psychological needs are not being met?

- Could a return to "authentic" Montessori environments cure this serious and rapidly increasing medical problem which is the scourge of our modern times?

A Love of Silence and Working Alone.

Another incredible change that Montessori and hundreds of visitors witnessed in the children was that they began to love quietness and working alone.

This phenomenon is still one of the hardest things for people who have never witnessed a true Montessori school to believe, but it is an undeniable fact.

We think of little children as being noisy and lovers of noise. When they first come to school they are often like this. The children of the first Casa had been described as vandals. Montessori however, found again and again that when little children become fully engaged in an activity they become quiet and peaceful and often select to work alone rather than in a group.

Note: This is also a very significant discovery. Very few early years professionals are aware that young children have a great need and love for periods of quietness and working alone during their daily activities. If adults don't know this, they will fail to facilitate it, thereby failing to meet an important psychological need in the young child.

A Need for Free Choice.

Another curious characteristic that Montessori observed in these small children was that young as they were, they had a need to select for themselves the activities they were going to work on. If they were handed an activity they often took no interest in it, but if they selected an activity for themselves, they tended to stick with it and became engrossed in it.

When they had free choice to select an activity, they chose slowly and carefully. It was as though they were being guided by some inner directive to select the activity which matched exactly their developmental needs at that specific time.

Note: This discovery of the young child's need for free choice is also a finding of great significance because it was the availability of free choice that lead these children to select activities which exactly matched their developmental needs at a specific period in time. What Montessori discovered here was that nature appears to guide the child to select the specific activity he needs for his optimum development at any given time.

A Need for Independence.

One of the most striking characteristics in the children was that, after a short period in the Casa they began to show a desire, one might even say a desperate desire to become independent of adults.

The children relished doing everyday tasks such as washing, dressing, preparing meals, sweeping, dusting, polishing, arranging flowers, cleaning tables et cetera all by themselves.

As they became more independent of adults they became more confident, more self assured, and more joyful. People even started to refer to them as the "joyful children".

Note: This is a very significant discovery about the link between independence and the development of self-esteem. Even in today's "enlightened" society, many people, don't understand this.

No Rewards, No Punishments.

One of the most profound changes that Montessori and the hundreds of independent witnesses saw in the children was what we might call a spiritual change.

These children, once they became focused and attentive, began to display what can only be described as a truly uncorrupted spirit. They showed, through their behaviour, that they were above the level where rewards and punishments have any meaning.

Again and again Montessori saw the futility of rewards and punishments and she finally abolished both rewards and punishments from the Casa, being convinced that they make no sense to young children. Work, is its own reward, she concluded and the absence of work is a punishment.

Note: This is another very significant discovery, yet despite its clarity, many schools for young children still use rewards in the form of stickers, gold star charts etc. and many child 'experts' encourage the use of such charts in the home to reward good behaviour. Yet studies have shown clearly that 'Extrinsic rewards not only decrease interest in an activity, they are also associated with less learning and creativity.' (Lillard, A. Montessori: The Science Behind The Genius). p191.

SOCIAL CHANGES IN THE CHILDREN

The Children Became Sociable.

Perhaps one of the most astonishing changes in the children was what we might call a social change. Initially, when the children came to the Casa in January 1907, Montessori said they were frightened, tearful children.

Yet within a matter of weeks, there were very positive social changes in the children. From being shy and tearful, they became friendly, more confident and more communicative. They were full of life and energy. They exuded a sense of happiness, they showed no shyness or timidity yet they were full of courtesy and good manners.

They loved having visitors to the Casa. Many witnesses said the children offered the visitors chairs, thanked them for coming and behaved impeccably without any one training them in social behaviour.

Note: This is surely a very significant finding. Nowadays, too much emphasis is placed on forcing the socialisation of young children. Here, the evidence shows that children become social naturally, when they are placed in an environment suited to their needs.

There Was a Distinct Lack of Bullying.

One of the most striking facts about the children's behaviour was that there was a distinct lack of aggressive or bullying behaviour among the children. This fact is quite extraordinary when we remind ourselves why the Casa was set up in the first place. These children had been described as vandals who were destroying the tenement buildings. Yet here they were, just a short time later and their behaviour was distinctly non-aggressive.

Note: This is surely another significant discovery for us in a day and age when bullying is rampant in many schools. Dr. Angeline Lillard's research published in Science Magazine in 2006 is very important in relation to this. That research showed that contemporary Montessori schools still have significantly less 'ambiguous rough play' (i.e. aggressive actions) than non Montessori schools. The questions we need to ask are:

- Why are children in "authentic" Montessori schools less inclined to engage in "ambiguous rough play"?

- Are "authentic" Montessori schools providing a type of psychological health to children which causes them not to feel the need to be aggressive?

- Do non-Montessori schools fail to provide the type of psychological health to children that they need, causing them to behave aggressively as a result?

Spontaneous Self-Discipline.

Perhaps the most amazing phenomenon that Montessori and hundreds of visitors witnessed in the Case was, that young children, when given a certain type of environment, develop a spontaneous self-discipline which is so remarkable, that it has to be seen to be believed.

The children went about their daily business, in a quiet and orderly manner. They took pride in the Casa. They helped to keep it clean and tidy by dusting and sweeping daily. They showed respect to the teacher and the other children. They delighted in their work and enjoyed being part of a community.

They helped each other in practical ways by washing, dressing and serving food to each other. The older children automatically helped the younger children and took pride in their achievements and they spontaneously took on the job of peer teaching.

Note: This is another hugely significant discovery. It proves that self -discipline arises spontaneously when children are placed in an environment suitable to their needs. So much heartache for both child and adult could be avoided if people knew that true discipline does not come from external rules and threats. The greatest discipline, that which emanates from the individual himself appears spontaneously when the human being is placed in an environment suited to his needs.

New Children.

One of the most noticeable changes in the children was the change in their emotional well-being. When these children first came to the Casa, Montessori described them as being frightened children. Now, they were no longer frightened. What stood out about these children is that they were not just happy, not just satisfied, they were joyful and that's what so captivated everyone who witnessed them and that's why people called them the "new children".

Note: This also is a phenomenon of great importance and significance and it is surely something we cannot afford to just skip over. These children were touched to their innermost beings. Surely an education that can achieve this deserves close examination.

PHYSICAL CHANGES IN THE CHILDREN

Rapid Improvement in Physical Health.

One of the most noticeable and amazing changes in the children was the rapid improvement to their physical health after just a short time in the Casa.

When the children first arrived at the Casa in January 1907, Montessori said that everyone could see that they suffered from malnutrition. They were in urgent need of food and sunlight.

Yet in a short period of time, having had no change in diet and no medical treatment, the children's health showed a huge improvement.

Note: Once again this is a phenomenon of great significance. Nowadays, many doctors have made the connection between mental well-being and good physical health. Here, Montessori, a medical doctor herself, saw categorically that the physical health of the human being is inseparable from his mental well-being. This is something we cannot afford to ignore in education today.

The Children Became Energised by the Work.

Another extraordinary phenomenon that occurred was that the children became energised by the work itself. This phenomenon was witnessed by hundreds of independent visitors to the Casa and it was a source of astonishment to most of them.

When the children finished their tasks, they appeared to be rested, happy and joyful, as if the work itself was a mental tonic.

They were never tired out by self chosen activities, no matter how many times they repeated them. In fact, the more they repeated things the more invigorated and energised they seemed to become.

Note: This is surely a finding of huge significance for educators in every generation. Real education does not tire the human being, it energises him.

3

COULD THIS BE JUST A FLUKE?

(A scientific response)

Montessori was first and foremost a scientist. So when she witnessed these extraordinary changes in the children, she responded with the mind of a scientist. At first, she couldn't believe what she was seeing. She needed to be sure that the things she was witnessing were not just a fluke. She needed scientific certainty, so she posed the following questions:

- Was this a new phenomenon in the true scientific sense?

- Could it be replicated with children in similar economic circumstances?

- Could it be replicated with children in better economic circumstances?

- Could it be replicated with older children?

- Could it be replicated with children from different cultures?

- If it was a new phenomenon, what were the conditions which brought it about?

She then set out to answer these questions.

The answer to the first question was a definite yes. Montessori pointed out that in physics and medicine there are rigorous standards governing the criteria for what constitutes a new phenomenon.

A new phenomenon, she pointed out, is an initial discovery of facts which had been previously unknown and consequently unsuspected.

Montessori was Professor of pedagogical anthropology, which means she was well acquainted with the history of education going back hundreds of years. Therefore she knew, with certainty, that no one had ever documented anything like these changes in children of this age on this scale before. She also knew, with certainty, that her findings ticked the box, for the discovery of a new phenomenon, in the strict scientific sense.

The answer to the second question was also yes .The phenomenon could be replicated with children in similar economic circumstances. This was proven later on in the same year when Montessori opened a second Casa in San Lorenzo. The children were the same; poor, deprived, sullen, disorderly, unfocused, unhappy, lacking in social skills and physically unwell.

The results were the same. Within a short period of time, the children showed an identical transformation. They became focused and started to concentrate on the activities. They became sociable, communicative, happy and were performing very well academically. Physically, they were looking bright and healthy. They were blossoming in their personalities.

In October 1908, Montessori opened another Casa dei Bambini for poor children, this time in Milan. The Casa was a success and in time many more Case were opened and funded by the Umanitaria organisation which funded this one.

The success of these Case was further proof that the phenomenon could be replicated with children in similar economic circumstances to those of the poor children of San Lorenzo.

The answer to the third question was also yes. The phenomenon could be replicated with children who were not poor. Evidence of this came early on when, in 1908, the British ambassador, started a Casa dei Bambini in the British Embassy in Rome for wealthy embassy children. The Casa was hugely successful and grew rapidly.

The answer to the fourth question was also yes. The phenomenon could be replicated with children from other cultures. When word spread about the success of the embassy school, more and more foreign diplomats wanted to have a Montessori school for their children. So the embassy school moved to a larger premises, a villa on the Pincian Hill in Rome. The children of diplomats from many different embassies started to come to this school. These children were from different countries, they spoke different languages and they came from different cultural backgrounds.

Initially, according to one journalist, it was like the Tower of Babel, but within a month, this school became a community of happy, busy children.

So Montessori had clear proof that the phenomenon could be replicated even among children from different nationalities and cultures, who didn't even speak the same language.

The answer to the fifth question was also yes. The phenomenon could be replicated with older children. According to an early eyewitness, Dr. Dorothy Canfield Fisher, Montessori was experimenting with the application of her ideas with older children in the 6 to 9 age range and her experiments were proving to be hugely successful.

So the final question, if this was a new phenomenon in the strict scientific sense, what were the conditions which brought it about? Montessori, with meticulous attention to detail, retraced her steps in an effort to pin down the essential conditions which brought about this phenomenon, and caused it to be repeated in each of the Case in succession. In her important book, The Secret of Childhood, she identified the three conditions which she believed had fused together to contribute to the extraordinary results in the Casa. These conditions were:

A suitable environment.

Scientific materials.

Humility in the teacher.

Explaining the Science:

By 1909, it was clear to Montessori and to discerning eyewitnesses that this new phenomenon was no fluke. This was scientific. This was a method of education that produced what people were now calling "new" children i.e. superior children, children with higher than average social, cognitive, physical, emotional and spiritual characteristics. People could see that these new children could be produced as as surely as you could produce good apples by giving them the right environmental conditions and removing the obstacles to their development.

The truth was out there and the public, especially teachers, were clamouring for information on the principles of this new method.

Montessori was at pains to point out that she did not have a mechanical method for churning out great children. The extraordinary results in her "children's houses" came about as a result of a combination of factors, some of which were so mysterious that she claimed she didn't fully comprehend them herself at this point. Montessori kept emphasising that she just followed the child and allowed his spontaneous behaviours to give her a glimpse into what she called "the unexplored depths of the child's mind". This she said, was how she gradually built up a picture of how children actually develop and learn.

Convinced that these findings had huge significance for the whole of humanity, Montessori's close friends urged her to write a scientific account of them.

So, in the summer of 1909, in response to public demand and the urging of her close friends, Montessori made two very important decisions:

- To give her first training course on this scientific method.

- To write her first book on this scientific method.

She gave the training course to over 100 students, most of them teachers, some of them her pupils from the women's training college. She then wrote her first book, in the space of a month, entitled, in Italian, Il Metodo della Pedagogia Scientifica applicato all'educazione infantile nelle Case dei Bambini. (The Method of Scientific Pedagogy Applied To The Education of Young Children in the Casa dei Bambini). Three years later, in 1912, the English translation was published, as "The Montessori Method". The book had instant success and had a very wide circulation. It was very soon translated into French, Spanish, German, Russian, Polish, Romanian, Dutch, Danish, Japanese and Chinese and eventually into more than twenty different languages. What had started out as a small experiment in the slums of San Lorenzo had now become something huge which had grasped the attention of the entire world.

4

THEY CAME, THEY SAW AND THEY WERE CONQUERED

(Independent Verification)

From 1908 onwards, independent verification of the extraordinary capabilities of and character changes in the children in the Case dei Bambini began to appear from several sources. These included:

- Eyewitness accounts

- The Italian Press

- The International Press

- Peer Reviews

Eyewitness accounts:

As news began to spread about the extraordinary capabilities of the children in the Case dei Bambini at San Lorenzo, huge numbers of people started to visit the Case to see things for themselves. People came, not just from Italy, but from all over the world. Among these people were professors of education, writers, journalists, diplomats from foreign embassies, social workers, doctors, teachers, people from religious orders, philanthropists and those whose curiosity urged them to just come and see for themselves.

For many of these eyewitnesses, the effect on them, of seeing the children's behaviour in the Case, changed the course of their whole lives and indeed their very philosophy of life.

One of the very early eyewitnesses of the San Lorenzo experiment was none other than the Queen Mother of Italy, Queen Margarita. The Queen spent many hours in the Case just observing the children at work. She was so deeply affected by what she observed that she wrote:

"I prophesy that a new philosophy of life will emerge from what we are learning from these little children." (Circa 1907/1908).

The Italian Press:

The Italian Press had been reporting the story of the happenings at San Lorenzo since 1907. In fact, press reports on the behaviour of these children aroused such public interest that visitor passes had to be issued to control the numbers of people turning up at the Case wanting to see things for themselves. And the public interest in the Case, fuelled by the Italian press reports, did not diminish with time, but, in fact, increased. Eventually the number of curious visitors arriving at the Case in San Lorenzo was so huge that it caused a serious dispute between the directors of the building society who had started the project and Montessori herself. This dispute was so serious that it resulted in Montessori finding herself "locked out" of the Case in San Lorenzo only two years after she had opened them!

Years later, in 1947, in a European newspaper article, Montessori recounted this extraordinary turn of events. She said that because her work with the children in the Case at San Lorenzo was causing such a "newspaper sensation," the building society who had paid for the project, claimed she was using the project as a "personal advertising campaign" and they instructed the porter not to allow her into the building any more!

The International Press:

It wasn't just the Italian newspapers who wrote about Dr Montessori. News of the amazing children was spreading through the International Press.

In an article published in the New York Times in 1912, it was stated:

"There is scarcely a country on the face of the globe that has not sent its emissary to visit Dr. Montessori and her schools."

McClure's Magazine:

The Italian Press and the International Press made Montessori famous, but it was S.S. McClure's magazine that made Montessori a global superstar.

Samuel McClure was one of the most influential journalists of his time. His literary and political magazine started the trend of what we now call "investigative" journalism. It was also the instrument which serialised chapters from such famous authors as Arthur Conan Doyle, Rudyard Kipling, Robert Louis Stevenson and Mark Twain.

In the spring of 1911 and the winter of 1911/1912, SS McClure, in a series of articles on Montessori education caused the "Montessori Approach" to teaching and learning to explode upon the American public imagination like a firecracker out of a box. So great was the interest aroused by the first magazine articles which included 17 pages of photographs, that second editions of the magazine had to be printed. This was an unprecedented event in journalism. The Montessori "phenomenon," already known to quite a few American educational experts was now placed before the general public.

McClure had been warned by his colleagues that an article about an Italian educational experiment would hold no interest for the American public, but his "gut feeling" for what would and would not attract American interest was always right. In this case, he was very, very right.

In response to the first article, McClure received hundreds of letters from ordinary readers who wanted to know more. They wanted to know where they could study and train in this "method," how they could introduce it to their own children, where they could get hold of the materials etc. Many of these people described themselves as "converts," "disciples" and "followers" in these letters.

Peer Reviews:

Following the press publicity and the articles in McClure's Magazines, prominent professors of education started to arrive at the Case in Rome to see the children for themselves and to meet with Dr. Montessori .

They came from Harvard, Princeton, Columbia, Pennsylvania, Miami, California, Arkansas, Michigan and other universities. Then peer reviews of Dr. Montessori's work began to appear rapidly from some of the academics who had travelled to Rome to see things for themselves and from other academics who read about the method.

Professor Henry Holmes. Harvard University.

In February 1911, Professor Henry W. Holmes of the education department of Harvard, contacted Montessori offering to write an introduction to an English edition of "Il Metodo". She agreed, so the English edition went ahead under the auspices of Harvard's Division of Education and was published in April 1912. The translation of "Il Metodo" from Italian to English was undertaken by Anne George and Dr. Dorothy Canfield Fisher. Miss George was, at that time, the only American who had been trained by Montessori herself, having gone to Italy in 1909 to meet with her and subsequently study under her.

In his introduction, Professor Holmes wrote: "..it is wholly within the bounds of safe judgement to call Dr. Montessori's work remarkable, novel, and important". He wrote: "... as a system it is the novel product of a single woman's creative genius". He also stated that "..all who are fair-minded will admit the genius that shines from the pages which follow". He concluded that "..no student of elementary education ought to ignore it".

Dr. Theodate L. Smith. Clark University.

In August 1912, Dr. Theodate L. Smith of Clark University, published "The Montessori System In Theory and Practice; An Introduction To The Pedagogic Methods of Dr. Maria Montessori".

In his introduction he summarised the academic interest that Montessori's work was attracting. He wrote:

"Harvard University, through Professors Henry W. Holmes and Arthur O.Norton, was probably first in this country to devote serious study to the Montessori System. It has been studied with care at Clark University. Columbia University has sent three members of the faculty to Rome for the examination of Madame Montessori's work, and several other universities are investigating the method".

Professor Edward P. Culverwell. Trinity College Dublin.

In 1913, Professor Edward P. Culverwell, professor of education at Trinity College Dublin, published another book length study of the Montessori approach. It was entitled "The Montessori Principles and Practice".

This book immediately stimulated a huge interest in the Montessori method in Ireland. In Dublin, Professor Culverwell's lectures attracted as many as a thousand teachers at a time.

His book was balanced, moderate and very favourable to the Montessori approach.

In his preface he stated that: "If the principles which she has applied more fully than any other educationalist are recognised in early education, they cannot fail to react on all education".

He said: "The careful attention to the individual child rather than to the group, and especially the respect paid to his individuality and his right to self-development, cannot fail to react on later education and life," and "assist in forming a healthy public opinion,"...."through which many of the injustices and inequalities of our social system may be alleviated". pxiv.

This man really grasped it. He really understood that this was not about spellings and sums, it was about helping the child who becomes the man, who becomes the government, who becomes the force, that rules the world, that man built.

So, if we want to eradicate inequality and injustice in our social systems, we must start with an education that builds individuality, that enables people to think for themselves, not just at 3, but at 6, 12, 18, 25, 30, 40, 50, 60, and so on.

It must be the type of education that 'assists in forming a healthy public opinion'.

He recognised that that is exactly what Montessori education does. (incidentally, so did Hitler and Mussolini some years later, that's why they burned her books and closed down her schools.)

Professor Culverwell's book gave serious academic support to Montessori's ideas.

He described Montessori as a "new light" in the "educational world" and said that the "remarkable advance made by Dr Montessori.... will ultimately place her name..... as one of the greatest in the history of educational progress".

Professor Florence Ward. Iowa State Teacher's College.

In 1913, Professor Florence Elizabeth Ward of Iowa State Teacher's College published a book entitled "The Montessori Method and the American School". This book came about as a result of her direct observations of the Case in Rome. Miss Ward, was a Professor of kindergarten education. In the spring of 1912, having heard of the transformation of the young children in Montessori's Casa dei Bambini, she decided to travel to Italy to see things for herself.

While on the very long boat journey from the United States to Italy, Professor Ward recalls: "..we received on shipboard one of the first copies of the English translation of Dr. Montessori's book as it came from the press". She says, "this book we read with eagerness, and by the time we had reached Naples its pages were well-worn from lending, as many passengers desired a peep into the book whose publication had been looked for with keen anticipation by American students of child life".

She says that: "On arriving in Rome, we found ourselves surrounded by Americans whose purpose was the same as our own, but we soon realised that one's presence there did not insure illumination on the subject of the Montessori method".

She says of Montessori that she was "no respecter of persons" with regard to those who came to see her. Whether one was a university professor, a reporter or a photographer, all were left waiting, often for days, "at the threshold of this quiet, unassuming originator".

But, she wrote, "once admitted, one was treated with the greatest cordiality".

She said, Montessori stated frankly, "I am willing to see those who are here in search of truth," but she was not interested in time wasters who only called out of idle curiosity. She said, Montessori "proves on acquaintance to be an untiring seeker after truth," and that "Personal recognition, and especially sensational notoriety, are apparently farthest from her desire". Professor Ward also stated that "she makes no sweeping claims of originality but gives full credit to other workers in the same field". (p11)

Professor Ward returned to America and gave an extremely favourable report on the Montessori method to the NEA (National Education Association) and followed up her report with the publication of her full-length book in 1913, which strongly recommended that the Montessori approach should be applied to the education of children in American schools. She wrote:

"A careful consideration of the Montessori method will convince all those who seek to be fair and candid that it contains principles of vital worth and that the schools offer object lessons which we cannot afford to ignore". p230.

Professor William Heard Kilpatrick. Columbia University.

Most of the professors and academics who visited the Case in Rome wrote very favourable reports about Montessori and her work, but there was one professor who wrote a very damning report. His name was Professor William Heard Kilpatrick. He was professor at the University of Columbia's prestigious Teachers College. He was known as "the million dollar professor," because he attracted so many students to his courses. Professor Kilpatrick came to Rome for one week, visited the Case, and took a dim view of everything he saw there. He returned to the US after just a week in Rome and he wrote a short book entitled, "The Montessori System Examined" (1914). In this book, he dismissed Montessori's thought as being fifty years behind the times, and called her methods mechanical, formal, and restricting. He wrote: "So narrow and limited a range of activity cannot go far in satisfying the normal child".

One hundred years later, we think it is safe to say that thousands of children around the world would have to disagree with him.

Dr. Jessie White:

Another eyewitness who published a full-length book on Montessori's work was an educationist named Dr. Jessie White.

Dr. White:

- Was vice-principal of a kindergarten training college in England.

- Had a scientific training and had been a science teacher for many years.

- Had attended a number of Montessori's lectures in London

- Had been inspired by reading the English translation of Dr Montessori's book.

In 1913, Dr. White decided to take a trip to Italy to see the schools in person.

Dr. White travelled to Rome in April 1913 and spent three months in Italy visiting Dr. Montessori's schools. No less than thirteen Montessori schools were visited throughout Italy and upon the return to England the findings were published in a book entitled:

"Montessori Schools As Seen In The Early Summer of 1913"

As a scientist, Dr. White was determined to describe Montessori's schools in as objective and scientific a fashion as possible. In the prologue to the publication, the good doctor wrote:

"Having had a scientific training and been a science teacher for a considerable number of years, I was fully aware of the qualifications necessary for sound observational work. For an observer of schools these qualifications, I think, may be stated as follows: acquaintance with other methods employed for children of the same age so that novel points may not escape notice, the psychological knowledge necessary for appreciating the results of the method, impartiality of judgement in estimating the value of the results, patience in studying the phenomena so that the impression formed one day may, if necessary, be corrected by later impressions, carefulness in weighing the judgements arrived at and in expressing them verbally....."

"One merit alone I claim, that I spared no pains in my attempt to see truly, and in writing out my observations have taken equal pains to convey, as far as possible, this truth unfalsified".

Dr. White's book is very informative. It describes the schools in minute detail. The book spares no one's feelings. It is dispassionately truthful. In general, the book is very favourable towards Montessori education. Dr. White returned to the UK with a very positive impression of the schools that were visited and hoped that the method would now be incorporated into English schools.

Dr. Dorothy Canfield Fisher:

One of the most influential people to publish a full-length book on Montessori's work was a lady named Dorothy Canfield Fisher. She was an educational reformer, social activist and best selling author.

Mrs. Fisher was an extraordinary woman in her own right. She was named by Eleanor Roosevelt as one of the ten most influential women in the United States.

Bio.

- She was born in Kansas USA in 1879.

- She was awarded a Ph.D. from Columbia University in 1904.

- She turned down a professorship for family reasons.

- She spoke five languages fluently.

- She was a wife and mother of two sons.

- She was awarded 13 further PhD's.

- She oversaw the first adult education program in the USA.

- She published a best-selling novel.

- She published 21 more works of fiction.

- She published 18 volumes of non-fiction.

- She met Montessori in Rome in 1911/1912.

- She published A Montessori Mother in 1912.

- She published The Montessori Manual in 1913.

Dr. Canfield Fisher's publications on the Montessori approach attracted huge attention in the United States and like McClure's magazines, were instrumental in making Montessori into a global superstar.

Not surprisingly, Dr. Montessori was not a bit pleased with Dr. Canfield Fisher's publications because she felt they over-simplified her method and consequently she denounced them publicly.

When Montessori published her own manual of the materials in 1914, entitled "Dr Montessori's Own Handbook," she wrote a letter to the Times Educational Supplement, which stated: "I hope my system will not be held responsible for any lack of success that may arise out of the use of other books than my own in connection with the Montessori apparatus".

Her response seems a little ungrateful and harsh towards Dr. Canfield Fisher who described Montessori as a "genius" and the Montessori approach as something that offers the "promise of a new future for us all".

Dr. Canfield Fisher's books did attempt to simplify the Montessori approach because, as she candidly stated: "it's usefulness to the race depends upon its comprehension by the greatest number of ordinary human beings".

Notably, despite her many PhDs, Mrs Fisher, referred to herself, the author of these books, as "an ordinary American parent, desiring above all else the best possible chance for her children".

Regardless of Montessori's feelings on the matter, because Dorothy Canfield Fisher was such a highly respected and influential person in her own right, her opinions held great weight. Her factual and intelligent appraisal of Dr Montessori's work was hugely instrumental in spreading interest in Montessori's ideas throughout the US and beyond.

5

THE TRUTH BEFORE THE WATCHING WORLD

(The Glass Classroom-San Francisco 1915)

If you believe that you've made a discovery of monumental importance, there is surely no better way to present it to the world than by allowing the world to witness it with its own eyes.

This is exactly what Dr. Montessori did in San Francisco in 1915 when she erected a glass-walled demonstration classroom in the Palace of Education at the Panama Pacific Exposition.

The exposition, which lasted for nine months, was opened in early 1915. Its official purpose was to celebrate the completion of the Panama Canal, but its obvious secondary purpose was economic, commercial and social. The aim was to boost the economy of San Francisco by attracting visitors from all over the world, and to act as a morale booster at a time of war and economic depression.

During the nine months it was open, more than 18 million people visited the exposition. Many of the exhibits were hugely impressive and ranged from the scientific, commercial and academic to the purely recreational. Concerts, food fares and purely fun exhibits were all part and parcel of the exposition.

One of the more serious associations participating in the exposition was the National Educational Association which held its annual convention during the exposition. This convention attracted 15,000 teachers and it welcomed delegates and speakers from over 30 different countries.

Montessori was one of the invitees to this convention. She was asked to speak and she was invited to set up a model Montessori classroom to be organised and conducted under her personal supervision throughout four of the months of the exposition .

For various reasons, including financial considerations, Montessori decided to erect a glass-walled classroom to be her demonstration school at the exposition.

She selected 30 children from thousands of applicants to be the pupils. The children were between two and a half and six years of age. The only stipulation she insisted on was that the children must never have attended any form of school previously.

The class took place daily from 9 to 12 noon. Montessori would have liked to conduct the class herself, but couldn't because she was booked, among other things, to give her Third International Training course in San Francisco. So, Montessori nominated Helen Parkhurst, her former pupil and protege to be the directress of the classroom.

Tiers of seats were arranged around the three glass walls so that hundreds of spectators could watch the children. Each day spectators had to arrive early to be sure of getting a seat in the viewing gallery, others were happy just to get standing room with a good view .

The spectators were fascinated by the level of concentration evident in these very young children who seemed oblivious to the crowd of observers peering in at them. Undisturbed, they showed unbroken concentration on their work with the Montessori materials.

Concentration is the key word here. This is what singled out these children and this classroom as being different from any classroom ever seen before.

Just as in the Case in San Lorenzo, these children began to demonstrate levels of concentration that were unexpected in children so young. Even the hundreds of visitors peering in at them couldn't distract them. They would look up from time to time, but then calmly and serenely go back to their work.

Newspaper accounts of the children in the glass classroom consistently reported how the children seemed to be above the level of distraction.

In one of the first newspaper articles on the Glass Classroom, it was remarked that the children appeared "oblivious" to the watching crowds.

(The San Francisco Chronicle)

One publication on the exposition stated that for long stretches the children hardly noticed the spectators because "their wits were so concentered on their work". (Todd The Story of the Exposition).

What the spectators witnessed and were fascinated by, was the spectacle of very young children who were captivated and transfixed by their work and whose personalities seemed to be elevated to a higher level by this concentration on their tasks.

This level of concentration was not commonplace to anyone except Dr. Maria Montessori who had witnessed this phenomenon over and over again in the Case in San Lorenzo.

The Glass Classroom proved to be one of the major attractions at the Exposition.

Lunchtime was especially fascinating to the spectators when these young children could be seen sitting at the long elegant dining table they had prepared themselves, set with candles, fine china, and beautiful linen napkins while a number of the children served lunch. Afterwards, the children washed the dishes, tidied away and rearranged the tables for the next day's class.

When the exposition ended, the Glass Classroom received not just one, but two, of the only two gold medals awarded in the field of education.

6

THE GREAT DISCOVERY

(What was it? In a nutshell)

- Was it simply the discovery that street urchins become better behaved when given a nice room to play in?

- Was it simply the discovery that children do better at their sums and spellings if you give them special materials?

- Was it simply the discovery that children can learn to read and write earlier than was previously expected?

- Or was it simply the discovery of another alternative type of education?

The truth is, it was none of these things.

Montessori's discovery was epoch making. It was timeless and monumentally important and it still is.

It is hugely relevant to today's world and therefore we cannot afford to ignore it.

You see, something very extraordinary happened to the children of San Lorenzo. They were evidently transformed mentally, psychologically, socially, emotionally, physically, intellectually and spiritually.

The transformation in the children posed more questions than answers. When Montessori first witnessed the children's behaviour and capabilities in 1907 and 1908 she found herself full of questions, questions such as:

- Why, after such a short time in the Casa, did the children develop a love for work, i.e. challenging activity rather than just amuse themselves with toys and play?

- Why after just a short time in the Casa, did the children develop a love for order and routines rather than the chaotic lifestyle they used to have?

- Why after just a short time in the Casa, did the children develop a love, almost a passion to be independent and do things for themselves?

- What were these children really doing? Beyond the pink towers, the cylinders and button frames, what were these children trying to achieve?

Then suddenly, the answer came to Montessori. These children were "constructing" themselves. They were literally building their own brains and perfecting their own bodies by selecting and completing activities. They were involved in self-construction. They were captivated by it, consumed by it and invigorated by it.

Once recognised, there was no denying it. What a discovery! It was comparable to Newton's discovery of gravity, he didn't invent it, it was always there, but no one had ever recognised it.

Similarly, this self construction in children, must have been there since the beginning of time, but no one had ever really taken note of it.

Then Montessori was faced with another question. If these children were in the process of constructing themselves, who was guiding them? It certainly wasn't any adult. After all, there were fifty or more children in the first Casa and only one teacher and one assistant. So who was directing the children's learning? Were some invisible laws of development at work? Were the children following the urging of some inner guide, some invisible teacher? If this was the case what were these laws of development?

Then other vital questions came to Montessori's mind, questions such as: if the children are now following some invisible laws of development and are now successfully constructing themselves, why weren't they doing that before they came into the Casa? Why had they previously been engaged in purely negative behaviour such as vandalising the tenement buildings?

Had something been preventing them from following these invisible laws of development, and if so, what was it?

Had there been obstacles in the way of the children's development and if so, what were these obstacles?

This led inevitably to the next question. Had the conditions in the Casa inadvertently been instrumental in removing the obstacles which had been impeding the children's development?

If this was the case, and the Casa had, even if it was inadvertently, removed the obstacles which were impeding the children's development, what was the essential ingredient which had caused all these various children to begin to normalise, i.e to become calm, social, industrious, helpful, kind and joyful members of a little community? These were burning questions, but the most crucial question of all was this: had these wonderful characteristics such as love of work, love of order, generosity of spirit, spontaneous self-discipline, been manufactured by Montessori's method or was there some other explanation for their appearance? This seemed to Montessori to be the pivotal question.

So, what was the answer?

In her intriguing book, The Secret of Childhood, Montessori answers this question. Despite the fact that people all over the world were now singing the praises of what they called the "Montessori Method," Montessori replied with extraordinary truthfulness and humility. She stated categorically that the wonderful characteristics that had emerged in the children of San Lorenzo and were now emerging in Casa after Casa, were NOT created or manufactured by her method of education. First of all, she pointed out that when these characteristics first began to appear in the children of San Lorenzo, she actually had no "method" of education. Secondly, as these characteristics began to appear in Casa after Casa, Montessori became convinced that these wonderful traits, amazing as it may seem, are, in fact,

"The normal characteristics of childhood".

And just as colours belong naturally to birds and fragrances belong naturally to flowers, so too these wonderful characteristics belong naturally to the child. They cannot be artificially created by anyone or by any educational method, but, and this is the vital point, these natural characteristics can be cultivated, can be protected by an educational approach that seeks to assist their development.

Just as the horticulturalist can protect and even improve on the natural fragrances, colours and shapes of flowers, so too, can the scientific educator, protect and nurture and help to develop the natural characteristics of the child, by removing the obstacles which are impeding his normal development and by giving him the freedom to follow the natural laws which seek to guide his development.

So, what was Montessori's great discovery? It was the discovery of "the normal characteristics of childhood." In fact, Montessori went so far as to say that it was "the discovery of the child," the true child, the normalised child, who had been hidden, buried, under a pile of deviations. In The Secret of Childhood, she said that there is a hidden child, a buried human being who must be liberated, and she saw this liberation of the "hidden child" as being the first urgent task of education.

She was certain that her method, although it was still in its early stages, had liberated both the poor and the wealthy children of San Lorenzo and had removed the obstacles impeding their development. It had given them the freedom to respond to the "invisible laws" of development leading them back on track from a state of chaotic behaviour to a state of normality so that they began to reveal the normal characteristics of childhood.

To use a medical metaphor, Montessori came to the conclusion that she had, almost by accident, created conditions in the Casa which had cured the children of all their psychological maladies just as a doctor cures a child of his physical maladies. And, to continue with this metaphor, just as the child, when he is cured of his physical illnesses, is left with the normal physical characteristics of childhood, e.g fresh complexion, shiny hair, good skin; so too, when the child is cured of his psychological maladies, he is left with the normal psychological characteristics of childhood, which are, joy, love of work, love of order, concentration, self- discipline, etc.

What this implies then is, that the other characteristics we frequently see in children, e.g. lack of focus, inability to concentrate, dislike of work, dislike of order etc etc, are actually deviations from the norm, the psychological equivalent of physical illness.

This was Montessori's great discovery. It was revolutionary then and it is revolutionary even now. What it implies is that everything we have come to accept as being normal in young children, things like, poor concentration span, inability to focus, dislike of work, temper tantrums, chaotic behaviour, instability of character, are all signs of abnormality, whereas the opposite traits, love of work, love of order, self-control, sociability are all signs of normality and psychological good health. What it also means is that our understanding of children is so poor that we have come to accept the pathology as the norm.

Now, the obvious question is, if these wonderful characteristics are actually the normal characteristics of childhood that we should be seeing in every child everyday, how come we don't see them every day? How come they are so rare?

Montessori's answer is threefold:

(1) We don't see the normal psychological characteristics of childhood everyday in every child everywhere because we constantly give children unsuitable environments in which to grow, which actually hide and repress the normal characteristics of children and prevent them from revealing themselves. We do this to both poor and wealthy children alike.

(2) From the moment of birth, children are constantly confronted with obstacles which act as roadblocks forcing them off the main road which leads to normal development and making them go down side roads which lead to deviations, i.e. defects in their personalities.

(3) Because these deviations occur in most children, during the early years, it is widely believed that these behavioural defects are normal and to be expected. People talk of the "terrible twos" and typical three year old tantrums etc, and so children are abandoned to their deviations because the general public are led to believe that this behaviour is normal. People say "ignore him and he'll get over it," as a child throws a tantrum, not knowing that the tantrum is an aberration and is the result of the child having been pushed off course by some obstacle. Therefore the child does not get the help he needs. No one knows that these deviations can be cured by the phenomenon which Montessori witnessed in the Case, a phenomenon she came to call "normalisation through work," and which she described as being "the most important single result of our whole work".

(The Absorbent Mind) p204

So, in a nutshell, Montessori's great discovery was the discovery of the normal characteristics of childhood, the discovery of the reasons why they are buried/hidden and the discovery of the key to digging them up and revealing them.

7

THE BLUEPRINT FOR HUMAN DEVELOPMENT

What makes a woman who had struggled so hard to get into medicine decide to cross her own name off the list of practising physicians and give up medicine for ever?

What makes a woman who ably held not just one, but two highly prestigious academic posts, i.e. Professor of Anthropology at the University of Rome and the Chair of Hygiene at the Women's Training College, decide to resign and devote the rest of her life to the study of children and childhood?

The answer is clear. Montessori was convinced, from what she was observing in Casa after Casa, that she had, almost by accident, made a scientific discovery of monumental importance. She was certain that she had made a discovery which had the potential to change the world by producing a higher, more responsible, more productive, more creative, more intelligent, more innovative, human being.

She was convinced that she had discovered "the blueprint" for normal human development which had been there since the dawn of time but which had never really been recognised.

She came to the conclusion that generation after generation had fumbled in the dark with the construction of the human being, trying now this approach and now that, not knowing that there is, in fact, a "blueprint" for the construction of the human being.

Her experience with the children of San Lorenzo and subsequently with children from many different nationalities, cultures and creeds, convinced Montessori that:

- Human development does not unfold haphazardly.

- There is a "Blueprint" for the unfolding of human life.

- There are laws of development laid down since the beginning of time.

- These laws have been placed there for the protection of normalcy in humans.

- If we obey these laws we will build normal human beings.

- If we ignore these laws we will build maladjusted human beings, damaged, sick human beings, people who are unable to attain peace and fulfilment in their lives, no matter what they do, or what they achieve.

- The very survival of our species depends upon us recognising and obeying these universal laws of development.

- Education must be revolutionised. It must become something that aids the human being and allows him to follow the natural laws of development from birth to adulthood.

PART TWO

HOW LONG DOES IT TAKE TO BUILD A HUMAN BEING?

8

WHY DOESN'T THE HUMAN BEING COME READY MADE?

Let's face it. - There is something very peculiar about every human being at birth.

We only notice this peculiarity when we compare the newborn human with the newborn animal.

Since most of us never do this, we never really notice this peculiarity, but it's there and it's very significant.

To put it simply:

When an animal is born, it is able, either from birth or shortly after birth, to become everything it is to be, e.g.

> The fish can swim.
> The bird can fly.
> The horse can gallop.

Similarly, when an animal is born, it is able, either from birth or shortly after birth, to make its own sound, e.g.

> The dog can bark.
> The cat can meow.
> The cow can moo.

However, when a human child is born, it is a different story. It will be many months before the child can walk and sometimes much longer before the child can talk.

Why is this? Montessori asked.

> "Why should it be necessary for the human being to endure so long and so laborious a babyhood. None of the animals has so hard an infancy. What happens while it is going on?"
>
> (The Absorbent Mind)P 23

This is the key question. What happens while the prolonged infancy of the human being is going on?

The answer became clear to Montessori, from her painstaking observations of babies and children worldwide; and it is this:

During the prolonged infancy of the human being, the natural process of "self-construction" begins. This is no accident, nature has planned it this way. This process is at its most critical stage during the early years.

Montessori discovered that "self-construction" is the task that faces every human being from birth. It is a task which is not imposed on any other species, only human beings are faced with it. In fact, it is this very task which distinguishes the human species from the animal species. In short, it means that the human child, as he lies helpless and dependent during that prolonged infancy, must begin to construct:

- *his intellectual self:*
  he must build his own brain, his own intellect, his own memories, his own connections between things. For this he relies on two things, his genetic inheritance and his environmental experiences.

- *his physical self:*
  as he perfects his movements teaching himself to sit up, crawl, walk, balance, run, climb and manipulate things with his hands.

- *his social self:*
  as he integrates into the daily hustle and bustle of family life and extended social life.

- *his cultural self:*
  as he listens to the language of his people and takes in their customs and traditions.

- *his emotional self:*
  as he is nurtured by his mother and thereby builds a primary attachment, and gradually reaches out to attach to others.

- *his spiritual self:*
  as he soaks in the atmosphere which surrounds him.

This then is nature's plan. The prolonged infancy of man is not by accident but by design. It allows the human infant the time he needs to absorb the language, culture, customs and traditions of the country he is born into, so that he can adapt himself to the time, place and civilisation that he finds himself in.

As Montessori put it-

"He enters upon life and begins his mysterious task, little by little to build up the wondrous powers of a person adapted to his country and its times. He constructs his mind, step-by-step till it becomes possessed of memory, the power to understand, the ability to think."

(The Absorbent Mind) p27.

Now the vital question in all of this is WHY?
Why is the human being given the task of self construction? As, we've stated already, the animals don't have to do it, they are complete at birth, they just get bigger and stronger.

Why is the human being so "unfinished" at birth, with so many areas to build up year after year?

The answer Montessori arrived at was simple yet profound. The human being is a NEW SPECIES, with a new role in life, a NEW DESTINY and it is our very ability to construct ourselves into unique human beings that sets us apart as a species and makes us unique creatures in the whole of creation.

<blockquote>"What a piece of work is man."</blockquote>

said Shakespeare, and how right he was.

Montessori wrote-

"Man is that superior being who is endowed with intelligence, and is destined to do a great task on earth. He must transform it, conquer it, utilise it and construct a new world full of marvels which surpasses and over-rules the wonders of nature. It is man who creates civilisation."

(The Formation of Man) p 96

She said,

"The prolonged infancy of man separates him entirely from the animals, and this is the meaning we must give to it. It forms a complete barrier, whereby man is seen as a being different from all others. His powers are neither continuations, nor derivations from those of the animals. His appearance on earth was a jump in life: the starting point for new destinies."

(The Absorbent Mind) p 60

"the human species....is built to a new design, and has a great destiny in relation to the other creatures."   (The Absorbent Mind) p 61

And so, nature has planned it that the human being cannot talk at birth because he is built to a new design, there is a new plan for him.

You see, although the dog can bark and the cow can moo, shortly after birth, these are the only sounds they will ever make. The cow born in China, will never moo in Chinese nor will the dog born in Italy, bark in Italian, but the human infant born in any country of the world will, within a year or two, learn to speak fluently, the language of that country. He will have absorbed its sounds, its phonemes, its grammar, its syntax.

The human infant has the capacity to speak any language no matter how different its sounds are. All he needs is the time to absorb it. This is why he cannot speak at birth. He is not pre-programmed like the animals.

Similarly, nature has planned it that the human being cannot walk at birth because he needs time for his brain to develop sufficiently so that it can direct the random movements of his limbs and bring them under its control, in order to give them that precision that makes human movements so different to those of the animals.

So, although we can admire the beauty of an eagle in flight, or the beauty of a horse in full gallop, the human being is unsurpassed in the variety and range of physical movements that he has perfected.

It is only among humans that we witness the skill of the surgeon's hand, the accuracy of the pianist's fingers, the precision of the dancer's feet.

Dr. Montessori was right. The human being is a new creature with a new destiny.

- It is the human being who creates cultures and traditions, philosophy, architecture, dance, music, literature, sculpture, and so on, in response to the needs of the human spirit.

- It is the human being who creates cities, civilisations and social structures.

- It is the human being who strives to build a better world, who fights for human rights and civil liberties.

- It is the human being who struggles to end poverty, injustice and cruelty in the world.

The human being is "unfinished" at birth, for a very good reason, and it is this: whereas the animals will never be more than instinctual creatures, following their impulses, i.e. what they are at birth is pretty much what they will always be, the human being, is made to a different design.

He has the potential to become just about anything. So he is not born with a "ready-made" mind but rather one that he himself will build.

So the tiny, helpless, human creature at birth may grow up to become anything. He is limited only by his genetics and his environment.

He has the capacity to adapt to any language, culture, country, climate, or period in history that he is born into and he has extraordinary potential. So, to answer our original question, THIS is why the human being doesn't come "ready-made".

9

HOW LONG DOES THE CONSTRUCTION WORK TAKE?

Some years ago, we conducted a survey in a busy shopping mall. We asked ordinary people to sketch on a small piece of paper, a diagram of how they saw the development of human life from birth to adulthood. All of them, without exception, drew something like this.

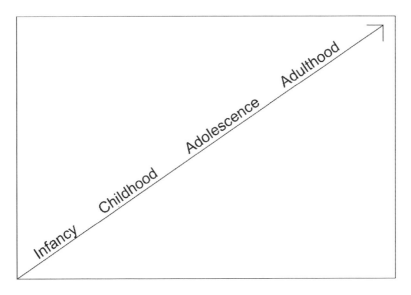

In other words, ordinary people see the development of human life as a steady progression, a line of ascent, from birth to adulthood.

From our brief conversations with these people we found out that the vast majority of people assume that the human infant is born "complete," "fully finished," "fully formed," and he just needs to get bigger, stronger and more skilful in order to grow successfully from birth to adulthood.

Moreover, most people believed this process of developing from child to adult ended at the age of 18 years. Some middle aged people even laughed and said they remembered their birthday cards with the "key" on them symbolising that they were now old enough to have the key of the house so they could come and go as they pleased. (Others remembered the glass of champagne on the card as having more significance!)

Well, if this is how most ordinary people "see" human development, they are in good company, because all through history, it has always been assumed that human development occurred like this, and generation after generation did not question it.

This view implies that human development occurs as a steady rise from birth to adulthood and that the infant, the child, the adolescent, the young adult, should be growing bigger, stronger, more intelligent, more responsible, more capable as every year goes by.

Because we accept this model and assume that the human being develops in a steady line, rising from birth to adulthood, we have devised a model of education to match this idea of human development.

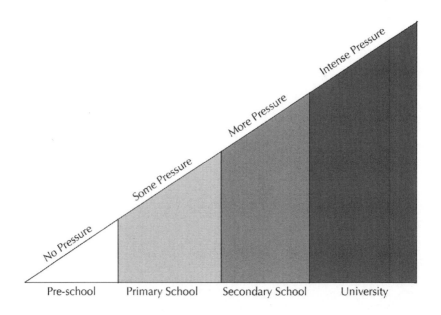

So we have developed a model of education which looks like the one above.

This model of education assumes that as the child gets older and older he should be able to cope with more pressure, more work, more academic demands on him, and we are shocked and disappointed when he can't cope with our expectations.

Montessori says that both of these models are fundamentally wrong.

She says, firstly, that human development does not occur in a steady rise from birth to adulthood at all, and secondly, because we have accepted an incorrect model of human development, we have compounded our errors by devising a system of education based upon a mistaken idea of how the human being actually develops in the first place.

As a result, our educational model is wrong and therefore is doomed to failure because it is not based on how human beings actually develop in real life.

What then is Montessori's theory or model of human development?

To put it simply, Montessori was convinced, from her meticulous observations of babies, children, adolescents and young adults, that human development is not like the growth of a tree which simply gets bigger and stronger each year until it reaches maturity, but is more like the growth of a butterfly which goes through distinct stages, which, although they are independent from each other, actually build upon each other to produce the final result e.g.

> The larvae stage
> The caterpillar stage
> The cocoon stage
> The butterfly stage

Each stage is so different from the one before and after it that we could be forgiven for thinking that the larvae, the caterpillar, the cocoon and the butterfly are unrelated creatures despite the fact that they are all part of the one unity.

Montessori was convinced that the story is the same in human development.
She wrote: "..man, even though he passes through independent phases- is nonetheless a single entity". Notwithstanding this, the infant, the child, the adolescent and the young adult are so different that one could almost believe they are different species at times.

Moreover, Montessori was convinced, from her observations that human development, does not occur in a straight line of ascent, but in a series of up and down stages or planes with highs and lows, progressions and regressions which are all part and parcel of "normal" human development.

So, she saw the model of human development as being not like this:

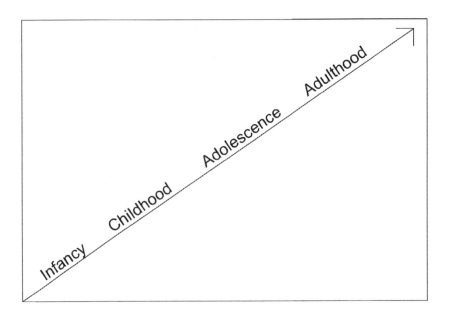

But more like this:

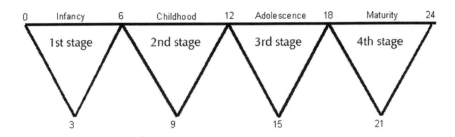

She called these four stages, the Four Planes of Development and she stated that they should be paired up with Four Planes of Education, so that education could act as an "aid" to life, something that works like a hand and a glove, at each stage of the human being's development.

Her view was this. If education fails to match the planes of development that the human being is going through, then it fails full-stop and it may even be harmful to the human being's growth.

So, when do the planes begin and when do they end?

Duration of the Planes

The first plane starts at birth and lasts until age 6
It is called the period of Infancy.

The second plane starts at 6 and lasts until age 12
It is called the period of Childhood.

The third plane starts at 12 and lasts until age 18
It is called the period of Adolescence.

The fourth plane starts at 18 and lasts until age 24
It is called the period of Maturity.

How do we know this? Because nature heralds the beginning and end of a plane by bringing about physical changes in the human body i.e.

- the milk teeth loosen and fall out around 6 years of age, which is the marker for the end of the first plane of development.

- puberty begins around age 12 bringing all sorts of physical changes to the human body, which is the marker for the end of the second plane of development.

- physical growth reaches a peek around age 18, which is the marker for the end of the third stage of development.

- brain development is completed around age twenty-four which is the marker for the end of the fourth stage of development.

So, there you have it, 24 years, that's "how long" the "construction work" takes.

Now, when Montessori presented these findings to the world many years ago, they were regarded as revolutionary. Indeed, some of her peers, discounted them as un-scientific.

However, in recent years, with the aid of neurology and the invention of functional magnetic resonance imaging (fMRI) brain scans it has been shown that the brain is indeed under construction for 24 or more years and the prefrontal cortex is not complete until the mid 20s just as Montessori had proposed. How she could have worked this out without the aid of modern brain scan technology is astounding.

Now, the implications of these findings are huge. How many of us ever approach a child or an adolescent with the conscious realisation that he/she is "unfinished" and is, in fact, still "under construction" and actually in the process of building him/herself? Probably very few of us. Most of us unconsciously hold the presumption that the child is already fully formed and just has to mature like a good cheese or a fine wine.

But that's not what Montessori was saying. She was saying that the human being is not actually "finished" at birth but is, in fact incomplete, and must spend 24 years building himself and adapting to the time and place that he finds himself in.

This was a revolutionary idea then and it is an equally revolutionary idea now. The significance of these findings, both Montessori's of many years ago and the confirmation of them by modern neuroscience, cannot be underestimated.

They should affect not only how we educate children and adolescents but also how we legislate for children and adolescents.

These findings will surely have huge implications in the future in the areas of family law, childcare law and criminal law.

For this reason, it is crucial for all of us to know with as much certainty as possible, precisely how long the "construction work" takes.

10

WHAT'S GOING ON DURING THE BUILDING PROCESS?

From her observations of children and adolescents, Montessori became certain that something very significant is going on during the building process. She discovered that each plane of development has:

- A purpose to fulfil

- A goal to reach

- An aim to achieve

The Purpose of Each Plane
The purpose of the 1st plane (0-6) is the Construction of the Child.
The purpose of the 2nd plane (6-12) is the Completion of the Child.
The purpose of the 3rd plane (12-18) is the Construction of the Adult.
The purpose of the 4th plane (18-24) is the Completion of the Adult.

The Goal of Each Plane
The goal of the 1st plane (0-6) is Physical Independence.
The goal of the 2nd plane (6-12) is Intellectual Independence.
The goal of the 3rd plane (12-18) is Social Independence.
The goal of the 4th plane (18-24) is Spiritual and Moral Independence.

The Aim of Each Plane
The 1st plane (0-6) aims to aid the self-construction of the human being into a Unique Individual.
The 2nd plane (6-12) aims to consolidate that construction.
The 3rd plane (12-18) aims to aid the self-construction of the human being into a Member of Society.
The 4th plane (18-24) aims to consolidate that construction.

How To Build a Human Being

Let's see this plane by plane.

The First Plane of Development (0 - 6)

Purpose: The Construction of the Child (This is a period of Creation)

Goal: Physical Independence

Aim: To aid the self-construction of the human being into a Unique Individual.

The Second Plane of Development (6 - 12)

Purpose: The Completion of the Child (This is a period of Consolidation)

Goal: Intellectual Independence

Aim: To consolidate the self-construction of the Human Being into a Unique Individual.

The Third Plane of Development (12 - 18)

Purpose: The Construction of the Adult (This is a period of Creation)

Goal: Social and Emotional Independence

Aim: To aid the self-construction of the Human Being into a Member of Society.

The Fourth Plane of Development (18 - 24)

Purpose: The Completion of the Adult (This is a period of Consolidation)

Goal: Total Independence which includes Spiritual and Moral Independence

Aim: To consolidate the self-construction of the human being into a Member of society.

11

DOES NATURE OFFER A HELPING HAND IN THE CONSTRUCTION?

The short answer is "yes". From her meticulous observations, Montessori became certain that nature provides the developing human being with "aids" at each plane of his development. These "aids" take the form of psychological impulses or drives which cause the human being to focus his attention on areas that are vital to his normal development at specific points in his growth.

- For example, during the first plane, nature gives the child specific "aids" which take the form of psychological drives which make him focus his attention on:

  Order
  Language
  Movement
  The senses
  Social life
  Small details

- Then, during the second plane, nature gives the child different "aids" or psychological impulses which cause him to focus his attention on fairness and justice and so are instrumental in building his moral character, which is vital for his development at this point in his life. Also during the second plane, nature gives the growing child enhanced reasoning and imaginative powers which are instrumental in helping him to attain mental and intellectual independence, and the ability to think and rationalise, which is the goal of this plane of development.

- Similarly, during the third plane, nature provides the adolescent with a totally new set of psychological drives which cause him to focus his attention on human relationships and life as a member of society. These "aids" are instrumental in helping the adolescent to attain social independence which is the goal of this plane of development.

- Finally, during the fourth plane, nature provides the young adult with a new sensitivity towards matters of civil rights/civil liberties which are underpinned by a new sensitivity towards the spiritual and moral side of life.

- At this stage, the young adult often becomes involved in politics, because he believes that certain practices are "morally" wrong. He speaks out, against injustices in society, ranging from such things as high taxes to world poverty. these "aids" are instrumental in helping the young adult to attain spiritual and moral independence which is the goal of this plane of development.

Montessori summarised the matter like this-

"It is all very clear really. A subconscious impulse during the period of growth, that is of the construction of the individual, urges it to realise its growth.......The outer world has value only in so much as it offers the necessary means to reach the goal set by nature." (The Formation of Man) p47

Montessori was here speaking specifically of the young child, but what she states applies to all the planes of development.

It's as simple as this :

- Nature gives "aids" at every stage of the human being's growth.

- These "aids" take the form of psychological drives or impulses.

- These "aids" are nature's way of aiding the baby, the child, the adolescent and the young adult towards the purpose, the goal and the aim of each specific plane of development.

Nature is practical, if the human being builds a good foundation during the first stage, the second stage stands a better chance of a good "completion." Similarly, if the human being builds a good foundation during the third stage, the fourth stage stands a better chance of a good "completion," because each plane rests on the achievements of the plane that goes before it.

It is nature's plan to produce at age 24 -

- Firstly: People who are strong individuals.

- Secondly: People who are rational and moral.

- Thirdly: People who have a strong sense of themselves as members of society.

- Fourthly: People who have a spiritual dimension and a sense of their role in the unfolding drama of human history.

A Word of Warning.

Montessori recognised that nature's "aids" are not just "little extras" that we can take or leave on our journey from birth to adulthood. She saw that these "aids" are part of a natural law, as real as the law of gravity. Just because we can't see something doesn't mean it's not there, or that it's not important.

Montessori was convinced that the growth and development of every human being is directed by these hidden but very real laws of nature which take the form of psychological drives such as we have described.

She saw that they apply to every being on the planet, in every geographical location and every era in history.

It was Montessori's firm conviction that these natural laws exist to aid the survival and continuation of a sane and a healthy species, and if we flaunt or ignore them, we do so at our peril.

She wrote -

"Life is divided into well defined periods. Each period develops properties the construction of which are guided by "laws of nature". If these laws are not respected, the construction of the individual may become abnormal, even monstrous. But if we take care of them, are interested in discovering them and co-operate with them, unknown and surprising character features, which we never even suspected, may result."

(The Formation of Man) p91

Montessori was convinced that the secret behind the extraordinary transformation of the children in the San Lorenzo experiment lay in the freedom they were given to respond to the laws of nature, which laws were instrumental in helping them attain the purpose, the goal and the aim of their particular plane of development.

The result was that these children became joyful, happy, sane, peaceful, calm, kind, generous and restored to mental and physical good health, because they were working with nature rather than against it.

Montessori regarded the discovery of guiding instincts, sensitive periods and laws of nature as amongst the most important discoveries ever made about human life.

She said:

"To trace the guiding instincts in man is one of the most important subjects of research for the present day."

(The Secret of Childhood) p225

She was adamant that it is:

" vitally necessary for everyone to know the laws of development."

(The Absorbent Mind) p14

She wrote:

"If we want to help life, the first condition of success is that we shall know the laws which govern it."   (The Absorbent Mind) p13

So, to answer our question:

"Does nature offer a helping hand in the construction?"

we must reply - "yes, absolutely, probably the most important hand in the mix".

12

SUMMARY OF DR. MONTESSORI'S MODEL OF HUMAN DEVELOPMENT

- Human development does not unfold haphazardly.

- All human beings are born in an "unfinished" state.

- This is not by accident but by design to allow for the growth of our unique individuality as human beings.

- Human development does not occur in a linear ascent from birth to adulthood, it occurs in four stages/planes.(0-6), (6-12), (12-18), (18-24).

- Nature heralds the beginning and end of a stage by providing visible changes which act as markers for the end of each stage.

- At each stage the human being has very specific characteristics, sensitivities, interests and needs.

- Nature has planned it that each stage has-

A purpose to fulfil.

A goal to reach.

An aim to achieve.

- Nature provides the human being with "aids" often in the form of sensitive periods at each stage or plane, which cause the human being to focus his attention and energies on areas that are vital to his normal development at that particular point in his growth.

- These "sensitive periods" are part of the "laws of nature" and are placed there by nature to ensure the development and continuation of a sane and a healthy species.
- If we ignore, repress or remain ignorant of the "laws of nature" we do so at our peril, because the human being will construct himself incorrectly, possibly creating a monster instead of a man.

- Educators must match The Four Planes of Development with Four Planes of Education.

- The most important research for the benefit of mankind is the study of the "laws of nature" as they relate to each stage of the human being's development and the publication and dissemination of all findings.

13

HOW CAN WE BUILD A HUMAN BEING?

The answer is simple, we can't. Every human being must build himself. But here's what we can do, to help the human being to build himself.

Firstly, we need to make it our priority to understand:
- The purpose
- The goal
- The aim

of each particular plane of development. Then we must help the human being to:

- Fulfil that purpose
- Reach that goal
- Achieve that aim

In doing this, we are "aiding" the natural development of the human being so that he can grow and develop as nature intended and hopefully become everything he has the potential to be.

Secondly, we need to make it our priority to understand:

- The particular characteristics
- The particular needs
- The particular psychological drives

of each developmental stage.

Thirdly, we need to make it our priority to understand the particular obstacles which can be strewn across the pathway of the developing human being forcing him to go "off course".

Fourthly, we need to make it our priority to understand the "deviations" i.e. behaviour problems, that can arise as a result of the human being, being forced "off course" because of obstacles on his pathway.

Fifthly, we need to make it our priority to find out about nature's "remedy" i.e. (normalisation) for getting the human being "back on track" when he has been forced to deviate "off course" because of obstacles.

Sixthly, we must prepare tailor-made environments, which match, like a hand to a glove, the characteristics, needs and drives of the human being at each stage of his development. This is what education should be, "a help to life," an aid to human development. If it is less than this, then it is useless.

Montessori said,

"Either education contributes to a movement of universal liberation by showing the way to defend and raise humanity, or it becomes like one of those organs which have shrivelled up by not being used during the evolution of the organism." (The Formation of Man) p18

Finally, if we genuinely want to help the human being in the course of his construction, we must pay heed once again to Montessori's admonition:

"If we want to help life, the first condition of success is that we shall know the laws which govern it." (The Absorbent Mind) p13

But we must also pay heed to Montessori's warning that:

"It is not enough merely to know them, for if we stopped there, we should remain exclusively in the field of psychology. We should never go further and become educators." (The Absorbent Mind) p14

The developing human being needs "educators" not just psychologists. He needs adults who understand his characteristics, needs and drives and who also know how to prepare environments to match these characteristics, needs and drives.

The names we place on these environments are irrelevant. We can call them communities, schools or homes, it doesn't much matter. What matters is that they match the particular developmental characteristics, needs and drives of the human being at each specific stage of development.

It is our hope that this book will reveal to the reader, how Dr. Montessori, in her lifetime, created environments to match most of the planes of development and how we, in our generation should expand on this, if we are really serious about wanting to help in the building of the human being.

PART THREE

HOW DOES THE CHILD CONSTRUCT HIMSELF?

(The Years 0 to 6) (The Age of Absorption)

14

HOW DOES HE TAKE IT ALL IN?

(The Absorbent Mind)

We all begin life the same way, we are plunged from the safety and comfort of the womb, into this strange, noisy, dazzling world. We arrive with no language, no memory, no knowledge of the world that we have entered into.

It is not an easy experience for any of us and much has been written about the trauma of birth, but in general, we don't have mental breakdowns.

Instead, we immediately begin to adapt to our new environment. In three short years, we move from being fragile, helpless, crying, uncomprehending infants, to boisterous toddlers, able to walk and talk.

We are able to speak the language of our country with a perfect accent we are happy to eat with chopsticks, spoons, or our fingers according to the customs of our country.

By the age of six, we can think and reason. We can make decisions and choices. We now have a memory and a database of knowledge about our world.

By six years of age, we have come a long way from the helpless, crying infants we were at birth.

How does this amazing feat come about?

Montessori said it came about through nature's aid to the young child, a special type of mind, which only exists in the first six years of life.

She called it the "Absorbent Mind".

The Absorbent Mind.

From her observations of babies and young children all over the world, Dr. Maria Montessori was convinced that:

- All children, during the first six years of life, have a mind which is totally different to that of the adult's mind.

- It is a mind which possesses special powers or skills which help it to adapt to whatever world it finds itself in.

- Whether he is born in the Stone Age or the 21st century, whether he is born in a Third World culture or a modern city culture, the child has a mind which can adapt by simply absorbing the culture it finds itself in.

- It is a mind which can absorb without effort or fatigue, all that is there in the surrounding environment.

- Montessori identified two stages to this absorption of the environment:

    * An unconscious stage: (birth to 3 years)
    * A conscious stage: (three to 6 years)

- In the first stage, the child is not aware that he is doing anything, he simply takes in all that is around him.

- In the second stage, the child is very aware of what he is doing, his activities are deliberate and self chosen. He knows what he wants and he goes after it .

- The absorbent mind is not rigid, it is plastic i.e. it alters itself with each new experience. It is formed and reformed with every impression that impinges on it. Therefore the actual physiology of the brain is altered as the child interacts with his environment.

- The absorbent mind is short lived. It only lasts for the first six years of life.

THE UNCONSCIOUS ABSORBENT MIND (0-3 years)

Montessori became certain that from birth to about three years of age, the young child has an unconscious absorbent mind. This is a mind that is constantly taking in, or absorbing, every aspect of the surrounding environment simply by living in it. It is an effortless and an unconscious process.

The child is unaware that he is doing anything. Yet as he lies in his cot, or crawls around the room, he sees, hears, smells, touches and tastes, and begins to build up a picture of the world which surrounds him.

The example of language.

The most striking proof that the child possesses an absorbent mind lies in the way every child learns language. If an adult wishes to learn a language, he needs at least to have a dictionary, a grammar book, possibly a teacher and maybe even language tapes. He also needs to have one language to start with so that he can use one language as a vehicle for learning another, e.g. if he is learning French and his native language is English he can say 'lait' means milk, 'vin' means wine etc. The child, however, has no language to start with, he merely absorbs his native tongue by living in an environment where it is spoken. No parent has ever sat down with a grammar book in one arm and an infant in the other and said, "now baby, today we will learn verbs and tomorrow we will learn nouns." Yet the child learns to speak his language fluently and with a perfect accent.

Moreover, when the child starts to speak he doesn't make the sounds of washing machines or car engines or dogs or cats, he speaks human language. This is something we take for granted but it is an amazing feat of intelligence that the child is able to distinguish from the host of noises all around him what is language and what is background noise.

Montessori saw this as ample proof that the child possesses a mind equipped with a special built in skill for learning any language. This was many years before the American linguist, Noam Chomsky, put forward a similar theory calling it a Language Acquisition Device. (LAD).

Montessori pointed out that this skill disappears as the child approaches his sixth year and the absorbent mind slips away. Certainly, no adult can learn language the way the child does. It is well known that most adult emigrants to other countries always retain a foreign accent no matter how long they live in their adopted country.

The child's mind then, during this period from birth to 3 years, unconsciously soaks up whatever is there in his environment, whether it is good or bad, whether it is gentle or violent, whether it is damaging or up-lifting. The child's mind does not select or filter experiences, he just "takes it all in." As Montessori put it:

"The things he sees are not just remembered, they form part of his soul. He incarnates in himself all in the world about him that his eyes see and his ears hear. In us the same things produce no change, but the child is transformed by them."   (The Absorbent Mind p62)

THE CONSCIOUS ABSORBENT MIND (3-6 years)

"First, he takes in the world as a whole, then he analyses it."

The passing from the unconscious stage of the absorbent mind to the conscious stage is a gradual thing. The child does not wake up on his third birthday and suddenly act in a different way. However, from around 3 to 6 years, there is definitely a marked change in the way that the child approaches his environment.

New Mental Faculties Emerge:

From birth to 3 years as we have already stated, the child takes in the surrounding environment unconsciously, without ever being aware that he is doing anything. Now, as he approaches three years, certain faculties which have been quietly developing over the last few years come to the foreground,.

The reasoning faculties, and the will, combine with the child's growing language skills, so that, at around three years, the child seems suddenly to be able to bring into consciousness what his unconscious mind has already absorbed. So, as he handles a toy, turning it over and over, he goes over in his mind the impressions that he has previously absorbed unconsciously, e.g impressions of colour, shape, size, texture, etc and he begins to remember that the colour of the toy he is handling is the same colour he saw before, or the feel of the toy he is handling is the same as an object he felt some other day.

As he approaches three years and as his language develops he can put names on things and so begins to classify them and put them into categories.

Whereas at first, the world was one big, noisy, dazzling place with objects of all shapes and sizes which the child's mind merely absorbed, now the child begins to see that there are categories of colour, categories of shape, categories of people e.g. mommies, daddies, boys, girls, babies.

It is at this age that the child announces constantly, with great seriousness and excitement, "I'm a boy" or "I'm a girl" and "that's a girl over there," and "I'm a girl too". We often fail to realise why the child is so excited when he makes these announcements, but we need to understand that the child has just discovered, that he is now part of a category, the category of persons, and this is a matter of real excitement to him.

This classification and categorisation is now made possible by the fact that the child's memory, which has been developing slowly from birth to 3 years, is now sufficiently formed for him to remember, i.e. to call up in his mind, things that he has experienced before.

In a similar way, during the first three years, the reasoning faculties and the will have been quietly and slowly developing so that, at around three years, the child seems suddenly to be able to confront his environment in a deliberate and conscious fashion, in an effort to gain mastery of it.

He begins to select and pursue things which interest him in a very deliberate way.

He shows very definite preferences when it comes to activities, food, and even toys. He seems to know exactly what he wants, and when he decides he wants to do something he sets out intentionally and deliberately to do it.

His mind's ability to soak in every aspect of the environment, without effort and without fatigue is still there.

He can learn immense amounts of information rapidly and effortlessly. However, the child from 3 to 6 years, tends to be more active in his absorption of the environment now. He uses his hands all the time as vehicles for the transporting of knowledge and information from the environment to his brain. He does this by touching, feeling, examining and manipulating puzzles, learning materials, and ordinary everyday objects.

THE CONSTRUCTION OF THE MIND

How experiences shape the developing mind. (birth to 6 years)

The crucial point that Montessori made about the child's absorbent mind during both the unconscious and conscious periods of development, is its ability to be moulded and altered by experiences. She wrote:

"Impressions pour into us (adults) and we store them in our minds: but we ourselves remain apart from them, just as a vase keeps separate from the water it contains. Instead the child undergoes a transformation. Impressions do not merely enter his mind; they form it."   (The Absorbent Mind p25)

This is the crucial difference between the mind of a child in both the unconscious and conscious stages of development, and the mind of an adult. The child's mind does not just receive impressions and store them like the adult does. Instead the child's mind acts like a mechanism which can absorb impressions through the senses and then combine these impressions into itself altering itself as it does so.

Medical Science Proves Dr. Montessori Was Right.

When Dr Montessori first put forward these ideas of how the young child's mind was actually altered by experiences, she was accused by some of being unscientific and vague, but in reality, she was correct, and was, in fact, about 100 years ahead of her time. Nowadays, modern medicine has the technology to view the living brain in action and it shows that the actual physiology, in other words the structure of the brain IS altered as the child interacts with his environment, just as Montessori had said. With each new experience, the brain's neurological network is altered and expanded, or as Montessori put it:

"A kind of mental chemistry goes on within him.... The child creates his own "mental muscles", using for this what he finds in the world about him. We have named this type of mentality, The Absorbent Mind."

(The Absorbent Mind p25)

15

HOW DOES SHE KNOW WHAT TO FOCUS ON?

(Sensitive Periods in Development)

The Porthesia butterfly is a very interesting creature. It lays its eggs at the fork of the tree where the branches part from the trunk.

This is a concealed area of the tree, offering protection to the eggs from predators.

Unfortunately though, it is an area of the tree that has no leaves and therefore no food for the caterpillars which will soon hatch from these eggs.

To make matters worse, the caterpillars which will soon hatch from these eggs will be small and delicate with mouthparts so fragile that they will only be able to digestive young and tender leaves.

Now, the tree does have young and tender leaves, but, wouldn't you know it, they are growing at the very tips of the branches, at the furthest remove from the fork of the tree where the baby caterpillars are soon to hatch.

So, what's going to happen when these caterpillars hatch? Who will tell them where the delicate leaves that they so desperately need for their very survival are?

Well, nature has supplied the answer. As soon as these caterpillars are hatched, nature tells them "what to focus on."

Nature gives them a special sensitivity towards light. They are fascinated by light, attracted to it as if by an irresistible force.

As soon as they are hatched, they wriggle towards the light, driven by an uncontrollable impulse.

In doing so, they make their way from the rough bark, along the tree branches, until they come to the tips of the branches where the tender green new shoots grow that will give them all the nourishment that they so desperately need at this stage in their development. And so the feasting begins.

This in itself is amazing, but later, something even more amazing happens.

When the caterpillar becomes big and strong from feasting on the tender leaves and now has the ability to digest any kind of leaf, it suddenly loses its sensitivity to light, so it no longer follows the light and begins to nourish itself from the ample stores of tougher leaves that grow all over the tree.

Now, the disappearance of the sensitivity to light is just as vital to the caterpillar as its appearance was, because it allows the caterpillar to eat from the huge range of leaves that grow on the tree, something that is now vital for its survival as an older caterpillar.

These amazing facts were discovered by the Dutch biologist Hugo De Vries. He called the caterpillar's sensitivity to light, a sensitive period in development.

He interpreted sensitive periods as temporary phases in development when nature draws the creature's attention to something that is vital to his survival and healthy development at a particular time, but which wanes and fizzles out when the creature has outgrown this vital need, never to appear again.

From her observations of children, Dr. Maria Montessori became convinced that exactly the same phenomenon is going on in human life and is particularly crucial during the period birth to 6 years.

Her observations convinced her that just as in the case of the caterpillar, the construction of the human child, birth to 6 years is not left to chance, but is a process watched over vigilantly by nature and guided by invisible but very real forces of nature which tell the child "what to focus on" and direct the child towards areas that are vital for his normal development.

Montessori was invited by Hugo De Vries to borrow his term sensitive periods in development to describe the phenomenon that she was discovering in young children.

Montessori defined sensitive periods as:

Critical periods.
Montessori recognised that sensitive periods are blocks of time in a child's life when nature directs him to focus his attention on areas that are vital, crucial and indispensable to his normal development.

Temporary phases.
Montessori saw that sensitive periods are temporary. They last for a specific period only. When nature reckons that the child has been given adequate time to focus his attention on the vital area, the sensitive period starts to wane and then fizzles out.

Windows of opportunity.
Montessori saw that sensitive periods provide the child with windows of opportunity for learning because during each of the sensitive periods the child experiences an intense and extraordinary interest in the area that nature directs him to focus on. As a result of this extraordinary interest, the child is able to focus so completely on a particular area that he can reach levels of concentration and skill that are truly astonishing.

Montessori was the first to recognise the educational value of sensitive periods. She quickly saw the importance of making use of the child's sensitive periods for educational purposes, because the child will never again experience the level of interest, concentration or devotion to a specific area that he experiences while under the influence of a sensitive period in development.

Montessori identified six sensitive periods in development, taking place during the first stage of development birth to 6 years. These are:

- A sensitive period for order.

- A sensitive period for language.

- A sensitive period for movement.

- A sensitive period for learning through the senses.

- A sensitive period for the social aspects of life.

- A sensitive period for small objects or details.

"Don't Mess With My Map".

(The Sensitive Period for Order)

- Jason is three years old. Every day his aunt Jenny brings him to preschool and his mummy collects him. He loves both of them dearly.

  Today his mummy got unexpectedly delayed and she sent his aunt Jenny to collect him.

  Jason's response: he took one look at his aunt and burst into tears saying " no, mummy has to come, not auntie Jenny."

  It took over 10 minutes for auntie Jenny to persuade him to go with her. He eventually left, tearful and upset still saying "mummy has to come, not auntie Jenny."

- Maria is 18 months old. Every day her mummy turns right at the traffic lights en route to her big brother's school.

  Today, the road is being dug up and mummy has to follow a detour to the left and go a different way to the school.

  Maria is frantic her car seat. She keeps pointing out the window sobbing "this way, this way." She will not even listen to mummy's attempt to explain why there is a detour.

- Mark is 12 months old. His parents get the chance of a cheap mid week break in a five star hotel. They pack up the car, put Mark into his baby seat and off they go.

  First night, Mark is very unsettled. Second night, Mark is so fretful, they believe he must be ill. They call a doctor. The doctor can't find anything physically wrong with Mark. Next day, his condition worsens.

  Finally, the couple decide to go back home and take Mark to their own doctor. They arrive home late at night. They put Mark in his cot, in his bedroom. He opens his tearstained eyes and looks around. Suddenly all the crying stops. He squeals with excitement and then falls into a deep sleep.

  Next morning, no need for a doctor, Mark is fine.

These stories, and one could relate hundreds more, reveal something about the young child that is of crucial importance. The young child from birth to 6 years, has a need for order and routine that the average adult cannot even begin to understand. This need for routine, for things to always happen in the same way is so strong that for most young children, lack of it brings upset and tears and for many, lack of it brings severe distress to the point of illness. It is an area of child development that has been under explained by most experts with just a chapter or two on the importance of routine for young children, but without any attempt to explain why routine is so crucial to the young child.

Montessori was very interested in the why. Why does the young child gets so upset when the order of events is changed? Why does he try to hold onto sameness. Why does he want events to happen in the exact same sequence each day? Clearly, order and routine mean something very different to the child than they do to the adult.

What Order means to the Adult VERSUS What Order means to the Child.

For the adult, order is merely a pleasant thing. We like a bit of routine, a bit of structure. However, if a routine has to be changed, it doesn't threaten our whole sense of well-being. We don't burst into tears, scream or have a tantrum. (Well, most of us don't!)

The reason, we as adults, can deal with a certain amount of change, is because we've already established our understanding of the world. We are not trying to build up a concept of what life on planet Earth is all about. We've already done this in our own early childhood.

For the child, order is vital. It is as important as food and drink. Why? Because the child has not been on the earth before. He doesn't know what anyone or anything is. From the moment of birth, he tries to orient himself, i.e. he tries to build up a picture in his mind of where he is and what goes on each day. He begins to make up a kind of map in which he starts to place landmarks. This map is unique to every child. His landmarks are things like:

This is my mummy, she always feed me:

This is my bedroom, I always sleep here:

This is my playroom, I always play here:

Naturally, if someone starts to move the landmarks, i.e. to change the order and routines that he has struggled to pin down, the child is bound to become confused and upset, and hence the screams, cries and hysterical outbursts so common in one, two and three year olds.

Psychologists call these outbursts tantrums, as if they were just naughty behaviours on the part of young children caused by some immature wilfulness. Montessori says the psychologists are wrong. These outbursts happen when the child is literally crying out for order, crying out for the landmarks which he has struggled to pin down, to be kept in place.

Appreciating The Child's Vital Need for Order.

As adults, it is very difficult for us to really appreciate the child's vital need for order because:

- We have forgotten what it was like when we were very young and the world seemed like a great big jumbled up jigsaw puzzle.

- We have forgotten how we went around each day trying to put the pieces of that great big, muddled, jigsaw puzzle together.

- We have forgotten how happy and contented we were when the pieces started to fit together, when we began to see patterns, themes, structures, order, rather than chaos.

- We have forgotten how utterly devastated we were when for no apparent reason, the patterns, routines and structures that we had just gotten used to, were changed.

What Is Nature Trying To Do During the Sensitive Period for Order?

Well, let's think about that caterpillar again. Why does the caterpillar have an irresistible attraction towards the light? Because it leads him to something vital for his survival, i.e. food. It is not the light he needs but the food which the light leads him to.

In the same way, Montessori was convinced that nature programs a young child to focus on order, patterns, routines and sequences in his daily life in order to lead him towards something that is vital for his survival. What is this? It is the orderly construction of his mind, healthy brain development, that is the vital thing that nature is urging the child towards because everything else hinges on this.

Remember Montessori pointed out that the child is born incomplete. His first task is to construct his own mind and he constructs his mind from what he finds in his immediate surroundings. If his surroundings are chaotic, he will construct a chaotic mind. If his surroundings are ordered, he will construct an ordered mind.

Montessori was convinced that nature hovers vigilantly over her charges. She needs the child to construct a healthy sane mind and so she directs him to look for order because it is vital to his normal healthy development, and his normal development is vital for the continuation of a healthy, normal, sane species.

Why and When Does the Sensitive Period for Order Fizzle Out?

When nature reckons that the child has been given enough time firstly to build up a picture of his external world, and secondly to construct his mind into a structure strong enough to build on, nature withdraws and causes the powerful sensitivity to order to wane and eventually fizzle out, so that the child is no longer frantic about changes in routine. This happens around four or five years of age.

Where does the child look for order? The short answer is everywhere. He is programmed by nature to search for order everywhere. Close observation of the young child shows that he is:

- Crying out for order in the family unit: parenting

- Searching for order in the home: routines .

- Looking for order in the school: structure.

Practical Points.

How can we help the child who is going through a sensitive period for order and routine?

- Try to make his daily life an ordered one. Try to have regular times for meals baths, sleep etc.

- Try to keep household objects such as furniture, clothes and toys in the same place from day to day.

- Try not to pass the child from one minder to another.

- If some upheaval is necessary and unavoidable such is moving house, going on holiday, a parent returning to work etc. be patient and sympathetic with the child. Remember, what the adult sees as a happy event e.g. a foreign holiday, may simply mean an uncomfortable change of routine for the child.

- The sensitive period for order and routine starts just after birth, peaks at two years and subsides around four or five years of age.

"He Never Misses a Trick".

(The Sensitive Period for Noticing Small Objects/Small Details)

The best way to explain this sensitive period is by giving a few examples.

Scenario one.

You have a two-year-old child sitting beside you as you leaf through a big, colourful book, full of illustrations of large elephants, tall giraffes and fat hippos. But, instead of noticing the huge bright, orange tiger, the child starts asking you about the "lollipop". You eventually notice, after you've used your magnifying glass, that at the bottom of the page, over in the corner, is a tiny girl, crying because she's dropped her even tinier lollipop. This, not the huge tiger, is what the child is interested in.

Scenario two.

You've just paid a fairly hefty price to go into the Pet Farm with your three year old child. There are all sorts of animals in pens there which your child has seen pictures of at the entrance door. However, you can't get your child to budge beyond the entrance. Why? Because just inside the entrance gate, your child has noticed something moving on the ground. It is an anthill. Tiny little ants are scurrying around, up and down a mound of earth. Now, your child is down on all fours, watching the antics of the ants and he won't budge any further. The tiny creatures fascinate him and he can't even hear your requests to move on to the "real" animals.

Explaining what lies beneath the child's interest in small details.

What is the reason for the child's preoccupation with and interest in small objects and small details? The answer lies in nature. The young child's tendency to notice small objects and small details is something placed in him by nature to ensure that every child learns two essential skills: - (i) to focus and concentrate and (ii) to pay close attention.

Learning to focus and concentrate:
Perhaps the most important fact about the sensitive period for small detail is that unknown to the child, this preoccupation with small objects and small details teaches him how to concentrate. A child will sit for long periods watching a small caterpillar crawling along a leaf or a spider weaving a web, and will be

totally absorbed when doing this, unaware that he is building up his skills of concentration, attention and ability to focus all at the same time.

Concentration is the key requirement for all learning. So nature had to find a way of teaching the child to focus, to be still, to give all his attention to something, and this is achieved through the sensitive period for noticing small objects and small details.

Learning to pay close attention:
Another important fact about the sensitive period for noticing small objects and small details is that the child learns to pay close attention to the world around him by not just looking at the big, gaudy, loud things which jump out at him, but by looking at the small, seemingly insignificant things which are often so important.

Small details form a necessary part of everyday actions. So, in order that the child might learn even intricate skills, nature draws his attention to small details. In other words, by following small, detailed steps, a child can learn such complex things as:

- The grammar of a language.

- The sequence of steps needed to walk, feed oneself, dress oneself, etc.

Practical Points.

How can we help a child during the sensitive period for small details?

- Give the child jigsaw puzzles which depict small details e.g. a park scene where many different things are happening, i.e. a girl on a swing, a boy dropping his ice cream, a mother giving a baby his bottle etc. As a general rule do not give puzzles with one large object and no activities going on. A puzzle with several diverse activities going on simultaneously seems to better captivate a child who is going through this sensitive period.

- Use the child's interest in small details to teach him the things he wants to learn, such as how to do his buttons, his zips, his buckles and how to lace his shoes.

- This sensitive period starts at about two years and ends at about four years, but his may differ from child to child.

"Why Won't He Just Sit Still?"

(The Sensitive Period for Perfecting Dexterity of Movement)

When our youngest child was about two years old we took her on her first trip to the zoo. We were in the zoo for more than half an hour and still had not seen any animals. Why? Because, just inside the entrance, there was a set of steps leading from one level of the zoo to another and these were the first things to catch our youngster's eye when we entered. She climbed up and down the twenty or more steps over and over again. She had eyes for nothing else. With great intensity and seriousness she climbed up and down the steps muttering to herself "I'm nearly there," "up another bit," and then, "now back down again." Our six year old son who was with us was becoming very bored waiting for her to move on. He had gone up and down the steps also but was bored after one or two rounds. He tried to entice her away from the steps with the promise of ice cream at a nearby stall. But no, she could not be tempted, not even by the promise of her favourite food, so great was the pleasure she was deriving from climbing up and down the steps. Eventually, feeling the need to do something to get her to move along, we made a suggestion. We suggested that if we moved on we might find more steps further along. Our two-year-old thought carefully about this suggestion, and replied, " yes, that's a great idea, one more turn here and then we'll go". True to her word, she had one more trip up and down the steps, and then she beamed at us and said, "let's go find more steps, then we be so happy."

A common tale:
Many parents have told us similar stories. In her book, The Secret of Childhood, Dr. Montessori gives examples of two and three-year-olds she knew personally who would spend over an hour just going up and down steps, or walking along low walls. Similarly, toddlers from 18 months onwards often walk distances of over a mile and clearly derive great joy from the exercise and do not get tired by it.

Working through a Sensitive Period is not tiring, but energising:
Over the years, we have seen children of three and four years of age, who had become so fascinated by the hand dexterity needed for writing letters of the alphabet, that once they started writing the letters, they wouldn't stop. We can remember many children of less than four years who, on various different occasions, wrote over twenty sheets of alphabetical letters in one sitting, for the sheer pleasure of perfecting their movements. When finished they showed no signs of tiredness, but rather seemed energised and full of joy.

The interesting point about these children was that, at this time, they showed no interest in writing actual words, nor did they show any interest in reading words, it was the sheer joy of perfecting their hand movements when writing individual letters that gripped them.

Explanation:
Why is this? The answer lies in the sensitive period for the coordination or the perfection of movements. Here again, nature urges the child to repeat these exercises in order to perfect his physical dexterity.

Sensitive periods don't last long:
This sensitive period is a transient, temporary phase. It begins immediately after the child learns to walk and continues until the child is about four years old. Then it disappears and never returns again. Long walks now become a bore and writing pages and pages of alphabetical letters becomes a chore, not entered into lightly. Older children will, of course climb and walk but not with the repetition and intensity of a child who is going through this sensitive period for coordination of movement.

Practical Points.

How can we help the child who is going through the sensitive period for perfecting dexterity of movement?

- Let the child take you for a walk. Go where he goes. Walk at his pace. Slow down with him when he stops to examine stones or bugs.

- Where possible, allow the child to repeat his movements, even if this means standing by while he climbs up and down steps twenty times over. It may bore you but it gives the child an inner joy and satisfaction as he responds to nature's urging to perfect his physical movements.

- Remember that this is a temporary, passing phase which ends when the child is about four years old.

"Could You Pass The Caviar Please Jeeves?"

(The Sensitive Period for the Social Aspects of life)

Many years ago I had an acquaintance who was very brilliant academically but who felt very inept socially to the extent that he avoided social gatherings because he was always afraid that he wouldn't use the correct knife or fork, or would make some faux pas which would expose his lack of social graces. Despite his superior intellect, he found it very difficult to overcome this problem.

Montessori discovered that there is a period in life when it is easiest for us to learn the social graces of our particular culture. She called this the sensitive period for the social aspects of life.

Around three years of age, the child, without any prodding from anyone, becomes very interested in social customs and habits. He wants to learn how to greet others. He looks for opportunities to shake hands, to say hello, to say goodbye, to say please and thank you, to say pardon me, to say excuse me, sorry for interrupting you etc. He also becomes very interested in manners and meal-time customs. It is a stage when young children begin to model themselves on adult behaviour.

Now, if that was all there was to it, it really wouldn't be much of a sensitive period. However, its real significance is huge. Montessori recommended that we should use this "window of opportunity" to teach children, not just how to meet and greet, not just how to say please and thank you, but, in effect, how to treat other people with respect and kindness.

So, through the Montessori lessons of "grace and courtesy," by teaching the child the "physical action" of stepping aside to allow someone to pass by, or the physical action of closing the door quietly so as not to deafen someone, we are, in effect, ingraining in his "procedural memory" the "know how"of how to show respect and kindness to others. We are teaching him how to treat others as he would wish to be treated.

Now, what does all this mean? Well, it means that we are laying the bedrock for preventing: bullying in childhood, bullying and cyber bullying in adolescence and bullying in the workplace in adulthood.

It has already been proven scientifically, by the research of Dr Angeline Lillard, published in science magazine (2006), that Montessori schools have significantly less "ambiguous rough play" (i.e aggression) than non-Montessori schools.

This is most likely because of the emphasis on the "exercises of grace and courtesy" which take place in authentic Montessori schools. These are very different from the constant admonitions to "share," "be nice," etc that most playschools dish out to the children in their care. These are very well thought out physical exercises which help a child to learn how to treat others. Now the really significant point about these "exercises of grace and courtesy" that has never really been fully understood by most people, teachers included, is that by making these exercises "physical actions" rather than just "admonitions" they become part of the child's "procedural memory", i.e the "knowing how" memory. This is very important because current research on memory suggests that procedural memory actually forms a person's "character".

The basis of this theory is that the physical learning of certain behaviours or responses causes them to become unconscious, automatic behaviours and responses, which become so "hard-wired" into our psyches that it very difficult to change them. They become "who we are." In the Montessori class these "exercises" are not rules. The child can choose to carry out these exercises or not. But the social atmosphere in the classroom encourages him to carry them out.

The fact is, when children are exposed daily to opportunities to "physically" show kindness, respect, and courtesy to others (e.g by closing a door quietly) during this period between two and six years, when they are most open to it, something significant happens in their personalities. These children, as Dr. Lillard's research shows are much less likely to engage in negative or bullying behaviour towards others.

So, anyone who thinks that the sensitive period for the social aspects of life is only about 'could you pass the caviar please Jeeves' is missing the point. The point is, nature has, once again, placed a protective element, in the species, an anti-bullying element you might say, and it is precisely this - the sensitive period for the social aspects of life.

Imagine a world where bullying didn't exist, where people were respected and people treated others as they would wish to be treated. It seems unimaginable. Yet nature, hovering vigilantly over the human being, has placed this sensitive period in all of us during the tender years of approximately 2 to 6, in order to give us a window of opportunity to learn to be kind to our fellow man.

In this era of mass bullying, can we really afford to be ignorant about the aim and the potential of this hugely important sensitive period in development?

Practical Points.

How can we help a child who is going through the sensitive period for the social aspects of life?

- Give the child, as much as possible, a varied and balanced social life. Don't restrict the child to the company of children of the same age, let him spend time with older children, and adults.

- Be aware of your own behaviour, as the child will model his social behaviour on yours.

- Always be as courteous to a child as you would be to an adult.

- Teach the child through "physical" actions how to treat other people with respect and consideration. Teach him how to say please, thank you etc (but do not force him to use the phrases). Teach the child how to greet people so he knows what to say when he wants to greet someone.

- This sensitive period starts at about two years of age and ends at about five years of age.

"Why Does He Never Stop Talking?"

(The Sensitive Period for Language)

The sensitive period for the acquisition of language is the longest of the sensitive periods. It starts at birth and remains in a heightened state of alert until about age 6 years. During this time, nature tunes the baby's ear towards the human voice and language, so that between birth and six years, the child will move from a silent creature who knows no language, to a fluent speaker of either Chinese, Russian, English, French, Romanian, Arabic, or whatever the native language is that surrounds the child. The child has the capacity to learn any language, he merely needs to be exposed to that language during the first six years of life.

The Process:

From infancy, the baby will focus his attention on his mother's mouth as she speaks to him. He'll watch and eventually mimic the movements made by her mouth and lips as she speaks and he'll listen to the sounds made by these "facial gymnastics". As time goes on he 'internalises' these gestures. This simply means, that something goes on internally within the child's mind, something we can't see where the child works out what's going on, works out the connection between these funny grimaces we make with our mouths and these sounds that we emit. After a period of "internalisation" (i.e. little conferences going on in the child's head), little signs begin to appear of the new skill that's being acquired i.e. language. A few ga ga 's and gu gu 's appear. The sensitive period is doing its job. It is focusing the child's attention on a specific area i.e. language, in order that a new skill may be acquired. Gradually, the child begins to speak words, short sentences, language. He picks up the sounds, the phonemes, the intonations, the nuances, the dialect of his mother tongue.

Without any formal lessons, he learns, sentence structure, syntax and basic grammatical structures. There will be more to learn and perfect as the years go by, but in essence, during the first six years of life, the child becomes a fluent speaker of his native tongue.

Exposure to language is essential:

The child must be exposed to language during this sensitive period for language development or it will not develop at all. Montessori was very aware of the story of the wild boy of Aveyron, a child about 12 years old, who was found wandering in the forest of Aveyron in France. It would appear that he had been abandoned from infancy. He was brought to Dr Itard, the famous French physician who was a great influence on Maria Montessori. Dr Itard managed to civilise the boy in many ways, taking him from his wild animal state to that of a human being, but regrettably, he could not teach him language. Dr Itard, had to accept that the boy had passed the critical or sensitive period when the brain can construct language.

More recent examples of language deprivation in childhood have emerged in recent years. There is the horrific case of Genie and the terrible examples of orphans and abandoned "feral" children in various parts of the world. The results are still the same. If a child is not exposed to language, during the critical period when the brain constructs speech, language cannot be acquired.

Thankfully, these extreme cases of language deprivation are relatively rare and nature provides a long window of opportunity for language development so that most children are almost certain to be given the opportunity for their language skills to be stimulated and developed.

Practical Points.

How can we help a child who is going through a sensitive period for language?

- Talk to the child in clear, correct language, not baby talk. Point out things to him and call them by their correct names.

- Take your child with you as much as possible so that the child will hear other people talking to you.

- Describe to your child what is happening, for example, say things like, "Here we are at the supermarket". "Now I'm going to peel the potatoes." etc.

- Sing rhymes and songs to your child.

- Read books to your child and point to the various pictures while saying the corresponding words.

- This sensitive period starts at birth and ends at about six years of age.

"Why Must He Poke And Prod Everything?"

(The Sensitive Period for Learning through the Senses)

"Don't touch."
"Put that back."
"Leave that alone."
"Stop shaking that bottle."
"Don't squish those marshmallows."

Walk down a supermarket aisle any day of the week and you will hear similar admonitions, coming from fraught, demented mothers, trying to weave their trolleys through the aisles as their octopus-like two or three year old tries to touch, feel, squeeze, shake and possibly "sample" everything within reach.

It's a trying time. Our own son has left us with many thrilling memories! This is what Montessori described as a sensitive period for learning through the senses. What a parent needs to know is that during this period of time, nature itself urges the child to explore everything with his five senses. This is nature's plan to help the child to develop his knowledge of the world around him. So, what does this mean in practice. Well, it means that the child feels the need to examine everything. He feels the need to shake, bang, squeeze, poke, pull, push, lick, chew, throw, and otherwise investigate the objects around him. During this period of time, the child's five senses i.e. touch, taste, smell, hearing, sight, are in a heightened state. (So are your nerves!)

Practical Points:

- Provide the child with a rich variety of sensory objects which he can touch and smell. Baskets of fabrics and natural materials are a good idea, as are stones, leaves, shells, pinecones, acorns etc.

- Offer the child opportunities to play with water, sand and play-dough.

- Invent games where children can shut their eyes and feel and identify sensory objects. Invent games for listening and naming objects in the environment.

- Try not to say "don't touch" all the time.

- Put dangerous objects out of reach.

- This temporary phase starts at birth and ends around age five or six years.

16

WHY ARE THEY SO SELF-OBSESSED?

(Self-Construction in Early Childhood)

"I'm going to be an astronaut".
"I'm going to be a ballerina".
"I'm going to be a tight rope walker".

One of the joys of working with little children is to be every day in the company of people who are filled with excitement, with expectancy, with the knowledge that each day they are becoming more and more able, more and more accomplished.

Young children are not concerned about world events, they don't interest themselves in tsunamis, earthquakes, or the price of oil. All they know about is what they feel inside, a burning passion to construct themselves, to build themselves, to develop their own little hands, to strengthen their own little legs, to build their own bodies and their own brains by undertaking more and more challenging tasks.

All day long you hear them say:

"Look at me."

"See how fast I can run."

"See how high I can jump."

The young child can hardly sleep with excitement about his accomplishments. His brain is buzzing with the thrill of it all.

When he's asleep, he often tosses and turns, no doubt thinking about all he is achieving. When he awakes, he dives out of bed looking for more challenges, maybe it's a banister rail to slide down, or a ladder to climb up!

Now, what Montessori observed, as she worked with children all over the world, was that, during the period birth to 6 years, the child is completely focused on himself, as an individual. He is not inclined to say

"See how high we can jump" or

"See how fast we can run."

The concept of "we" is alien to him at this period of life. Something seems to tell him that this period of life is all about his skills, his achievements, his accomplishments, his individuality. What others can do doesn't really interest him.

Modern child experts often refer to this self-centred characteristic in young children by stating things like:

"The young child is very egocentric"

and then they go on to give us techniques on how to get him out of this egocentric disposition. One thing they never attempt to explain is why the young child is so self-absorbed.

Montessori was very interested in the why. When she witnessed this egocentric characteristic in children, all over the world, she became convinced that there must be a purpose for it, and that we, as adults, need to understand what this purpose is, in order to help and support the young child.

So the big question is, "why is the young child so obsessed with himself as an individual?"

The answer, Montessori said, is simple. Nature has planned it this way for a very specific reason, and the reason is this:

The human being needs to develop as an individual first and a social being second.

Let's say that again. The human being needs to develop as an individual first and a social being second.

Nature, in her wisdom, has planned it that the young child should focus on himself as an individual during the years birth to six, focus on the attainment of his skills, the mastery of his abilities, in order to aid him in his task of self construction.

This is a law of nature.

And as nature urges the child to develop his skills, strengthen his muscles, construct his brain, he cannot help but be self-focused, self-obsessed, self-centred. There is no way around this.

Now, if this was a permanent state of affairs it would be disastrous. The world would be filled with millions of self-obsessed human beings.

We would have no society, just countless throngs of self-absorbed creatures. But, it is not permanent. It is a temporary period with a specific aim and that is, to aid the self construction of the human being into a unique individual. After the first six years it declines. Why?

Montessori, with incredible insight, tells us why. Society is made up of individuals and a society is therefore only as strong as the individuals who compose it.

It is necessary therefore for the child to be given the chance to develop himself as a strong, capable, independent individual before he comes forward to offer himself, in adulthood, to society, with something to contribute to the group as a whole.

Nature needs to ensure that the child builds his unique individual self to the best of his ability, because the next planes of development will stand or fall depending on how strong the foundation plane is.

So what is the result of all this self-centred activity? Does the child at six years of age show himself to be a selfish, self-obsessed individual?

Absolutely not. Indeed quite the opposite happens if the child is allowed to develop as nature intended..

In the space of six short years, the child will manage to construct himself from being a helpless, dependent infant, into a strong, capable individual who is independent, capable of communicating, capable of performing practical and intelligent tasks, capable of making decisions and choices, someone with a sense of who he is, someone who is strong in character.

In fact, we end up with the person that nature intended, a child that is strong, fair-minded, kind, well-balanced, confident, unafraid, happy, joyful and ready to move smoothly into the next plane of development, bringing him closer and closer to the social man, the man who has the capacity to take humanity forward into the next generation.

But for now, nature has planned it that the young child should use these first six years of life to build his unique self, so that at a later period of life he will have something to offer to the group.

This, according to Montessori, is nature's plan for the first plane of development, the construction of the human individual, not the social man, that is the task of a later period of life, a later plane of development.

17

WHY WON'T SHE DO IT THE EASY WAY?

(The Law of Work)

When our first child was just a toddler, about 12 or 18 months old, her favourite activity was to carry a very large, heavy, cardboard box of disposable nappies from one end of the room to the other.

In those days, long, long ago, they didn't do compact boxes. The box was as big as the child herself. So she would puff and pant as she half carried, half dragged the heavy box across the room.

When she eventually reached the other side of the room, she would rest for a few moments and then, without further ado, lift up the heavy box and begin the whole process all over again, puffing and panting her way to the other side of the room until she was right back where she had started from.

We lost count of how many times she did this in an evening. (By the way, we did buy her toys! But this game captivated her more than the toys).

Now, whenever visitors came and witnessed this nappy box activity they always responded same way.

They would notice the child's struggle with the big box, rush over to her, take the heavy box out of her arms and carry it for her over to the other side of the room, saying something like "there you go, my love," clearly thinking that they had done her a great favour .

Our child, always responded in the same way. She would burst into tears and try to push the visitor away from the box, making it clear that the favour had not been appreciated.

The visitor was always left embarrassed, hurt and confused and was always at a loss to understand what had gone wrong. Well, what had gone wrong?

The answer is simple. The visitor had completely misunderstood the child's motive. The visitor assumed that the whole point of the exercise was to put the heavy box on the other side of the room, the end result, if you will.

However, for the child, the whole point of the activity was the process itself not the end result. The point of the activity was the struggle, the effort, the challenge or what Montessori called "the law of work."

Understanding That Work is a Vital Instinct.

Why? We may well ask, does the child feel this irresistible urge towards work? Why does he feel this urge to struggle, to put himself through such huge effort and exertion?

The answer, according to Montessori is simple. The urge to seek work i.e. challenging activity, is a human tendency, something in our DNA, something that separates us and marks us out from other species, something that is essentially human. She called it a vital instinct, the characteristic instinct of the human species. She discovered that it is a universal phenomenon among human beings. So, just like Robinson Crusoe, if we were stranded on a desert island, one of the first things we would do, is try to create meaningful work for ourselves.

Montessori discovered that human tendencies are placed in us by nature for a specific purpose and this urge to work, to exert effort, is no exception to the rule. So now we must pose the question: what is the specific purpose of this urge to work?

Discovering That The Child Builds Himself Through Work.

Montessori discovered that the specific purpose of this urge towards work is self-construction. The child builds himself through work. He deliberately chooses hard work because nature tells him that this is how he builds himself, this is how he develops his own dexterity, coordination, balance, strength, endurance, character.

In short, this is how the child builds the man, the adult he is to be. Nature is practical. Society needs adult human beings who are skilful, capable and strong.

But it is not just dexterity and strength that are built up by work, it is also the very personality, the very character of the human being which is built up by work.

Montessori discovered that without work, i.e. meaningful, challenging activity, the human personality cannot organise itself normally and so it deviates from what she called the normal lines of construction.

She discovered that something very sinister and very destructive happens to the human being if he is deprived of work i.e. challenging activity at the period when he most needs it. (See section 20 on "Deviations from Normal Development".)

Recognising That The Child Is Always Looking for Work.

Even a few moments of observation of the small child will reveal to you that he is always looking for work, something challenging to do. He cannot stay idle.

It is as if mother nature is constantly whispering in his ear, encouraging him to use his surroundings to create challenging activities in order to build himself. Indeed the whispering is so strong and so compelling that he risks a telling off or worse for climbing on chairs, jumping off sofas, sliding down banisters in an effort to build himself.

Recently, I was sitting in a popular fast food outlet with some of my family. At the table opposite us, a mother sat her two children down. They were, a boy about six years old and a girl about four years old. With a wag of her finger, she warned them not to move while she joined the queue to get "happy meals".

Within minutes, the young boy, like a marine on a mission, indicated through hand signals to his little sister his intention to stand up on the seat and peep through the partition wall above their heads to see if he could spy on mummy without her seeing him. He stealthily carried out his mission. He was successful. Now, with more hand signals, he helped his little sister to do the same.

The queue was long. For nearly ten minutes the children played a skilful game of standing up on their seats, peeping through the partition and darting back down into their seats again. The young boy's kindness and helpfulness to his little sister was remarkable. So was their skilfulness, speed and precision of movement. I don't believe I could have done what they were doing without being caught. I was fascinated by them. I couldn't take my eyes off them.

However, all good things must come to an end. Mother arrived with a tray of food, caught a glimpse of movement, slammed the tray down on the table and with scary wagging of the finger in front of nervous faces, snapped out a lecture about unacceptable behaviour etc. etc. etc.

The children, with bowed heads and subdued faces, ate their not so very "happy meals".

Look around you and you'll see this scenario played out every minute of every day. The adult has no idea that the child is always looking for challenging activity, because nature is telling him to do this, and so the adult is affronted, threatened, completely thrown by the child's constant urge to do something.

When I was leaving the outlet, I felt compelled to go over to the mother and briefly speak to her. I told her that she had two beautiful children and that they were everything that children should be. Her eyes filled with tears and she thanked me.

What a pity that the general public doesn't know that the child is always looking for work.

Outdoors, the story is the same. If there is a stone on the pavement, the child will try to kick it and direct it to a particular spot or goal.

If he is near a hill, he will try to run up to the highest point. If he walks past a low wall, he will try to walk along it, attempting to balance, sometimes on one foot. If there is a shortcut across the grass verge, he will opt for the longer path.

In all his actions, he looks for challenge, he searches for difficulty, he follows the law of maximum effort.

He does these things instinctively. No one asks him to struggle but he opts to struggle, because nature whispers to him "look for work."

Looking At The Child's Attitude Towards Work.

Clearly the child has a different attitude towards work to that of the adult. Recently, I watched a 3 year old carrying out the job of replacing five jigsaw puzzles, which had been all muddled up, back into their slim, wooden box. First he painstakingly completed each puzzle on his table. Then he took each puzzle one at a time and replaced them, piece by piece into the box. He stacked each completed puzzle on top of another so that they all fitted neatly back into the slim, wooden box. He then replaced the sliding lid and sat staring at the box for a few seconds with a look of pleasure and satisfaction, whispering to himself "all done, all tidy."

Then, without further comment, he slid off the lid, poured out all the jigsaw puzzles onto the table and said "Again, me do it again."

He then proceeded to do the whole activity all over again.

If any adult did this, I feel sure it would raise questions about his sanity. When an adult goes to the trouble of carefully tidying something up, he certainly does not undo the task seconds later with the comment "I'll do it again."

If we observe children, freely at work, we will witness them constantly carrying out painstakingly careful tasks, only to undo everything minutes later and start the whole process all over again. It is only by observing the child freely and without interruption as he carries out his tasks that we learn something about the child's attitude towards work, and it becomes clear that the child's attitude towards work is very different to that of the adult.

Comparing The Child's Work To The Adult's Work.

Goals:

The adult works to get the job done. If the adult had tidied up the five puzzles in the scenario above, he would have put the tidied box back on the shelf and left it there. He certainly would not have poured out the puzzles and done the task all over again.

The child works for the process. His aim, though he is not consciously aware of this, is the perfection of skills and the development of character. So nature urges him to repeat tasks over and over so that he develops precision, exactitude, order.

- The adult's goal when he works is short term.
  He aims to get the job done.

- The child's goal when he works is long term.
  He aims to build skills and character.

Attitude:

The adult looks for ways to make his work easier. If the adult had the task of tidying up the five puzzles in the scenario above he would welcome help from someone to make his work easier i.e. he would willingly share his work. The child however cannot share his work because his unconscious aim is to perfect himself through work. Therefore he feels compelled to do the work unaided.

- The adult's attitude to work encourages him to share the task.

- The child's attitude to work discourages him from sharing the task.

Tempo:

The adult does the job as fast as he can to get it over with. He doesn't drag out the job. However, the child works at a leisurely pace as he relishes the process of the work.

One of the best examples one can give here is hand washing. Observe an adult and a child washing their hands and all will be revealed. The adult washes, dries and is finished. The child, if he is left alone and not interrupted will leisurely relish the feeling of the water on his hands, the soap between his little fingers, the squishy sounds of the two soapy hands when rubbed together, the spectacle of small bubbles filled with colours as the light catches them, emanating from the movements of the two soapy hands. Indeed hand washing is a favourite activity among two and three year olds, often selected in preference to play with toys. A young child could spend 20 minutes washing his hands, an adult will spend 20 seconds.

- The adult's tempo at work is fast and efficient.

- The child's tempo at work is slow and leisurely.

Reward:

The adult often finds work to be a burden, he only does it for financial reward. The child finds work to be a pleasure, because he does it in response to nature's prompting, it is an inner need. He is supremely happy when he is allowed to just work away at his own choosing. The work is its own reward.

- The adult looks for rewards for his work.

- The child finds work to be a reward in itself.

Understanding What Work Does For The Child.

Here is a summary of what work i.e. meaningful activity actually does for the child.

- The child builds himself through work
- Work develops skills
- Work builds character
- Work develops patience
- Work promotes endurance
- Work develops concentration
- Work develops industriousness
- Work builds confidence
- Work promotes responsibility
- Work develops self-esteem
- Work encourages true self-knowledge

Montessori saw clearly that it is precisely because work is so vital to the child for the proper building of the human being that nature gives each and every normal child an irresistible urge towards work. This is the irresistible attraction to purposeful activity that all normal children are born with.

So the good news for parents and teachers is, we don't need to put pressure on children to produce the qualities listed above, because nature takes care of it all, if we let her, through "the law of work."

Discovering That Children Prefer Work to play.

From her earliest work with children in Italy to her later work with children all over the world, Montessori discovered something she herself found hard to believe, and that is, children prefer work to play. By work, she meant purposeful, challenging activity, and by play she meant activities which are enjoyable and diverting but not too challenging.

Taking a Controversial Stance on Work Versus Play.

Despite Dr. Maria Montessori's direct and honest reporting of this finding, child development experts have always had a problem with it. (Children have no problems with it!) Controversy has always surrounded Dr. Maria Montessori's straightforward assertion that children prefer work to play, and clearly find work more satisfying than the mere diversion of play. It is probable that the controversy is caused by a lack of understanding of what Montessori really meant by the word "work." Perhaps the following scenario will help to clear up the confusion.

Comparing Work to Play - A True Scenario

Activity :   going up and down a slide:

Child 1 :   aged two years.
Child 2 :   aged seven years.

Scenario:

Child 1:
The two year old climbs up the slide. He mounts each step with great effort and perseverance. Each step is a challenge to his short legs. He talks to himself as he struggles "up, up, a bit more, another bit." It takes a while for him to reach the top step, yet he refuses all help. If anyone tries to help him, he gets upset and starts to cry.

When he finally reaches the top, he sits on the platform and looks around him like a man who has just climbed Mount Everest. He beams with pride. He sits for a few moments to take in the whole experience, the sense of achievement. Behind him can be heard the frantic cries of the other, usually older children telling him to get a move on, to slide down. He ignores them all, he seems to be locked for a moment in his own little world .

Embarrassed parents threaten and cajole, "slide down, for Pete's sake," they say, "the other children want a turn."

Eventually, he slides down. He enjoys the slide, but the real enjoyment is the steps, he remembers them with excitement, and so he races back to the steps to begin the hard climb all over again, and again and again. They offer him challenge, effort, struggle.

Onlookers would describe what he is doing as play, yet if any adult put the same amount of struggle, effort and commitment into something, it would be called work, and that's what Montessori called it. For the child, climbing up that slide, is work, i.e. purposeful, challenging activity .

Child 2:
The seven-year-old races up the steps of the slide. He can't wait to get to the top. The steps mean nothing to him. He takes them two at a time, just to get to the top quicker. For him, they are just a necessary nuisance to bring him up high enough to make the slide down, a good thrill.

When he gets to the top, he wastes no time looking around, he feels none of the sense of achievement the two year old felt by mastering the steps. For him, it's all about the slide, the thrill. He takes two or three turns and then moves on to something else. This is play. It is a valid experience and a hugely important part of human life, but it is very different and has a wholly different effect on the human being to the experience of work.

Examining The Difference Between Work and Play.

Perhaps the most interesting point about this true scenario is that both children were engaged in the same activity i.e. going up and down the slide. Yet for the younger child this was work but for the older child this was play. What made the difference? Just this: for the two-year-old, it involved effort, struggle, challenge and it provided satisfaction and a real sense of achievement in return. For the seven-year-old it did not involve effort, struggle or challenge. It was amusing and diverting, it provided fun and a thrill, but it did not provide the sense of achievement that the younger child experienced. This probably explains why the older boy moved on quickly to something else.

It would seem then that whether an activity is work or play, satisfying or merely diverting does not depend on what the activity is but on how the child approaches it.

Almost anything can be used by a child for either work or play, but the rule is, if the activity involves:

- Free choice.
- Deep interest.
- A personal challenge set by the child himself.
- No interference from others.

it becomes work. When one of these factors is missing, it becomes play.

The Positive Effects of Work Versus Play on the Child's Personality.

What Montessori discovered was not simply that children prefer work to play but that work has a positive effect on their personalities and behaviour which play does not have.

This is probably something that has to be seen to be believed. We can attest to the validity of this finding having witnessed it ourselves for many years.

However, because this discovery is not generally known or publicised and because modern child experts are so biased in favour of play, children are frequently only offered toys and amusements and are told to "go and play."

It is worth noting that in many current TV programmes which feature young children with challenging behaviour whose parents are being taught techniques to control their behaviour, one can usually spot, in the background, play rooms full of expensive toys.

Presumably these children have plenty of opportunities to play, but perhaps few opportunities to carry out work, i.e. meaningful, challenging activities. Is this lack of "work" the chief cause of their challenging behaviour?

What Montessori discovered about work and play is hugely important. To put it simply, she discovered that children want and need purposeful activity as much as they want and need food and drink.

Without purposeful activity they cannot build themselves as nature intended and their growth becomes warped resulting in a deviation from normal development.

18

WHY WON'T HE LET ME HELP HIM?

(The Law of Independence)

Sometime ago I was walking through a shopping mall carrying two heavy bags. I sat down on a bench in the central aisle to rest my weary arms.

As I sat there a young mother with a child about two years old sat down on the other end of the bench. The conversation between them was heated.

The little boy was trying to do up his duffle coat and his mother, who was clearly in a hurry to do her shopping was trying to help him. Every time the mother managed to close a button, the child would cry "no, me do it," and he would undo the button and attempt to re-do it himself.

The mother was exasperated. She kept telling the child that she needed to get into the supermarket to get the shopping and she even tried to bribe the child with the promise of "choc choc's".

But the child could not be bribed. He took control of the buttons and would not give in. The scene became very tense and I felt sure that it would end in tears with the mother exerting her authority and greater strength over the child.

How right I was. Within minutes the mother grabbed the child and placed him kicking and screaming into the empty shopping trolley, with the buttons half done up.

The mother justified her action by loudly announcing over the child's sobs "you are becoming a very stubborn little boy and it will have to stop."

I swallowed hard, thinking how commonplace these heart-rending scenes have become.

Understanding That Nature Urges the Child to Become Independent.

So, what caused this three-year-old to refuse the offer of "choc choc's" in favour of fastening the buttons on his duffle coat? (I would have opted for the "choc chocs"!)

The answer is clear, the child feels a powerful unconscious instinct urging him to carry out tasks which help him to become independent.

It's as if mother nature whispers in his ear instructing him that it is vital that he does things for himself. Time and time again, we've witnessed young children, who, when engaged in a puzzle or some similar activity react fiercely when some well-meaning person puts a piece of his puzzle in place for him without asking. The child usually shows his displeasure by screaming or crying, then lifts out the piece, throws it in the pile of mixed up pieces, and then, when he's ready, puts it in place himself. Even the most mild-mannered of children will do this, which indicates that the fierce reaction is not caused by an aggressive temperament but by the child's sense that he must do the job himself. He is simply following the urge of nature telling him to become independent.

Recognising That the Urge Towards Independence Is a Healthy Sign.

Instead of getting ourselves uptight because of the child's urge to do things for himself, we need to recognise that the intense urge that the child feels to become independent is a healthy sign. Montessori pointed out that the child who is born normally and is developing normally strives to become independent. Unfortunately, it is the child who doesn't strive to become independent who may have a developmental problem.

Accepting that Tasks that Lead to Independence Cannot be Shared.

Some years ago, I heard a story about a lady on her driving test. Things were going reasonably well until the tester asked her to reverse. She put the car in gear and then thoughtlessly said to the tester: "We're all clear on my side, can you tell me how we're doing on your side before I reverse." The test came to an abrupt end and needless to say she failed. Why?- Because the test demands that she be able to do the task all by herself: some things just cannot be shared.

As adults most of us know instinctively that we have to master certain things in life all by ourselves. For example, if we want to learn to swim, we can observe our instructor watch our companions but it is not until we plunge into the water by ourselves and move our own arms and legs that we will actually learn how to swim .

Similarly, the young child seems to know instinctively that in order to achieve independence he must carry out his tasks all by himself, he cannot share them. For this reason, his constant refrain is, "let me do it, let me do it," and he will defend his need to do things for himself quite aggressively, even pushing the well-meaning adult away as the adult tries to lend a helping hand.

The child knows instinctively that he cannot become independent by sharing the tasks that lead to independence. It's as if nature whispers in his ear - "you have to do it yourself."

The closest he can come to accepting help is when he physically can't do something and he asks - "help me to do it myself."

Understanding Why Independence is so Important for the Child.

Independence from adults is vital for the child because:

- It allows him to develop real skills.
- It brings confidence.
- It builds character.
- It results in self belief, self-esteem.
- It gives the child a realistic view of himself.
- It encourages the child to attempt greater challenges.
- It fosters growth and so helps the child to build himself.

Helping the Child to Achieve Independence.

We can help the child to achieve independence by:

- Allowing the child to do things for himself .
- Giving help only when needed and requested.
- Giving the least amount of help possible.
- Leaving the last stages of the task to the child.
  so that he gets a feeling of accomplishment.

Showing the Child Ways of Becoming Independent.

We can show the child ways of becoming independent by teaching him:

- To wash his hands.
- To brush his teeth.
- To dress himself.
- To comb his hair.

Providing the Child with the Means to be Independent.

We need to provide the child with :

- Low hooks to hang his coat, scarf and hat on.
- Low shelves to put his toys on.
- Low cabinets to put his clothes in.
- A low shelf in the fridge to put his snack on.
- A low shelf in the bathroom, so he can reach his toothbrush, facecloth, towel, independently.

19

RUNNING INTO TROUBLE

(Obstacles To Normal Development)

Some children are very fortunate. Right from the outset they get the very things that nature drives them towards i.e love, order, work and independence.

These children breeze through their twos and threes, without ever throwing a tantrum. They are content and joyful children, a pleasure to all they spend time with.

Other children are not so lucky. Although they often have very loving parents, and come from "good" homes, they often get very little of the kind of love, order, work and independence that they crave. "Obstacles," is what they get.

Montessori was convinced, from her observations, that even in the best of families, the child's course along the "road of normality" is often strewn with obstacles which eventually lead to deviations i.e. defects in his personality and behaviour problems.

When Something Blocks The Way.

From the time of conception, there stretches out before us what we might call "the road of normality". If everything in the first few years of life went smoothly, we would travel along this road calmly and peacefully and all would be perfect. As Montessori put it,

> "If at conception and during gestation, at birth and the period following birth, the child had been scientifically treated, he should at three be a model individual."
>
> (The Absorbent Mind p195)

However, she went on to say,

> "This ideal is never reached because, apart from other reasons, many obstacles intervene." (The Absorbent Mind p195)

In other words, even from conception, obstacles, both little and large, begin to get strewn across the child's roadway, preventing him from continuing with his ideal journey and forcing him ultimately down side roads of deviation.

Identifying the Obstacles to Development.

It is not difficult to identify the big obstacles which can confront a child. Events like death, separation, divorce, or a serious illness in the family, are obviously going to pose stumbling blocks for any child.

However Montessori was even more concerned about the less obvious obstacles which can cause huge problems for the child. These are often "invisible" things that no one ever suspects could have negative consequences for the child.

Rounding Up the Usual Suspects.

It may seem unbelievable, even unfair to state this, but often the greatest obstacles to the young child's normal development come from:

- The family.

- The home.

- The school .

Let us explain.

OBSTACLES IN THE FAMILY.

Obstacles in the family can be many and varied. The most serious obstacles are:

- High levels of stress in the mother during the pregnancy.
- Interference with the child's need to remain attached to his mother for the first two to three years after birth.

Close up on Obstacles posed by the Family Post-Natally.

Obstacles to the child's need to attach to his mother during the first two to three years after Birth.

In the entire history of the human species, certain essential facts have remained unchanged. These facts are; - in a "natural" (i.e not surrogate) pregnancy,

- It is the mother who carries the baby for nine months.

- It is the mother who goes through labour and birth.

- It is the mother's breasts that fill with milk making it practical and in some countries essential to keep the baby close to her for two years or more.

Why is this?
The answer is simple. It is nature's plan that the child should be primarily attached to his mother at least for the first two years of life.

This is not always possible, owing to the death, illness or circumstances of the mother, but it is still nature's plan.

In simple societies, this plan is accepted by men and women automatically. No one has to explain it or defend it, it is just understood as something natural in life, like the fact that men grow hair on their faces and chests and women don't. It is in more sophisticated societies that this plan of nature is questioned, argued against and often ousted.

The argument put forward by modern societies is this: yes, women carry the infant for nine months, yes, women go through labour and birth, yes, women lactate and produce breast milk, but breast milk can be put into bottles and fed to the baby by anyone, so why not have 50-50 parenting after the child's birth and get rid of this "old-fashioned" idea of the mother as the primary carer.

Well, this sounds like a valid argument. However, discoveries in neurology and neurobiology which confirm Dr Montessori's original findings (100 years ago) are revealing why this is not actually a valid argument at all and why prolonged periods of separation from the mother, during the first 2 to 3 years of life can be detrimental to the child's brain and general mental health development.

Let us explain.

In the early 1900s, Dr Maria Montessori, brain specialist, medical researcher, and professor of pedagogical anthropology, made an astonishing assertion. She asserted that the human being at birth is different from all other creatures. She claimed that he is "built to a new design," because he has a "double embryonic life". She wrote:

"Man seems to have two embryonic periods. One is prenatal, like that of the animals; the other is postnatal and only man has this".   (Absorbent Mind p60)

She asserted that during the nine months in the womb the child is a "physical embryo," but when he is born, he is not "finished," he is not "complete," he now must undergo a further period of foetal development which now takes place outside of the womb.

During this second period of foetal development, he is a 'spiritual embryo'. Both of these embryonic periods are like the two sides of the same coin. And during these two embryonic periods, the mother and child must not be separated as to do so will prevent the child from completing his formation.

Now, the vital question is, if the human child has a second "embryonic period", what is the purpose of that period? What part of the child is not "finished" yet? What part is not "complete" yet? He has all his arms, legs and body parts, so what's going on?

What's going on is 'invisible'. It is entirely to do with the heart and the brain, and the creation of the mental and psychological faculties. Montessori wrote:

"This baby, far from finished even physically, has to build himself up into the complex being that man is. .... although he is already born, he continues to carry on an embryonic life, by which he builds up what seems to be no less than a set of human instincts".   (The Absorbent Mind. p71)

"... he will have to make for himself all man's mental life".   (p71)

"He enters upon life and begins his mysterious task; little by little ....
He constructs his mind step-by-step.' (The Absorbent Mind. p27)

And what is the mother's role in all of this? Neurology is showing that she is the "master template". The mother, has been chosen by nature to be the actual tangible template that the infant uses "to make for himself all man's mental life" i.e. to build up his mental faculties. And that, in short, is why separation from the mother for prolonged periods during the first few years of life can have detrimental and long lasting consequences for the mental and psychological development of the child.

The American neurologist, Dr. Allan Shore, has shown that the baby's neuronal system learns from his mother's brain. Dr Shore maintains that the mother's brain acts as a kind of "brain-wave template" which teaches the baby's brain when to "wire and fire".

Remember, the baby is born with an exuberance of brain cells to allow it to adapt to whatever environment it finds itself in. It doesn't need to keep all these brain cells. It only needs to keep the ones it will use. These are the ones that need to be "wired and fired". The others need to "die off," as they are superfluous to requirements.

Now, how will the baby know which ones to wire and fire? Well, just like in our caterpillar story, nature has provided the answer. Nature has arranged it that as the child seeks out his mother primarily for milk, he (inadvertently) allows the mother to function as a "brain-wave template". The child just mimics his mother.

Eventually, says Dr Allen Shore, "the prefrontal cortex of the mother becomes the prefrontal cortex of the infant".

But, if the infant is separated from the mother, who is the "master template," the prefrontal cortex of the brain may not develop as nature intended it to, the reptilian brain, rather than the frontal cortex may be dominant in development.

Dr. Shore has traced many problems and psycho-pathologies in adolescence and adulthood right back to damage to the mother/child attachment bond in the first few years of life.

Furthermore, the American child development expert, Dr Joseph Chilton Pearce has shown that during the period after birth, the period that Dr. Montessori refers to as the second "embryonic" period, something extraordinary happens between mothers and babies which has to do with electromagnetic fields.

Most of us don't know this, but the human heart produces a very powerful electromagnetic field. This field surrounds the body and is so powerful that you can take an electrocardiogram reading from it as far as three feet away from the body. Now, the crucial thing is the way in which this electromagnetic field affects the brain. Research is showing that harm to the child's emotional life causes a corresponding harm to his brain development, which can be life-long.

Now, immediately after birth, the infant's electrical pattern mimics the pattern of his mother's electrical heart waves but only when she is close to him, especially during breastfeeding.

Dr. Chilton Pearce calls this mimicking phenomenon "entrainment". He says the heart waves of the infant are "entrained" with his mother's heart waves. This means that the electrical waves of the two are "together". Mother and child are literally "on the same wave-length".

We know this because of the work of researchers like Dr. Gary Schwartz of the University of Arizona who has been able to identify the EEG pattern of the mother encoded within the EEG of the child and vice-versa.

This evidence shows that the electrical patterns of a mother recorded on an electroencephalograph are encoded within the EEG pattern of the child. The waves are literally "in synchrony" with each other.

But when the child is separated from the mother for a prolonged period, the electrical waves become "discordant" or chaotic and only return to a state of "resonance" when the mother and child are reunited. Discordant heart waves are an indication of distress.

Now when this state of discord happens, cortisol is released by both mother and child and stress levels rocket in both. Excess cortisol is toxic to neural systems especially new ones, so both mother and baby are harmed.

This discovery is huge. It shows that "separation anxiety" is not just an unpleasant experience for a child, something he will get used to or overcome with time, it is actually toxic to brain development and the harm it causes can be carried through from childhood to adolescence and on into adulthood as Dr. Allen Shore's research shows.

Now, if it is so crucial for the child not to be separated from his mother during this second embryonic period, what provision has nature made to keep the mother close to the child during this critical second embryonic period?

The answer is obvious: lactation. Montessori wrote:

"Lactation is the tie which still keeps the spiritual embryo attached to its mother. This is a fact common to all races". (p91)

Montessori noted that in many countries:

"The mother carries the child in her arms and keeps him with her wherever she goes". (p95)

She noted:

"A French missionary who has studied especially the customs of the Bantu people in central Africa, was astonished at the fact that the mothers do not even think of detaching themselves from the child. They consider him as part of themselves. When attending a solemn royal installation that missionary saw the Queen arrive, child in arms, and she received the honours of a sovereign while keeping her child all the time with her. He also marvelled that Bantu women can keep up breastfeeding for so long a period. Generally it lasts two full years. In other words, it lasts for the whole epoch which nowadays is of such special interest to modern psychologists."
                                        (The Formation of Man p95)

Montessori also noted:

"It is really unnecessary for the body that the child should be fed its mother's milk for so long, but the mother follows an instinct of love by not detaching herself from her child and by carrying him with her all the time."
                                        (The Formation of Man p95)

You see, nature watching vigilantly over the newborn gives the mother guidance on "how to build a human being".

Montessori could see that the child needs to be primarily attached to his mother for mental and psychological reasons even more than physical reasons during the first two years of life. The child's brain may not develop as nature intended if he doesn't have that attachment.

We can like this statement, or be incensed by it, but that doesn't change the facts.

Society may have changed, but the human infant hasn't. His neurobiological needs are still the same as they were thousands of years ago.

Now, what are the obstacles that can stand in the way of this necessary primary attachment in the first two years of life?

Answer, there are many potential obstacles. The most common ones are:

- Death of the mother or illness in the mother keeping her in hospital or some place where she is detached from the child.

- Addiction problems in the mother, forcing her to be detached from the child.

- Depression or mental illness in the mother causing her not to want to "bond" with her child.

- The necessity for the mother to return to work very soon after the child is born.

- The reluctance by mothers in the western world to breastfeed their child which is nature's way of keeping the child close to them.

- Family Court Orders, stipulating that the custody of the child be divided between the homes of the mother and the father, forcing the child to be separated from his mother.

Nature has planned it that the child should be primarily attached to his mother for the first two years of life. If that doesn't fit in with our lifestyles then we need to change our lifestyles but we should not try to change nature.

Montessori wrote:

"Nature, wise nature, must be the basis on which a supra-nature still more perfect, can be constructed. It is certain that progress must surpass nature and adapt different forms. It may not, however, proceed by trampling upon nature".

(The Formation of Man p 96)

OBSTACLES IN THE HOME.

Obstacles in the home are usually threefold:

1) Obstacles to ORDER

2) Obstacles to WORK

3) Obstacles to INDEPENDENCE

1) Obstacles to ORDER in the Home.

Often, when a new baby arrives, he brings with him an uninvited companion, his name is "chaos." In the first few months of life with a new baby, "chaos" often, though not always, calls the shots. When the new baby has colic and won't settle, when the new mother has the blues and gets tearful, when the new father has had enough and runs to the pub, "chaos" sits smiling in the armchair. Chaos, for a few weeks is something we can get over, but it's when chaos refuses to leave that we have problems. The human child is wired to look for order. He searches for it everywhere, right from the start, and if he doesn't find it, he deviates off the main road. Remember, a lack of order in the home is an obstacle to the child's normal development.

Close-up on Obstacles to ORDER in the Home.

Lack of Routines:
A child needs routines. Why? because he is trying to make a map of his world. He needs routines for:

Waking up
Getting Fed
Getting Washed
Getting Dressed
Playing
Toilet/Nappy Changing
Outdoor Activities
Bath-time
Bedtime

Constantly Changing Routines:
A child needs routines to be fixed. If they chop and change they can cause as much harm as if there were no routines. The child is looking for constancy. If you mess with his map you cause huge upset and damage to the child often resulting in serious harm that shows itself in behavioural and speech abnormalities. A young child needs to know the "what," "when," "where" and "how" of things. He needs to know when things are going to happen, where they are going to happen and how they are going to happen i.e. what sequence they will come in, e.g. "bath, story, bed," and not "story, bath, bed," unless that is the usual sequence.

The young child cannot read clocks. He relies on routines like breakfast time, lunch time and dinner time to help him grasp the passage of time throughout the day. He doesn't yet understand things like hours in the day, days of the week, months of the year. He has no understanding of time initially and so we must facilitate this lack by supplying routines to mark the passage of time until his brain is sufficiently developed to learn how to read the clock.

Despite his inability to read the clock, the young child searches for patterns in his daily life. He searches for landmarks and routines that demonstrate pattern, in order to help him to understand how life works. This is why the young child actually loves routines and needs them for his mental health as he tries to make a mental map of his world.

* * *

2) Obstacles to WORK in the Home.
Even in the best of homes, obstacles to work (i.e challenging activity) abound. These obstacles can take the form of:

> Too much TV or video games.
> Too many toys.
> Too much interference from adults.
> Too much interference from siblings.

REMEMBER: A lack of opportunities for work in the home is an obstacle to the child's normal development.

Close-up on Obstacles to WORK in the Home.

Too much TV and video games.

This is something that can creep in accidentally. Most good parents don't consciously plan to allow their child to spend hours in front of the TV, but it can happen and once it does it can be very difficult to end.

Too many toys.

Advertising and marketing has a lot to do with this. Boys and girls are affected by advertising. Boys crave endless cars and trucks that they often just bash and crash. Girls crave endless dolls and fairy castles until they are virtually mesmerised into a fantasy world. Montessori recommended that we give children access to a variety of interesting activities using real tools and utensils. We need to offer children opportunities to do gardening, knitting, sewing, cooking, and general housekeeping activities, suitable to their particular capacities.

Too much interference in the child's work.

Montessori repeatedly advised that once a child has started to concentrate on something, we should back off and leave him alone. We should not interfere in the child's work unless he asks for help. Too much interference is an obstacle to the child's urge to work.

* * *

3) Obstacles to INDEPENDENCE in the Home.

Again, even in the best of homes, obstacles to independence abound. These often take the form of:

Too much unrequested adult help.

Too few supports to facilitate independence.

REMEMBER: A lack of opportunities in the home for the child to achieve independence is an obstacle to the child's development.

Close-up on Obstacles to INDEPENDENCE in the Home.

Too much unrequested adult help.

Montessori pointed out that too much adult assistance, far from being a help to the child, is an obstacle to the child's development. Often the adult, out of sheer love for the child, cannot bear to watch him struggle at something, and so jumps in too soon and gives help when it was not asked for and probably not needed. The result is usually tears. At first, the child protests and resists the adult's help, but the adult usually persists, thinking he knows best. The result, said Montessori is very serious. Eventually, the child, will give up his attempts to do things for himself and in time become lazy, lacking in initiative, and, more seriously, lacking in belief in himself. After all, the adult has made it clear to the child that he "can't do it," and so the child's favourite phrase becomes "I can't," and the awful truth is, he really believes he can't.

Too few supports to facilitate independence.

No low hangers to hang his coat on.

No shelves to put his toys on.

No low sink for him to brush his teeth at.

* * *

OBSTACLES IN THE SCHOOL.

Obstacles in the school are usually threefold:

1) Obstacles to ORDER

2) Obstacles to WORK

3) Obstacles to INDEPENDENCE

1) Obstacles to ORDER in the School.

Even in the best of schools and preschools, obstacles to order and structure can creep in unnoticed. These obstacles often take the form of :

Noise in the classroom.

Crowding in the classroom.

Disorganisation in the classroom.

Close up on obstacles to ORDER in the School.

Noise in the classroom.

Noise is a very real obstacle to the child's need for order. Noisy schools can have very negative outcomes for the child. Research shows that:

- Quieter environments are associated with more positive developmental outcomes in children than noisy ones.

- Noisy environments are associated with negative developmental outcomes in children.

- To put it simply, quietness is better than noise when it comes to better outcomes in preschool and junior school classrooms.

For details of this research, the reader is directed to Dr Angeline Lillard's book Montessori The Science Behind the Genius (chapter 9).

Crowding in the classroom.

Crowding is a very real obstacle to the child's need for order. Research shows that in crowded conditions children show:
Higher levels of:

. Stress

. Tension

. Annoyance

. Discomfort

127

Research also shows that in crowded conditions, children show:

Lower levels of:

. Academic achievement.

. Independence.

. Task persistence.

. Mental and physical health.

For details on this research, the reader is again directed to Dr Angeline Lillard's book, Montessori The Science Behind the Genius (chapter 9)

Disorganisation in the classroom.

Disorganisation is a very real obstacle to the child's need for order. Research shows that, with regard to physical order i.e. the layout of the environments,

Children from organised environments performed better on,

. Cognitive tests

. Language tests

than those from less organised environments.

Children in disorganised environments showed a range of negative outcomes such as:

. "Poor cognitive competence".

. "Less adequate language".

. "More difficult temperaments".

. "Lower mastery motivation".

Again, for further details of this research, the reader is directed to Dr Angeline Lillard's excellent book, Montessori The Science Behind the Genius (chapter 9).

Preschools and nurseries, therefore, which are disorganised in their layout (i.e. which have toys and games all over the place), are an obstacle to the young child's development.

* * *

2) Obstacles to WORK in the School.
Even in the best preschools, obstacles to the child's need to work, especially, to complete a cycle of activity, abound. These obstacles often take the form of:

- Too many interruptions to the child's work cycle.

- Too much emphasis on group activity rather than individual activity.

Close-up on Obstacles to WORK in the School.

Too many interruptions to the child's work cycle.

Many schools make the mistake of constantly interrupting the child's work cycle with:

. Song-time

. Circle time

. Story- time

. Art-time

. This time

. That time

This stems from a failure to understand as Montessori did, the child's desperate need to concentrate on a task, for out of this concentration, his whole character will develop.

Too much emphasis on group activity at the expense of individual activity.

Many preschools and nurseries overemphasise group activity. There is an obsession among preschool and nursery teachers with socialisation. The aim of so many of these teachers is to make the children socialise, make them share, make them find friends. However, this is all based on a very incorrect premise. It is, in fact, putting the cart before the horse. Montessori witnessed, from her lifetime of work, all around the world, with children of many nationalities, cultures and creeds, that all children, under six years of age, show a powerful need for individual activity. The child in the first six years of life needs to do a lot of individual activities before he is able for (or even interested in), group activity. Certainly, he likes to work/play alongside other children, but he needs to carry out activities from beginning to end, by himself.

REMEMBER, too much group activity, at the expense of individual activity is an obstacle to the child's urge to work.

* * *

3) Obstacles to INDEPENDENCE in the School.

Once again, even in the best of preschools, obstacles to the child's need for independence can creep in unnoticed. The easiest way for this to happen is via something innocuous, such as having too many adults helping out.

Close up on Obstacles to INDEPENDENCE in the School.

Too many adults helping out is an obstacle to the child's need to be independent.

Montessori was very firm about not having too many adults in the classroom, because she knew that it led to a type of helplessness in the children. Her arrangement, which actually came about by accident, is to have a three year age span between the children i.e. an age range of 3 to 6 years in the same class. This arrangement is ideal because children aged five and six years love to help the little three year olds, and three year olds love to imitate the six-year-olds, so mutual learning takes place. Montessori also noted, from her observations, that children are not as inclined to jump in too fast to offer help to a child the way an adult would. They seem to be better able to weigh up the situation, and only offer help when it is needed.

20

GOING OFF COURSE

(Deviations From Normal Development)

When a child meets "obstacles," which are, in fact like roadblocks on the "road of normal development," he can no longer stay on that road. He is forced, against his own wishes, to go down, what we might call, a side road. Unfortunately, all side roads deviate from the road of normality. This means that changes in behaviour and the beginnings of defects in character are inevitable. Montessori called these changes "deviations" i.e. behaviour problems.

Different Personalities, Different Deviations.

From her close observations, Montessori saw that children did not all develop the same type of deviations i.e behaviour problems in response to a specific obstacle. For example, two children from the same family, faced with the same obstacle, might develop different types of deviation i.e. behaviour problems. It all depends on the child's personality type. Montessori saw that children have either, what she called "strong" dominant personalities (i.e. the type who will not bow down to any obstacle,) or "weak" submissive personalities (i.e the type who will put up with anything for a quiet life.)

It would not be strange or unusual then to find two children in the same family, who, when faced with the same obstacle (for example, a lack of boundaries in the home) tend to show different responses.

One of them (the dominant one) might become out of control, wild, a law unto himself, while the other one (the submissive one) might become insecure, whiny and fretful much of the time.

Note. Montessori's terms "strong" and "weak" are open to confusion. She did not mean to imply that one personality type was better than the other (i.e. strong is better than weak). Far from it, both personality dispositions have their own problems, as we shall soon see.

Identifying the Deviations seen in Children with a Dominant Personality.

These children often demonstrate:

- fits of rage
- tendencies to violence
- insubordination and aggression
- disobedience
- destructive impulses
- possessiveness
- selfishness
- envy (tries to take other peoples possessions)
- inability to concentrate
- poor coordination
- mental confusion
- a tendency to shout and scream
- a tendency to be generally noisy
- a tendency to disturb and tease other children
- a tendency to be unkind to animals
- a tendency to be unkind to smaller children
- a tendency to be greedy

A child may show one or more of these tendencies.

Child experts call these tendencies "normal" traits in children. Montessori says the child experts are wrong. She says these tendencies are "deviations" they are what happens when a child has been forced "off course." Just as cancers etc. are seen as deviations from normal physical health, these traits should be seen as deviations from normal psychological health, because they do not appear in the normalised child.

Identifying the Deviations seen in Children with a Submissive Personality.

These are children who:

- cry for what they want
- try to get others to do things for them
- are always wishing to be entertained
- are easily bored
- are frequently idle
- are frightened by everything
- cling to adults

- are often untruthful
- often steal
- have imaginary illnesses
- refuse to eat
- sometimes eat excessively
- have disturbed sleep
- have nightmares
- fear the dark
- have nervous complaints
- live in a fantasy world

A child may show one or more of these tendencies.

Again, child experts regard most of these tendencies as normal traits in young children. Montessori disagrees. She says these are all deviations from the norm. They are what happens when a child has been forced off course by some obstacle blocking his way from the road to normality.

Deviations arising from a Lack of Order.

1) Lack of Order in the Family.

When a child cannot find ORDER in the family the following "deviations" may occur:

The "submissive" child may:

- feel insecure
(shows this through timidity)

- become clingy

- become shy

- become nasty sneakily

- become disobedient covertly

The "dominant" child may:

- feel insecure
(hides it through bravado)

- become out of control

- become aggressive

- become nasty blatantly

- become disobedient brazenly

2) Lack of Order in the Home.

When a child cannot find ORDER in the home (i.e. routines) the following deviations may occur:

The "submissive" child may:	The "dominant" child may:
• Develop eating problems. (eats very little)	• Develop eating problems. (eats too much)
• Develop sleep problems. (has nightmares)	• Develop sleep problems. (won't go to sleep)
• Develop chaotic behaviour (cries to eat, drink, play at very inappropriate times)	• Develop chaotic behaviour. (demands to eat,drink,play at very inappropriate times)
• Develop a chaotic mind. (show symptoms very similar to those of Autistic Spectrum Disorder. (A.S.D.)	• Develop a chaotic mind. (show symptoms very similar to those of Autistic Spectrum Disorder (A.S.D.)
• Show confused thinking.	• Show confused thinking.
• Lack confidence.	• Lack confidence.

3) Lack of Order in the School.

When a child cannot find order in the school, (i.e structure), the following "deviations" (behaviour problems) may occur:

The "submissive" child may become:

- timid
- idle, bored
- a victim
- unable to concentrate
- unnaturally quite
- untruthful
- lacking in appetite
- mentally confused

The "dominant" child may become:

- aggressive
- destructive
- a bully
- unable to concentrate
- extremely noisy
- untruthful
- greedy
- mentally confused

Deviations arising from A Lack Of "Work".

When a child cannot find opportunities to do "Work" (challenging activities), the following deviations may occur:

The "submissive" child may become

- Lazy
  (shows idleness and boredom)

- Apathetic
  (no interest in anything)

- Unable to concentrate
  (abandons activities)

The "dominant" child may become

- Lazy
  (shows anger and aggression)

- Destructive
  (interested in breaking things)

- Unable to concentrate
  (does not even try activities)

- Become babyish
  (selects infantile activities)

- Show a lack of confidence
  (because confidence comes
  from mastery of tasks.)

- Turn to fantasy
  (often quiet fairy stories)

- Become whiny and tearful

- Become reckless
  (meddles with adult jobs)

- Show a lack of confidence
  (because confidence comes
  from mastery of tasks.)

- Turn to fantasy
  (often loud super-heroes)

- Become whiny and aggressive

Deviations arising from a Lack of Independence.

When a child cannot find opportunities to become Independent, the following deviations may occur:

The "submissive" child may:

- Show dependence on adults.
  (rely heavily on adults).

- Become lacking in initiative.
  (will not even do activities
  that are targeted to his age)

The "dominant" child may:

- Show total disregard for adults..
  (become a law unto himself).

- Show misplaced initiative.
  (tries to do activities that are
  unsuitable for his age).

• Become lacking in drive and motivation.	• Show plenty of drive and motivation (but, directs it towards activities that are unsuitable for his age.)
• Refuse to do things for himself e,g, won't feed himself won't dress himself	• Only do the things he feels like doing i.e. he is driven by his whims,eg some days he may feed himself, some days he may dress himself,
• Constantly ask for help.	• Constantly refuse help even when he needs it.
• Constantly say "I can't".*	• Only say "I can't" when he is being lazy.
The child genuinely believes he can't do anything as a result of being prevented from doing things at an earlier period when nature urged him to do "work".	The child actually can do a lot of things but now has a lazy attitude as a result of being prevented from doing things for himself at an earlier period when nature urged him to do "work".
• Show signs of unhappiness (because happiness comes from challenging activity ie "work".)	• Show signs of unhappiness. (because happiness comes from challenging activity ie "work")

Calling a Spade a Spade. Deviations as a Cry for Help.

Montessori recognised that all the myriads of behavioural problems in children, whether they be the aggressive, destructive behaviours of the dominant child or the clingy, whiny, fearful behaviours of the submissive child, they all have one thing in common. They are all deviations, detours, a moving away from the main road of normal development, and most importantly, they are all a cry for help. The child does not engage in these behaviours because he enjoys them or because they make him happy. Indeed, these behaviours clearly make him very unhappy indeed. The problem is, he is only two, three or four years old. He doesn't know that he has deviated from the main road of normal development. He just knows that he is out of sorts, and sometimes he literally cries for help. The problem is, who is listening to his cries?

21

GETTING BACK ON TRACK

(Normalisation of Development)

When obstacles have forced the child off the main road of normal development and pushed him down side roads of deviation the big question is: can he ever get back on that road of normal development?

If the answer is yes then the next question is how?

Montessori discovered that the young child can be helped to get "back on track" if we do two things for him:

1) remove the obstacles that threw him off course in the first place.

2) normalise the conditions under which he lives.

So, the first step is to get rid of the obstacles which pushed the child off the main road in the first place. These obstacles usually lie in either:

- The family - Parenting issues
- The home - Routines
- The school - Structure

They always involve a breach of the child's need for order, work or independence.

Discovering the Phenomenon of Getting Back to Normal Through Work.

As explained earlier, Montessori first discovered the phenomenon of getting back to normal (normalisation) by accident. It was in the year 1907 in that first Casa dei Bambini, in Rome, when Montessori first confronted this extraordinary phenomenon.

When the children first arrived at the school, they displayed the usual traits commonly seen in young children, i.e some were noisy, disorderly and rough, while others were shy, frightened and very dependent.

Yet, within a relatively short period of time of having been in attendance at the school, where the obstacles to their development were removed, their character traits began to change. Within a short time, most of them became orderly, hard-working, focused, sociable, kind and joyful children.

Seeing is Believing - It's Too Good to be True.

At first, Montessori couldn't believe what she was witnessing. It all seemed too good to be true. However, as the weeks went by and more and more evidence of these extraordinary changes in the children continued, Montessori could see that normalisation was a phenomenon that could not be denied.

She later called it, "the most important single result of our whole work."

These children were casting off their behaviour problems all by themselves. They were becoming kinder to each other and more sociable but what was making it happen?

Searching For Clues - What Actually Causes Normalisation to Happen?

Montessori herself was astonished by these extraordinary changes in so many of the children's personalities.

She hadn't expected them and hadn't consciously done anything to obtain them, and yet they occurred.

Later she was to see these changes in children in her schools all over the world.

140

She realised that the obstacles which had caused the children's deviations had obviously been removed in her schools, making it possible for normalisation to happen.

Since Montessori was a scientist, she automatically started to analyse the situation. She retraced her steps and began to look for clues to explain what actually causes the phenomenon of normalisation to occur.

Revealing The Vital Ingredients Of Normalisation.

It didn't take long for Dr. Montessori to find the two vital ingredients which bring about normalisation. They were -"work and concentration." Montessori found that by concentrating hard on work i.e. challenging activity, the children's personalities began to normalise, i.e. their "deviations," i.e behaviour problems began to disappear and they became kinder and more sociable to their peers, while manifesting a newfound love for learning. The answer was in front of her:

"Normalisation comes about through concentration on a piece of work".
(TheAbsorbent Mind p206)

Examining The Process of Getting Back To Normal through Work.

The process of normalisation always follows the same pattern.

Scenario:

1) you have a child who has been forced off the main road, because some obstacle stood in his way.

2) the child has deviated from the road i.e. has behaviour problems.

3) the obstacle has now been removed but the child is still "off course" and needs to be brought back onto the main road of normal development.

Enter the child.
The particular location does not really matter. Normalisation can and does take place whenever and wherever the right conditions prevail.

• Initially, you have a child with no focus. He flits around, messes a bit with this occupation and then that. Nothing really takes his fancy.

- Then, for no apparent reason, either days or weeks later, he suddenly fixes his attention on a particular game or material, probably something that he has snubbed many times in the past.

- He very deliberately selects that material and carefully starts to work with it.

- He becomes so engrossed and involved with this particular material that he shuts out virtually all external stimuli. He appears not to notice anyone else, even the children sitting beside him.

- He works intently at his activity, sometimes repeating it over and over again.

- Then, all of a sudden, five minutes, ten minutes, half an hour later or whatever, he suddenly stops. Clearly he is finished. He often looks around him as though waking from a dream.

- He tidies up the game or material and puts it back where he got it from.

- Then he sits or walks around with an expression that indicates that he is contemplating a job well done. He appears satisfied and happy with himself.

- He seeks out another child who is not too busy and chats happily with him.

- Although he doesn't know it, this child has now placed his feet back on the main road, the road of normality. After this spell of deep concentration, the child is never really the same again. All he needs now is to have regular, hopefully daily opportunities to concentrate on other interesting tasks, until activity, freely chosen, becomes his regular way of living, and his behavioural problems, whatever they were, slowly, but surely, disappear.

Analysing the Conditions Necessary for the getting Back to Normal Phenomenon to Occur.

Montessori could see that normalisation did not just occur by accident. She could see that it was the presence of certain conditions that had caused it to occur in the Casa dei Bambini.

She began to analyse what those conditions were. She identified the following five conditions as the conditions most necessary for the occurrence of normalisation:

1) **Interesting activities.**

   The first essential is the provision of interesting activities for the child to work on. These cannot be just any old activities just thrown in the child's direction for him to amuse himself with. They need to be activities which:

   - Involve the hand and the brain working together.
     A simple example of this would be a game like the cylinders where the child has to slot wooden cylinders of varying dimensions into a block of wood drilled with matching sockets. The child has to use his brain to judge the dimensions of the cylinders in the sockets. Thought must accompany each action. This prevents the mind from wondering and makes the child concentrate on what he is doing. Every piece of material designed by Montessori involves this inseparable connection between the hand and the brain.

   - Induce concentration rather than fatigue.
     Certain activities fulfil this requirement better than others. We've always noticed that children who like jigsaw puzzles and elect to do them, always appear to be more energised after they have completed the puzzles than they were at the outset. Concentration on an interesting task is definitely energising, not tiring.

   - Arouse such an interest that they engage the child's whole personality. Normalisation only takes place when the child is fully engaged in the task, when it is a task that really grabs his interest.

   - Are not just chosen at random, but are planned by the adult who must organise a world of progression of interest. So for example, if the child takes an interest in the job of scrubbing a table, we must be ready to follow this up another day with the job of washing windows, or washing the car. In other words, we must offer him progressively more challenging tasks.

2) **Free choice.**

   Montessori stressed that the child must be free to choose from a range of possible activities. Normalisation will not take place if the adult imposes his choice of activity on the child.

3) **Concentration on a task.**

   Montessori pointed out that there is a world of difference between deep concentration and mere occupation. Only deep concentration on a task can bring about normalisation. Just going through mechanical motions i.e.

occupation with a task, without that intense interest which engages the child's whole personality, will not bring about normalisation.

True story.
I am reminded of the hours our first child used to spend working on her doll's house. She would organise all the furniture into categories, bathroom furniture, bedroom furniture, kitchen furniture, etc. and then place them all in the rooms.

Then she would organise the dolls into mothers, fathers, boys, girls and babies. Then the pets, she would place them into kennels, baskets, birdhouses etc. Then she would make little paper rugs, carpets, photos, paintings etc suitable for each of the rooms. She often was so engrossed in this activity that she had to be reminded to eat and drink.

On other occasions, when she had a friend with her, they would play with the doll's house and occupy themselves, but show none of the deep concentration just described above. Both types of activity are valid, both are normal, but only the first type with the deep concentration produces normalisation.

4) **A suitable environment.**
    Montessori stressed that the child needs a suitable environment in which to work. He needs-

- A reasonably peaceful environment i.e. no noisy din in the background.

- A reasonable space to work in. Clutter is bad.

5) **No interruptions.**
    Montessori stressed that the child needs an opportunity to work without constant interference and interruptions.

- Parents need to be aware of this so that when they need to dash to the shops, rush to the post office etc. they can plan it around Johnny or Mary's work periods.

- Schools need to be aware of this and they need to control their practice of circle times etc. which often intrude on the child's concentration.

The Characteristics of the Child who is Getting Back To Normal Through Work.

When a child starts the process of normalisation i.e. a return to his real normal self, which became deviated as a result of obstacles, four characteristics always appear.

They are:

- Love of work
- Concentration
- Self-discipline
- Sociability

1) Love of work
The child who used to flit from one thing to another without actually staying at anything, now develops a love of work. Work now deeply attracts him. He doesn't want to be idle any more. He wants to do things, to work with things, to struggle and master things. The drive towards work which had gone underground for a while, comes back again. The child searches for work and applies himself to it.

2) Concentration
Now the child who couldn't keep his mind focused on something for more than a minute or two, can concentrate deeply. He quickly becomes engrossed in his tasks. He may be working side-by-side another child, but he will hardly notice him for a while, as he carries out his self-selected work.

3) Self-discipline
Now, the child who had no self-discipline, no perseverance, no ability to stick at anything, suddenly shows the beginning of the development of character, of perseverance, of self-discipline. No one asks him to struggle with his task, to see things through to completion, but he does it anyway, driven on by some new found strength. He is most definitely on the path to normality.

4) Sociability
Montessori noticed that when children start the process of normalisation through work, they begin to show signs of social sentiment that previously they did not display. In other words, little Joey now starts smiling at other children instead of sticking his tongue out at them!

True story.

We will always remember a particular little four -year-old boy who attended our school, many years ago. He was a very grumpy little soul, for very understandable reasons. There had been a lot of problems in his family unit. He never smiled and was quite gruff in his manner. Although, it is many years ago now, we can still remember the day he first began the process of normalisation.

He selected a rather large puzzle of dinosaurs. Although he had not previously shown any great skill even with small puzzles, He began to work on this large puzzle.

He worked away on his own for what seemed like a very long time. Break time came and went, usually his only favourite time, but he never even noticed. He just went on with his work, totally absorbed in it. Finally, he stopped.

He looked around, but didn't seem to notice anyone. Then he stood up, stared at his completed puzzle and beamed. Next he went over to a few little children who were chatting together. He pointed to his finished puzzle.

They each complimented him saying well done. And then he did something which stunned everyone. He reached over and kissed the children he was talking to very tenderly.

This was a boy who had hardly ever said as much as hello to anyone, and who most children were wary of. But clearly something had happened to this child.

From that day on, this boy was different. He became friendly, happy and we would even say joyful. This boy had begun the process of normalisation (a return to his normal self) which had become deviated, as a result of the obstacles in his family life.

His display of social sentiment, as well as his concentration, perseverance and love of work, were clear indications of the process of normalisation at work.

22

SUMMARY OF THE CHARACTERISTICS OF THE CHILD FROM BIRTH - 6 YEARS.

The Period of Infancy.

A Period of Creation.

The Creation of the Child.

Duration: birth to 6 years.

Subdivision: 0 - 3 years.

                3 - 6 years.

General Description:

This is a period of huge transformation.

Physical Characteristics:

This is a period of tremendous growth. The human being develops from being a tiny helpless infant to a walking, speaking, independent child in six short years. It is a fragile time physically. The immune system is weak and there are frequent illnesses.

Neurological Characteristics:

Neurologically, something hugely important is going on in the infant's brain. The overproduction of brain cells which occurred in the womb and probably continued in the first 18 months of life is now being "pruned". In fact, research suggests that the infant "models" his prefrontal cortex on that of his mother during the first two years of life.

Mental Characteristics:

The child possesses an absorbent mind. From birth to 3 years the absorbent mind is unconscious. From 3 to 6 years the absorbent mind is conscious.

Social Characteristics:

This is the period for the development of the individual. The child is egocentric, and self-obsessed. The child's chief goal is self-development, self formation, self construction.

Emotional Characteristics:

The child relies very much on the love of his parents for protection, warmth, and understanding. He relies on this love for his emotional security and well-being.

Needs:

The child needs independence, freedom within limits, purposeful activities, and exposure to daily life and culture.

Sensitive Periods:

Montessori identified six sensitive periods during this period of development. They are sensitive periods for order, language, perfection of movements, learning through the senses, attraction to small objects/small details and the social aspects of life.

23

HOW CAN WE HELP THE HUMAN BEING DURING THE PERIOD BIRTH - 6 YEARS?

Given that we know that the human being between birth and six years needs love, order, work and independence, and the freedom to follow the guiding hand of nature as it leads him through the sensitive periods, our job then is to create environments in which all of this is possible.

This is exactly what Dr. Montessori did, although inadvertently at first. She created environments which matched like a glove fits a hand, the needs of the developing child. This is what the Case dei Bambini, were all about. Initially, Montessori started her schools with children over two years of age, but as time went on, she started to develop a programme which has come to be called, The Infant Community. This programme is geared towards the younger child from about 12 or 14 months to 3 years. This programme also gives advice to parents on matters of child-rearing from conception to 3 years.

So, back to the question, how can we help the human being during the period birth to six years? The answer is clear. We must create, as Dr. Montessori did, "prepared environments" to match the characteristics and needs of the human being during this period. This is best done by having:

- Montessori environments for the under threes: The Infant Community
- Montessori schools for children three to six years: The Children's House.

The Infant Community. (14 months to 3 years)

The infant community is a gathering of toddlers from about 14 months to 3 years who can walk independently. The aim of the infant community is to offer these very young children a nurturing environment in which a specially trained Montessori guide aids the development of the child's:

- independence
- language
- gross motor skills
- fine motor skills

The child is helped to develop a sense of belonging through the communal daily activities that are organised by the Montessori directresses such as:

- laying the table for lunch
- serving food to others
- washing little plates for meals
- sweeping up with small dustpans

These activities help the child to feel that he is part of a community.

The Children's House. (3 to 6 years)

The Children's House is a school for children between 3 and 6 years of age. It is based entirely on the characteristics, needs and sensitive periods of the human being from 3 to 6 years. It recognises the child's need for love, order, work and independence. Therefore, it is first and foremost:

- a nurturing environment:
  where the children are loved and cared for by kind and nurturing directresses.

- an ordered environment:
  where everything in the room is laid out in a precise and orderly arrangement.

- a working environment:
  where every object in the room calls the child to work, ie challenging activities.

- an independent environment:
  where everything in the room encourages independence. The materials are laid out on low shelves so that the child can reach everything without adult help.

The Curriculum.

The curriculum is based around the child's sensitive periods and needs. It is divided into 5 areas. These are: Practical Life Skills, Sensory Refinement, Mathematics, Language and Culture.

PART FOUR

HOW DOES THE CHILD COMPLETE HIMSELF?

(The Years 6-12) (The Age of Imagination)

24

WHERE HAS MY LITTLE BABY GONE TO?

(Physical Changes in Late Childhood)

Whether the child lives in China, Africa, England or Japan, at around six years of age, something very significant happens to him. What is it? It is this: he starts to lose his front teeth.

We are so used to this phenomenon that we don't give it a second thought, but it is a very significant phenomenon indeed.

It is a message from nature, a sign that a change is coming. Nature is heralding a new phase in the child's life, a new plane of development.

All over the world children undergo significant physical changes during the period 6 to 12 years.

It starts with the teeth. The cute little "pearly whites" start to get loose and fall out. They are replaced with big, often not so white, strong, deeply rooted teeth, that initially look odd in their small mouths.

Then it's the hair. The lovely curly locks start to straighten. The golden blonde streaks start to darken and the hair becomes less fine and it feels like each strand is becoming coarser and thicker.

Then it's the body shape that changes. The chubby fat legs of the three year old, become thinner, often scarily thinner and the child's whole body becomes leaner and thinner than it was.

Despite this, the child is robust and healthy. In fact the child usually experiences extraordinary good health during this stage of life. He gets taller by the day and seems to be able to shake off coughs and colds more easily now.

The child, in this period of life, is energetic, fit and strong. He wants to run, climb, cycle, swim, from morning to night. It is hard to keep up with him. He gets impatient at the adult's lethargy. He feels the need to move, to be active, to be alive.

He sets himself physical challenges all the time. He's not content to just ride his bike, he must practice racing it, he must practice falling off it, he must practice cycling with just one hand on the handlebars, then he must practice with no hands on the handlebars. If he's running, he'll make himself an obstacle course with a few jackets or coats to jump over. If he's swimming, he'll want to practice diving, forwards, backwards, sideways. He's brilliantly creative at thinking up new ways to challenge himself. He pretends to be "Tarzan" swinging from tree to tree.

All this physical activity builds his muscles. Although he is often skinny, he is very robust.

It is during this period that he literally gets "big and strong" and mothers all over the world ask "where has my little baby gone to?"

25

WHY DOES HE ASK SO MANY QUESTIONS?

(Cognitive and Neurological Changes in Late Childhood)

If you spend any time in the company of 6 to 12 year olds you can't help noticing that they never stop asking questions. They ask questions like-

- How much is 1 million multiplied by 1 trillion?

- How come the moon doesn't fall down on us

- Where have all the dinosaurs gone to?

- Who invented languages?

- Where did I come from?

- Why does snow melt?

- Why are rocks hard?

- What is a star?

- Is there a God?

- Do all dogs go to heaven?

These are BIG questions. They involve physics, chemistry, history, mathematics, linguistics, philosophy, geology, astronomy, theology etc.

When Montessori observed that children all over the world, from different countries cultures and creeds all ask these kinds of questions during this precise period in their growth, she became convinced that nature itself must be at work in the child urging him to ask all of these questions in order to develop in him a new type of mental capacity.

So, what's happening to the mind of the 6 to 12 year-old? Is the type of mind that he's had for six years changing? The answer is yes.

Nature itself is urging the child towards a new way of using his mind. Up until age six the child's mind has been entirely concrete. He explored the world one hundred per cent through his senses.

He needed to touch, see, hear, taste or smell things in order to hold them in his mind. Now, nature is helping him to make the passage from the concrete to the abstract. The child who has spent the last six years using his hands and his five senses to explore the world, will now begin to add to his repertoire. He will begin to use a newfound power to explore the world, a power granted to him by nature itself, the power of "abstraction".

The Passage of the Child's Mind from the Concrete to the Abstract.

From the outset, let's be very clear about this issue. The child at this age "adds" to his repertoire of skills to help him learn about the world. When nature gives the child the power of "abstraction," at this stage of development, she doesn't tie up his hands or remove his senses. The child does not stop using his hands or senses to explore the world during this period. He doesn't or shouldn't become a "head" as opposed to a whole person. The "Decartesian split" between mind and body which has been the ruination of many a child, was "man-made," not "nature made."

The mistake that adults have made since the advent of compulsory education is to assume that because the child is now able to "reason things out" he has no need of concrete objects in his learning. This is entirely wrong. What he actually needs is to use concrete objects to arrive at an understanding of abstract things.

When I went to primary school, (between five and 12 years of age), there were no concrete objects in our classroom. We had a pencil and an eraser. The teacher even kept the copybooks locked up. That was in the 70s. The belief was that children had to learn through their heads. Sitting at desks all day copying things from the blackboard was the norm. This was considered education. It's a tribute to the human spirit that anyone of us turned out normal having endured such deprivation of our natural urge to move, to touch, to manipulate objects. I have no doubt that most of us failed to reach our full potential, through no fault of our own, but rather through the fact that we were deprived of the opportunity to build our brains through the activity of the hand. Let us not allow anyone to misunderstand this period of life and make this cruel mistake again.

The change in cognitive development in the 6 to 12 year old is simply this: if we tell a three-year-old child that the goldfish died, he will be sad, maybe even cry, he'll ask can we bury the goldfish, draw a picture of the goldfish, perhaps even buy another goldfish, but the seven year old, will ask, why? Why did the goldfish die? What happened to it? Was it sick? Did it not get enough food? Did it drown? etc. As Montessori put it, "He is not satisfied with the mere collection of facts, he tries to discover their causes."   (From Childhood To Adolescence p36).

Then he will ask more questions such as, "why do things die?" "does everything die?", "what does "die" mean?". "is it sad to die?" "how many times can you die?" or my personal favourite, "did you ever die?'

But, the real question is: why does nature want the child to move from concrete thinking to abstract thinking? The answer is clear. Every invention of man, from the wheel to the Rolls-Royce, from the abacus to the iPhone, came about as a result of man's ability to think abstractly, to hold in his head thoughts about things that are not concrete realities.

If the world is to continue into the future, it is man's ability to think abstractly, to come up with creative solutions and ingenious ideas that we will be relying on, especially nowadays when the earth's resources are dwindling.

So nature is practical and is always gearing us up for the next stage of development. Since every human adult needs to be able to think beyond the concrete, needs to be able to conceptualise things that are not concrete, nature makes a start on this process of moving the human being towards abstract thought during this time period 6 to 12 years. And how does nature do this? By urging the child to ask a new type of question?

Montessori pointed out that, at this period of development, there is an unusual demand on the part of the child to know the reasons for everything. The child at this stage shows an almost daily increase in his powers of reasoning. He wants to find out the underlying causes of things.

This is clearly a newly awakened faculty. It is the reasoning mind and it is the hallmark of the child at this stage of development. Just as the child in the previous stage of development had to touch, pull, poke and probe concrete objects in order to understand them, now the child in this second stage has to probe abstract concepts in order to come to an understanding of them. How does he do this probing? Answer: through his questions. So, in answer to our original query, we would have to say, this is why the child, during this period of life, "asks so many questions."

Neurological Changes in Late Childhood.

In recent years, because of the intervention of fMRI scans, neurologists have been able to take a close look at the living growing brain, and what they found going on in late childhood has astonished them.

At around 11 or 12 years of age, in every child, there occurs what is described in neurology as an "exuberance" of brain cell production. This is a second wave of overproduction of brain cells. The first wave occurred in the womb and possibly during the early months of life, but no one, until recently, knew that it happened a second time.

What it means in effect is that the "grey matter," the thinking part of the brain, grows extra branches and connections on so huge a scale that the change is actually visible on a fMRI Scan. The "grey matter" in the brain of a 12-year-old actually thickens visibly. So there really is a time in life when it's good to be thick! So, if you're a pre-teen and someone tells you, "you're thick", or as my former primary teacher used to say to children "you're a thickhead" you can reply: "why thank you."

But, back to neurology.

This "exuberant" growth of brain cells at around age 12, which is like an enormous web of extra branches and connections in the brain gives indescribable potential to the human being. It is a building up phase of life. It gives the human being a foundation for the capacity to be skilled in many different areas. So much will depend on what the human being does with this potential in the next plane of development.

But for now, it is a time of plenty, plenty to think about, plenty to talk about and plenty to ask questions about. That's why the human being at this stage of development asks "so many questions".

26

WHY IS SHE SO OBSESSED WITH FAIRNESS?

(Moral and Ethical Changes in Late Childhood)

- We were playing snap and Susie took two turns instead of one, that wasn't fair, was it mom?

- The boys were playing cowboys and they wouldn't let me join in because I'm a girl, that's not fair, is it dad?

- Johnny's dog was put to sleep by the vet because it was old, that's not fair, is it mom?

- Some people in the world have no food and we have lots of food, that's not fair, is it dad?

- Molly goes to bed at 9 o'clock, but I have to go to bed at 8 o'clock, that's not fair, is it mom?

- Tom is allowed to go to the store on his own, but I'm not, so that's not fair, is it dad?

- The teacher said we mustn't shout at people, then she shouted at Mark, that's not fair, is it mom?

The examples could go on and on. Anyone, who spends time with children in this age range will be familiar with these sorts of observations and questions.

So, what's going on? Is the child becoming a "tell-tattler"and a whine? The answer is no.

What's happening is simple, but very very important. What's happening is this: nature, once again, is at work in the child, this time guiding his moral and ethical development.

The Awakening of the Moral Sensibility.

Montessori said: "A turning towards the intellectual and moral sides of life occurs at this age."...... "It is at seven years that one may note the beginning of an orientation towards moral questions, towards the judgement of acts."

One of the most interesting features of this age is that the child starts to notice things that he never noticed before, and they all have to do with justice and fairness. To put it simply: it is the awakening of a natural morality, a natural conscience.

The Importance of Being "Just" To Children .

Ask anybody between the ages of 50 and 99 to tell you something they remember from their childhood schooldays and it won't take long before you'll see a pattern in the anecdotes. Virtually all the anecdotes remembered will have a hidden theme and it is this:-"fairness" or "lack of fairness," "justice" or "lack of justice".

Elderly ladies will tell you how the teacher said, "I'm going to give prizes to the "good girls" at the end of class. But, at the end of class, she gave the prizes to her favourites, who sat in the front seats where she had placed them and just ignored the "good girls."

Elderly gentlemen will tell you about how they knew they'd never be picked to play rounders or hurley, so they didn't even volunteer because only the teacher's "cronies" got picked. This sense of injustice stayed with them all their lives.

I remember myself, walking home from school each day when I was about ten or twelve and going over in my mind all the injustices I had witnessed that day and talking out loud to myself I would say: "when I grow up, I will never allow anyone to do that to children."

I didn't actually suffer many of these injustices personally, because I was one of the "good girls" and so I escaped a lot, but I felt the pain and the humiliation that others in my class were put through because they were not bright, or attractive and didn't demonstrate any ability to the teacher (though most of them later grew up to be fine people.)

It cannot be emphasised enough how important it is for the child to experience "justice" at the hands of adults at this period in their lives when nature is leading them towards the development of a "moral sensibility."

If a child, at this age, constantly sees adults behaving unjustly, it will have a very damaging effect on his ability to grow up to become a just person himself.

In my own case, I had a sense of fairness and justice which I believe I got from my family's values. This helped me to see what was wrong about the way my teacher treated the children in my class.

The Concept of Justice: "Distributive Justice" versus "True Justice".

Montessori pointed out that: "It is at this age.... that the concept of justice is born..... The sense of justice, so often missing in man, is found during the development of the young child." She also pointed out that "It is the failure to recognise this fact that engenders a false idea of justice."

Most adults and even schoolteachers have "a false idea of justice." They equate justice with what Montessori called "distributive justice," i.e. "Jonny got three sweets, so I must give Susie three sweets". "I must not give special treatment to one child over another." This is "distributive justice", it is the kind of justice usually meted out in the school and in the home, but it is only an inferior version of "true justice".

"True justice" may demand that Susie be given six sweets, because of her particular circumstances. "True justice" may demand that we do give special treatment to one child over another. You see true justice is not "fair," it is "just".

Adults teach children about fairness, not justice, because they themselves have probably never grasped this important concept that true justice is not fair, it is simply just.

Now if you observe children who are allowed freedom within limits during this period of development, you will notice that nature tries to teach them "true justice," which comes about through what Montessori called "interior education".

But "distributive justice", which is what most parents and teachers try to inculcate in children through ceaseless admonitions like: " you had one turn, so now Jonny must get one turn," according to Montessori, destroys the "inborn, natural sense of true justice."

I remember witnessing an example of this phenomenon of "distributive justice" versus "true justice" many years ago as I sat on a bench outside a supermarket, waiting for a friend to finish her shopping.

There was a group of "traveller" children outside the supermarket who were begging for "loose change" from shoppers as they came out. The oldest girl was the "banker" of the money. She placed the pennies in a little purse tied around her neck. The younger girl and boy were the "workers" whose sad little faces got the most sympathy from the shoppers and therefore the most pennies.

Every ten minutes or so, the little ones would ask their big sister "Will we get the same as you?" At first she told them: "No, I'm the oldest so I will get the most." The two little ones moaned and groaned listing various reasons why they should get as much as their big sister. The arguments went on for some time.

Amazingly, at the end of it all, when it looked like the security man was about to move them on, the older sister sat down on the ground with the two younger ones beside her, poured out her purse of pennies onto the pavement and divided the money up.

To my surprise, she gave the largest amount to the young boy, because she decided that he had collected the most and he had been the one to suggest the location.

I have to admit, (to my shame), that I was astonished at this example of "true justice," particularly because these three children were travellers and my only experience of travellers had been negative ones where I was duped and my kindness had been taken advantage of by adult travellers.

But these were children not adults, and they were different. They were still young enough to feel the promptings of nature urging them towards a "natural law" where "true justice" meant that the little boy should receive the most pennies.

For me it was an incident which gave me a glimpse into the mysterious workings of nature. It showed me how nature which is eminently practical goes about helping the human being to develop what Montessori called an "inborn, natural sense of true justice" and an ability to judge what is morally right.

A Word of Warning:

What Dr Montessori is saying here is of crucial importance for the proper development of the "moral sensibility" in the human being. Like so much of what Montessori says, it has very serious implications not just for an individual human being but for the generations of humans that will come after him. So let's be very clear about what she said. She stated:

> "The principle of distributive justice and individual right, purely external, destroys the inborn, natural sense of true justice."

In childhood, distributive justice may simply mean that if Johnny gets three sweets, Susie gets three sweets.

But, in adulthood, distributive justice may mean that since you've bombed our country and killed our innocent civilians, we will bomb your country and kill your innocent civilians.

In adulthood, true justice may mean that poor countries should be absolved of debt, but rich countries shouldn't be. This is not fair, but it is just.

So when the child, during this period of development constantly plagues the adult with questions about what's fair, be aware that he is not being a whine, he is following the urge of nature prodding him to come to an understanding of justice, so he can develop his moral sensibility.

So when we notice an adult, becoming impatient with a child because the child wants to address some perceived injustice, dishing out severe retorts such as, "stop moaning, you got some sweets", or "get over it, you'll get something later" be aware that, it is precisely this dishing out of "distributive justice", that "destroys" the "inborn, natural sense of true justice."

So, when you hear on the news of people demanding "rights" when it is clear that they have no similar interest in "duties," or when you read in the media of the increase in white collar crime such as bank fraud, insider-trading or corruption in high places, don't be surprised, be reminded that this is exactly what Dr. Montessori predicted, the destruction of the inborn sense of "true justice."

It is not possible to over exaggerate just how crucial it is for the child to develop this "inborn natural sense of true justice." Obstacles to the proper development of the moral character in childhood will result in deviations of the worst kind in adulthood.

Some years ago, I read a summary of the legal defences put up by a number of priests who had been convicted of sexual abuse of children. A number of them blamed the fact that they had not been given sufficient "guidelines" telling them what was right and wrong in their contact with children.

It seemed incomprehensible to me that these people were actually saying that without "guidelines" they didn't know that it was wrong to rape and abuse children.

Nature sets out to prevent such ignorance and such wicked defences. Our courts would be a lot emptier and the court lists a lot shorter if more human beings had an "inborn, natural sense of true justice".

Our mistake, which Dr. Montessori pointed out, is to "think that the problem of morality only occurs later". This, according to Montessori, "is to overlook the change that is already going on".

Not only that, but as Montessori points out, later on, as the child gets older, "the moral problem becomes a good deal more difficult unless the child has been helped during the sensitive period." The help he needs in this period of life is that which will "encourage interior development."

Imagine a world where the vast majority of human beings had such a well established "interior development" that we didn't need to put up signs saying such things as: "Domestic violence is wrong," "Child abuse is a crime," "Speeding Kills". Such a world would be possible if the "interior" moral development of the human being was perfected before he reached adulthood.

Now, how could that come about? Answer, by giving the human being a sensitive period for the development of a moral sensibility early on in life.

Since moral and ethical standards take a long time to develop, the work must begin early on in life. That's exactly what nature has done. Nature, has planned it that the ground work on moral and ethical development should begin during the period 6 to 12 years.

So, to answer our original question: THIS is the reason why the child in this period of development appears to be "so obsessed with fairness".

27

WHY DOES HE FEEL SO "HEMMED IN"?

(Social Changes in Late Childhood)

Tommy is eight years old. His mom is at a loss to know what to do with him sometimes.

She brings him to extracurricular activities almost everyday after school. These activities include swimming lessons, gymnastics, music lessons and tennis/hockey coaching.

He's usually happy enough to participate in these activities, but when the lessons are over, he is frequently grumpy and bad humoured. He frequently seems "ill-at ease" with himself.

He constantly wants to "go out" but he doesn't really know where he wants to go or what he wants to do. He says he feels "hemmed in".

His mum remembers feeling this sense of being "ill at ease" when she was a child. Looking back, she thought it was the lack of extracurricular activities that must have caused her unsettled feelings. Yet these activities are clearly not doing much for her son.

So, why does he feel so unsettled? Why does he feel so "hemmed in"?

Well, the answer is explained very clearly by Dr. Maria Montessori. Montessori discovered, from her observations of children all over the world, that during the period 6 to 12 years the child goes through a re-birth.

"He has become a strong being, a being who is entering into a new world."
(From Childhood to Adolescence. p23)

Whereas in the first plane the child's motto was "let me do it myself," in the second plane his motto is "let me find out about it myself so that I can fully experience it myself".

The child does not want the benefit of anyone else's knowledge or experience at this period of life, he wants to find out everything for himself.

Nature is urging him towards the real goal of this plane which is, intellectual independence. Intellectual independence necessitates finding out things for yourself, this necessarily involves "wider boundaries" and a "larger field of action".

Dr. Montessori says "the adult finds this being, newly born to the world, a bit annoying."

He's annoying because we don't usually understand what's going on with him. Why doesn't he like school anymore? Why isn't he satisfied with swimming, music and tennis lessons?

Well, the answer is simple. "The closed school" is no longer sufficient for him. "Something is lacking for the full development of his personality." Montessori says "We note a certain regression in his character," but she pointed out that this is merely a reaction to "an environment that has become inadequate." p10 C to A

But we don't understand this. "We say that he is 'naughty' and correct him." "Most of the time we are unaware of the cause of his 'naughtiness.'"

But the child, by his very behaviour, demonstrates the problem. "The closed environment is felt as a constraint, and that is why he no longer wishes to go to school." "He prefers to catch frogs or play in the street." A "Huckleberry Finn" phase comes over him. Nature begins to whisper new things in his ears, things like:

"You need to spread your wings a bit now."

"You need to do adventurous things."

"You need to experience natural life."

"You need to hike through forests."

"You need to climb rock faces and hills."

"You need to camp under the stars."

"You need to fish and cook your catch over a wood-fire."

"You need to wash in a stream, not a bathroom."

"You need to do these things with your peers and mentors, not your family."

"You need to be part of an organised group, a "gang" with codes and rules.

"You need to distance yourself a little bit from your parents, yet know they are

nearby, in case you need them."

Montessori says that the child at this period "feels the need of something different, a more rigid environment with far wider social contacts."

She says the Boy Scout movement fits the bill, because it offers children at this stage of development "a more exacting environment," "wider social contacts" and "independence from their families". (The Four Planes)1937.

When I was growing up, one of my relatives joined the Boy Scouts. I was very puzzled by this because this particular boy disliked school, hated being told what to do by adults, and would have been regarded as a bit of a "tear-away". Yet he voluntarily joined the Boy Scouts, was very proud to wear the uniform and took the rules and duties very seriously.

Years later, I asked him why he loved the Boy Scouts so much considering he disliked school. The answer he gave me was almost exactly what Montessori said,

"In conforming to the rules of scouting, a new dignity is born in the child."(p18)

He said that the fact that joining was voluntarily, that the aim was to help and protect others, that no one made him obey the scoutmaster, as he voluntarily agreed to do this, along with many others who also volunteered to do the same, was what attracted him to scouting.

He said he did not feel confined as he did within the walls of a classroom. The only constraints on him were the "moral" principles of scouting that he freely chose to accept and abide by.

He said he remembers enjoying the rigours of the long walks and hikes and the nights in the open air.

He said he loved the challenges of setting up tents, lighting fires and the feeling of independence and dignity that comes from being able to survive without family for a few days and nights, and above all the sense of being part of "a gang", a crowd of like-minded people.

He said, although the school had brought his class on several "hikes," none of them gave him that feeling of dignity and self-sufficiency that the Boy Scout hikes afforded him, in fact most of them were unpleasant affairs full of rules that had to be followed without any choice or input.

Since the "boy Scout" type of social life is what the human being needs at this stage of development, is it any wonder that music lessons, gymnastic lessons and so on, don't "cut it" for the child.

The child needs to respond to nature's promptings at this period of life. These are promptings to: endure physical challenge, get a bit of distance from family, develop a moral conscience, make voluntary commitments, be part of a "gang" of like minded individuals, with codes and rules that they all voluntarily agree to.

However, because most of us are ignorant of "nature's promptings" we don't understand what the child needs. So we give him highly organised, heavily monitored, adult controlled activities, often indoors, with lists of dos and don'ts attached to them and often serious consequences for non-compliance.

Then we ask why does he feel so "hemmed in"?

28

SUMMARY OF THE CHARACTERISTICS OF THE CHILD 6 - 12 YEARS.

The Period of Childhood

A Period of Consolidation

The Consolidation of the Child

Duration: 6-12 Years

Subdivision: 6 - 9 Years

                9-12 Years

General Description:

This is a period of great stability.

Physical Characteristics:

Nature sends a sign that a new stage in development is occurring. The milk teeth fall out, the hair thickens, the child becomes leaner and taller. It is a period of robust good health. The child becomes "big and strong."

Mental Characteristics:

This is the real intellectual period. The child develops great reasoning faculties, and he is interested in learning about everything. He wants to know how everything came about, he asks the "big questions."

Neurological Characteristics:

Neurologically, something hugely significant occurs around age 12. A second wave of overproduction of brain cells occurs (the first overproduction occurred in the womb and possibly even in the first 18 months of life.) Now, in this period of development, the "grey matter," or thinking part of the brain, grows extra branches and connections on so huge a scale that the change is visible on a f MRI scan. This "exuberant" growth gives the brain enormous potential. This is a building up phase. It gives the human being a foundation for the capacity to be skilled in many different areas. So much will depend on what the human being does with this potential in the next plane of development.

Social Characteristics:

The child becomes less egocentric and now actively seeks the company of his peers. He loves to be part of a group. A herd instinct develops. Children at this period also develop their own rules for social life. They form clubs with secret passwords and membership codes.

Emotional Characteristics:

Children at this age begin to wean themselves away from their parents. They feel the need to distance themselves by joining the scouts etc.

Needs:

Intellectual stimulation. The child needs real exposure to grand ideas and big concepts. He needs to see the big picture. He needs exposure to other cultures and customs around the world.

Sensitive Periods:

Montessori claimed that nature gives every normal child between six and twelve years a sensitive period for imagination, a new reasoning ability and a sensitive period for the building of a moral conscience.

29

HOW CAN WE HELP THE HUMAN BEING DURING THE PERIOD
6 - 12 Years?

Physical Considerations:

Dr. Montessori pointed out that the period of life between six and twelve years, is generally a period of robust good health. The child is getting big and strong. He has energy. He is fit. He wants to run, climb, swim, cycle, do high jumps, do cartwheels, balance on trampolines etc.

Taking into account these physical considerations, Montessori recognised that the human being, during this period of life, has a great need for:

- physically challenging activities.

- opportunities to run, climb, cycle etc.

- opportunities to be in the outdoors,

- opportunities to be in natural environments.

Cognitive Considerations:

Montessori states: "The need for abstraction and intellectual activity makes itself felt around the seventh year." But she also states, in the same paragraph, that "the child needs to classify and absorb the exterior world by means of his senses." Montessori was aware that these are two sides to the same coin. The child between six and twelve years has an increased intellectual capacity and his mind is being directed by nature to move from a purely concrete understanding of things to abstractions, but he needs to arrive at abstract thought through the manipulation of concrete things. Montessori wrote: "Children show a great attachment to the abstract subjects when they arrive at them through manual activity."   (To Educate The Human Potential)p9.

Taking into account these intellectual considerations, Montessori recognised that the human being during this period of life needs:

- opportunities to continue "to learn through the activity of the hand."

- opportunities for the child's hands to work "side by side" with the child's intelligence.

- opportunities to come to grasp "abstract subjects" by arriving at them "through manual activity."

Montessori asked: "Must a man be classified either as a worker with his head or with his hands, instead of being allowed to function with his whole personality?"

She asked: "Where is the logic in the view that one-sided development can be beneficial to the whole?"

She strenuously emphasised the need for "mental functioning aided by manual activity."

Social Considerations:

Montessori recognised that the child from 6 to 12 years, needs to "enlarge his field of action." He needs "wider boundaries for his social experiences". He needs "to establish social relationships in a larger society."

Taking into account this newfound desire to widen his horizons and spread his wings, Montessori recognised that the human being, during the period 6 to 12 years needs:

- opportunities to have social events outside the school walls.

- opportunities to take control over these social experiences.

- opportunities to organise, plan and execute "going out" experiences.

- opportunities to join organisations like the Boy Scouts which are a good fit for the social needs of the human being at this period 6-12 years.

Emotional Considerations:

Montessori recognised that the child from 6 to 12 years feels a need to distance himself a little from his parents. If all has gone well with his prior emotional attachments, he will feel strong enough emotionally to break away a little from family life and spend an overnight with a relative or friend or even go away for a weekend with the Boy Scouts.

Taking into account this change in the emotional needs of the human being during the period 6 to 12 years, Montessori recognised that the human being during this period of life needs:

- opportunities to build emotional independence by having an occasional overnight or weekend away with friends or a club like the Boy Scouts.

(But this must never be forced or cajoled. It must come from the child.)

Economic Considerations:

Montessori recognised that at this period of life 6-12 years "it is necessary that he (the child) come to understand, among other realities, what money ought to represent." She said "It is therefore necessary that children have firsthand experience in buying objects themselves and that they come to realise what they can buy with a unit of the money of their country."

Taking into account this need for the child to understand the economic dimension to life, Montessori recognised that the human being, during this period needs:

- opportunities to buy and sell products, possibly goods they have made or grown themselves.

- opportunities to learn about the currency of their country, and what they can buy with a unit of currency.

Ethical and Moral Considerations:

Montessori pointed out that: "The 7 to 12 your old period, then, constitutes one of particular importance for moral education." She recognised the child's obsession with justice and fairness as a sensitive period in development. She pointed out that this is the age when: "the understanding of the relationship between one's acts and the needs of others" is born.

Taking into account this new sensitivity towards ethics and morals which appears in the human being during the period 6 to 12 years, Montessori recognised that the human being, during this period needs:

- to witness adults acting fairly and justly.

- opportunities to encourage "interior development".

- protection against the destruction of his "inborn, natural sense of true justice."

MONTESSORI'S SUGGESTIONS FOR A SUITABLE ENVIRONMENT

FOR THE HUMAN BEING 6-12 YEARS

When Montessori examined the physical, cognitive, social, emotional, spiritual and economic needs of the child in the period 6 to 12 years, she suggested what she believed would be a type of education that would embrace all of those needs. She called it "Cosmic Education". The word "cosmic," in this context, means comprehensive, all-inclusive, vast.

What is "Cosmic" Education?

Firstly, to put it into very straightforward language, cosmic education is an education which tries to give children a global vision. It is an education which aims to help children to ultimately, not immediately, come to an understanding and appreciation of their place, their role, their function, their task as human beings, in this huge, awesome universe that we find ourselves in.

It is an education which tries to help the child to come to an appreciation of all that has gone on before him. The child needs to know that things were not always as they are now. There was a time when even the simplest of things which we take for granted, e.g. the food that we eat, the clothes that we wear, the vehicles we drive around in, did not exist. And it is thanks to the work, the toil, the inventions and the creations of the many nameless and forgotten people who went before us that we have so much in our world today.

Cosmic education attempts to help the child, not only to come to feel a sense of appreciation, of respect, of awe, of gratitude to those nameless generations of people who toiled away before us, but also to feel a sense of confidence in the knowledge that, "if they could contribute something to mankind, well then, so can I."

Montessori believed that children need to know, indeed all of us need to know, that our lives have a purpose, and that we have a contribution to make to the world we live in. And the success or failure of cosmic education can be judged by whether or not it helps to produce people who feel this confidence, who feel this sense of purpose, who feel that they are part of the order of things, who feel that they are vital participants in the ongoing life of the universe.

Secondly, cosmic education is an education which aims to make children aware of the vital interdependence that exists in nature between one form of life and another, and this includes the interdependence of man with nature. Interdependence is the key word here.

In practical terms, it means showing the child that the little honeybee, as it goes about its business gathering nectar for its young, although totally unaware of it, is fulfilling a very vital role in the cycle of nature. Because, if it didn't feed on the nectar in the flower, its legs would not spread pollen from one plant to another and the colonisation of flowers would not occur. Without the spread of pollen from flower to flower, the fertilisation of flowers would not occur and so flowers would not produce seeds. Without seeds, new flowers would not grow to replace the ones which die and so flowers would simply die out and become extinct. If there were no flowers, then there would be no nectar for the bees and the bees would eventually die out.

In a lecture she gave at the peace Congress in Copenhagen in 1937, Montessori said,

"All creatures who live on earth have a cosmic role to play... the disappearance of one species in a certain place upsets the balance, because the lives of all species are interrelated".

So the central idea in cosmic education, is this idea of a cosmic plan in which all things, whether consciously or unconsciously, serve the great purpose of life.

So, cosmic education is about presenting the world to a child as something that makes sense, something that is not random or chaotic, something that reveals a great plan, and something that reveals the interconnectedness of all things. It is a philosophy of life which shows, that there is meaning out there. Life is not absurd or meaningless. All things are connected and interrelated for a purpose. For Montessori, there was not just a plan, but also a planner. For Montessori, it was the Christian God who was the planner but she recognised that all people, whether Christian, Hindu, Buddhist, Muslim or no religion, could still accept that there is a great plan and that we are all consciously or unconsciously involved in that plan.

Thirdly, cosmic education, is an education which tries to give the child a framework, a huge framework upon which to organise all that he has already absorbed and learned during the first six years of his life and all that he will observe and learn in the future, as he goes about his daily life living, breathing, sleeping, thinking, growing and developing.

This framework should be like a giant web. Information can be placed anywhere on it, there is no beginning, middle or end. Information can come in, and a bit can be placed here, and other bits can be placed there, and eventually, as the years go by, the links between the various areas will become clearer. As Montessori put it, "Since nothing exists that does not constitute a part of the whole, it is sufficient to choose one detail at random, which will then become a point of departure in the study of the whole." It will be like a giant "join the dots," except that the child is not asked to go from 1 to 2 to 3 etc. Instead, he may decide to start at number five then he may move to number nine, then he may decide to have a look at number two, and then number seven. But eventually, and maybe it will take some years, the dots will join up, revealing a picture, a clear picture of the universe with all its connections, and most importantly man's role within it.

Why "Cosmic" Education?

Montessori wrote,

"This plan of cosmic education..... is no new idea, for it has been the natural plan wherever there has been education in the real sense... for children first to be taught the creation of the world and man's place in it."

(To Educate The Human Potential p7)

So, it was always the practice, for children to be taught first about the creation of the world and man's place in it, before being taught anything else. So, what happened? Why did this practice full into disuse? And more importantly, what were the results of the discontinuance of this type of education?

Well, the answers to these questions lie in the history of philosophy and philosophical thought. There is a famous painting, a fresco, painted on the wall in the Vatican. It was painted by Raphael in 1510. This painting really explains this whole problem of education in a nutshell. The painting is called The School of Athens. It is a painting which depicts the famous Greek philosophers Plato and Aristotle talking together. In this painting, you can see Plato with one finger pointing upwards which indicates that he was pointing towards the absolutes or "ideals" as he called them. In contrast, in the painting, you can see Aristotle with his fingers spread wide and pointing downwards to the earth, which means that he is emphasising the "particulars," the individual things which are all around us.

This emphasis on the particulars rather than on the whole, was brought into the philosophy of the Middle Ages by St Thomas Aquinas. This set the stage for the humanistic elements of the Renaissance and the basic problems those humanistic elements created.

Now, to keep it very simple, the problem is this. If we begin our education with man alone, if we begin with only the individual things in the world, what Aristotle called the particulars, the problem we face is how to find any ultimate and adequate meaning for the individual things. Without some ultimate meaning for a person, what is the purpose of life and what would be the basis for morals, for values, for law?

Beginning from man alone, Renaissance humanism and humanism ever since, has found no way to arrive at universals which give meaning to existence and morals. There were many positive results to Acquinas's teaching, but the negative results of the teaching was that the individual things, the particulars, tended to be made independent, autonomous and consequently meaningless.

We can think of it like this. The individual things gradually and increasingly came to be seen as having meaning in and of themselves and not in relation to anything else. Man was seen as having meaning in and of himself and not in relation to anything else, and when this happens, slowly but surely, meaning itself is put in jeopardy and meaning itself disappears.

You can imagine it like this. Supposing a number of people receive an odd shaped piece of card in the post. They are each informed that the piece of card is valuable and must be studied. So, one person studies the shape of the card and writes a thesis all about the shape of this card. Another person studies the colour of the card and writes a thesis all about the colour of this card. Yet another person studies the texture of the card and writes a thesis all about the texture of this card. But what none of these people know, and what known of them can find out, is that each card is really only one piece of a very large and very important jigsaw puzzle. And if all of the pieces were put together, a pattern would emerge, a picture would appear. But none of the people know that their little individual piece of card is part of a big picture and so they don't even look for the big picture.

And so, to put it in a nutshell, if we offer the child an education which emphasises the particulars without showing how these particulars fit into the big picture, then the child doesn't ever come to see the big picture, he just sees meaningless fragments, he just sees those individual bits of card, and on their own, the bits of card are meaningless.

But, the child does not want meaninglessness. He is wired to look for meaning, to look for answers. He needs to hear what Scully said to Mulder in the X-Files, "The answers are out there Mulder, you just have to know where to look."

Cosmic education is necessary because, we need to tell children that the answers are out there, and we need to help children to know where to look for those answers.

As Montessori put it, "To bring detached notions (to the child) is to bring confusion ....We must determine ties between facts.....By determining.....the correlation between facts, we create for him a philosophy, and why can't the child do philosophy?"

Cosmic education helps the child to create a philosophy of life. Montessori wrote,

"Through long experimentation, we have now arrived at.......the possession of a key which can unlock for children the gates of a healthy and happy education. On our courage and perseverance in its use depends the future of humanity".

We believe that key is cosmic education.

How is "Cosmic" Education Presented To The Child?

Montessori saw that children all over the world during the years 6 to 12, are prompted by nature to ask the BIG questions, these are questions that involve philosophy, religion, mathematics, history, geography, astronomy, chemistry, physics, biology, geology etc.

Montessori also saw that the problem the 6 to 12 year old faces is this: nature urges him to ask many, many questions. However, because the child now thinks about so many vast areas, he can easily become confused. His mind wanders from one area to the next, it goes around in circles, causing his attention to wonder, his focus to be non-existent, and the child himself to become frustrated and exhausted from trying to figure it all out and make connections between things.

So, what's the solution?
The solution is to give him a scaffold to hang everything on. That scaffold is the universe itself, the big picture. Montessori suggested that we give to the child "a vision of the whole universe," because "all things are part of the universe," and are connected with each other to form a whole unity.

She said that this approach helps the mind of the child to stop wondering and allows him to place bits of knowledge onto the scaffold as he comes across them. This sounds like a great idea but how do we present the big picture, "the universe," to the child? The answer is simple. Montessori came up with the idea of presenting the big picture to the child as a series of thrilling tales. During her time in India, Maria Montessori and her son Mario, devised a number of short, fascinating stories, designed to arouse the child's imagination, causing him to ask questions about everything and causing him to look for answers to everything. These stories are known as the five great lessons. They are:

- The story of creation.
- The story of the coming of life.
- The story of the coming of humans.
- The story of language.
- The story of numbers.

These stories lead the child directly to studies in the area of physics, chemistry, biology, history, geography, astronomy, earth sciences, languages, ancient civilisations, mathematics, religion and philosophy.

And, as Montessori said, the child begins to ask questions such as:

Who am I?
Where do I come from?
What am I here for?
Where am I going to?

179

So, the child, even at the tender age of six years can be offered, not just cold, hard facts about how chemical reactions resulted in the formation of stars and planets, but can be offered an opportunity to ponder philosophical questions, even at the tender age of six, nine, and twelve. So that when he reaches 18 or 21 years, he won't be facing these questions for the first time, he will have been thinking and rethinking these questions over and over for many years, altering and adjusting his views as he gets older and is learning more and more about the world and as his emotional, social, intellectual and spiritual development progresses.

So, how can we go about presenting the five great stories to the child?

Again, the answer is simple. In Montessori schools for 6 to 12 year olds children are invited by the teacher to sit around a storyteller, almost like sitting around a campfire, to hear the first great story, which is the story of the creation of the universe.

The storyteller, presents the story as a fascinating tale, making it as dramatic and as exciting as possible, appealing always to the child's imagination.

For the telling of this first story, the creation of the universe, the teacher needs to set the scene. He needs to create the right atmosphere. He may choose to start off with a darkened room, because the story aims to make the child experience first hand that darkness enveloped the universe at the beginning. When the storyteller says "and then there was light," a single candle is lit in the darkened room.

The five great stories do not support any particular religious approach. They are neither creationist nor evolutionary in their depiction of the creation of the universe and the beginning of life. They are in fact, compatible with all major religions and theories of creation.

So, the storyteller tells the children the first story, in as dramatic and as exciting a way as possible. He accompanies the story with a few small experiments to aid the children's imaginations showing how minerals and chemicals first interacted with each other and formed the elements fire, water and air, and how matter transformed into solids, liquids and gases and how particles joined together and formed the earth and how heavier particles sank to the earth's core and volcanoes erupted sending molten rock, ashes and vapour into the atmosphere, how mountains were formed and the atmosphere condensed into rain, creating oceans, lakes and rivers. For this part of the story, the teacher uses fascinating charts, diagrams and illustrations.

The stories aim to take the child back in time, through the use of his imagination to allow him:

- To be there at the moment of creation.
- To be there when the stars and the planets were flung into space.
- To be there when the first life appeared on the earth.
- To be there to see the growth and spread of plant life over time.
- To be there to witness the coming of human life.
- To be there to see early man grow food, build homes, make tools etc .
- To be there to witness the beginnings of language.
- To be there to see the origins of writing.
- To be there to witness the beginnings of numeracy.
- To be there to see the human being as he learns to build civilisations.
- To be there to witness the great inventiveness of man from the wheel to the chariot, from the abacus to the iPad.

Then cosmic education leads the child to ask questions such as:

If the humans who went before me could achieve all this through their toil, their creativity, their ingenuity, what can I achieve through my intelligence, my creativity, my ingenuity?

Cosmic education leads a child to feel confidence, to feel hope, to feel excitement about the possibilities for every human being on the planet. It leads the child to feel, as Shakespeare put it:

What a piece of work is man.

Through cosmic education, the child is allowed to feel and to experience the greatness of man, and the child is brought to feel a sense of gratitude to the generations who went before him, who toiled to bring civilisations forward, and he feels a confidence in his place in time and history. He begins to feel certain that he too has a part to play, that the children of the future may look back on his generation's achievements with the same sense of gratitude that he now feels towards his predecessors. And so the child naturally starts to ask himself questions such as:

What is man's role in this wonderful universe?

What is my role in this wonderful universe?

Montessori pointed out that it is the child who starts to ask these philosophical questions not the teacher giving out homework assignments. The child is led by the great lessons to philosophise, to think about man and his role in the universe.

The five great lessons do not attempt to give the child all the information that could be given. They do not go into details about anything; that is the role of the Key Lessons, which follow later on. The Great Lessons just offer a skeleton, a framework. They give just enough information to spark the beginnings of an interest in the child so that the child starts to ask his own questions and then starts to look for his own answers.

This, is what real learning is all about, asking your own questions, looking for your own answers, learning to investigate things for yourself. In fact, this is the pathway to lifelong learning.

As the years go by, the child will take up these questions again and again and delve deeper into them. There is a kind of spiral structure to the type of education proposed by Montessori for 6 to 12 year olds. During the years 6 to 9 seeds are scattered. During these years the seeds are growing, maturing and this process continues during the years 9 to 12, when there is a kind of consolidation of the knowledge and understanding that was gained in the previous three years. So that by 12 years of age the child has mulled over things for a long time, adjusting his understanding over and over again as new information comes his way.

It is very important to note that in Montessori's approach, the teacher, having presented the story does not follow it up by requesting an essay or a piece of work from the children on anything relating to the story, instead the children are left free, to ponder on what they have heard .This is referred to as "the rest."

The children are free to explore, individually, or in small groups, any questions which have been prompted by the story. Some children will work with timelines, some may perform simple experiments which the teacher has prepared to support the story, others may gather information from library books. But, the real difference between traditional education and Montessori cosmic education is this: the children will not be compelled to do anything following a story. They will be allowed time to assimilate what has been enacted or narrated. This approach allows the story to steer up the child's imagination, so that, within days, he can't stop asking questions, wanting to know more, and so he gives himself classwork and homework, because he wants to learn more, he wants to find out more about these things which have now captivated his imagination.

The word imagination is crucial here because Montessori was convinced that it was the child's imagination that we must appeal to if we wish to present a vision of the cosmic plan.

She wrote:

"The secret of good teaching is to regard the child's intelligence as a fertile field in which seeds may be sown, to grow under the heat of flaming imagination."

"Our aim therefore is not merely to make the child understand, and still less to force him to memorise but so to touch his imagination as to enthuse him to his inmost core."   (To Educate The Human Potential.)

To summarise then, Montessori suggested a plan of education for the human being 6 to 12 years which she called Cosmic Education. Its aims are:

• To present the child with the Big Picture, starting with the creation of the Universe charting the development of life on earth, celebrating the coming of the human being with all his inventions and achievements from the wheel to the iPad.

• To allow the child to feel a sense of gratitude to the generations who went before him, on whose shoulders he now stands, and on whose toil and ingenuity he now builds.

• To allow the child to feel a sense of hope, a sense of excitement, a sense of "if they could achieve all that, what can I and my generation achieve?"

• To allow the child to see that all creatures have a Cosmic Task, a job to do on this earth, from the honey bee to the human being, because all life is interrelated and interdependent.

• To cause the child to ask: "What is my role in this amazing world that I find myself in?"

• To give the child a giant framework upon which to hang all the knowledge that he has absorbed during the first six years of his life and all the knowledge that he is taking in now, during this extraordinary period of intellectual growth, the period 6 to 12 years.

This then, is how we can help the human being during the period 6 to 12 years.

PART FIVE

HOW DOES THE ADOLESCENT CONSTRUCT HIMSELF?

(The Years 12 to 18) (The Age of Passion)

30

WHY ARE THEY SO SPOTTY?

(Physical Changes In Adolescence)

Facts:

- Acne affects over 60 million people in the US alone.

- Acne affects about 90% of adolescents.

- 92% of acne sufferers have felt depressed because of it.

- Acne breakouts peek at 14 to 17 years of age in girls.

- Acne breakouts peek at 16 to 19 years of age in boys.

- The global acne market is estimated to reach revenues of over 3 billion dollars by 2016.

Remember what happened to the human being at 6 years of age? His little pearly white teeth started to fall out, his body became thinner and longer and his lovely curly hair began to straighten and thicken. What was this all about?

It was nature heralding a change, giving us a physical sign that something remarkable was happening internally in the child, in the invisible recesses of the mind. The child was moving from the world of concrete reality to the world of abstractions. He was moving into a realm where he could now use his new "aids", i.e "abstraction," "reason" and "imagination" to grapple with the world he found himself in. In short, he was moving on to the next stage of growth, the second plane of development.

Now, six years later, something very similar is happening again. Nature, once more, heralds a period of change in human development. The human being is about to leave the second plane of development and move into the third plane.

This is a "critical period" in development because it represents a death and a re-birth. The human being must undergo the death of childhood and a re-birth into a period we call "adolescence," which is a type of "holding ground" on the way to adulthood. For a period of six years, the human being will be neither a child nor an adult.

This is not an accident, it is nature's design. The "prolonged adolescence" of the human being, parallels the "prolonged infancy" of the child, and just as there are very precise reasons to account for the "prolonged infancy" of the child, there are also very precise reasons for the "prolonged adolescence" of the human being. These reasons will be explained in the following pages.

Maria Montessori was a doctor, a brain specialist and an expert in disease. In her book, From Childhood to Adolescence, she made the following observations about the physical nature of adolescence:

- "This is a critical period"

- "The body grows rapidly, but not at a uniform pace, so that a functional imbalance results."

- "This results in an insufficiency of the heart which causes palpitations and the waning of the resistance of the lungs."

- "It is good to observe closely the growth of the adolescent.... as well as to make periodic checks of heart and lungs, even when the adolescent seems to be in perfect health."

- "Particular attention must be paid to diet. It must be both abundant and nutritious."

- "In rural locations where vegetables, fruits, eggs and milk products conserve all their value, foods such as raw vegetables and especially fruit accompanied by milk, milk substitutes, and eggs must abound in the menus."

- "The ordinary poisons, alcohol and tobacco, must be banished."

- "Life in the open air and sunshine, bathing and swimming ought to occur as frequently as possible, almost as in the sanatorium. Flat terrain, where long walks are easy, on the seashore or in the woods, is preferable to a high mountain where hikes may strain the heart at this stage of development when the chest is insufficiently developed."

From Childhood to Adolescence p 116/117

Montessori pointed out that adolescence, especially the period 12 to 15 years, has parallel features with the years 0 to 3 when the human being undergoes a huge physical transformation. Physical growth is rapid in both of these periods. Montessori pointed out that "it is easy to understand how rapid growth can weaken an individual." Both of these periods of life are periods of physical vulnerability. Sudden illnesses are common in both of them.

It is noteworthy that in the period birth to 3 years, sudden infant death, (SID) is a painful reality. In the period of adolescence, sudden adult death, (SAD) is now making headlines.

Perhaps we should pay careful heed to Montessori's admonition that the growth of adolescents should be observed closely and "periodic checks of heart and lungs" should be carried out "even when the adolescent seems to be in perfect health".

- Certain physical diseases are more common in adolescence e.g. meningitis, glandular fever and acne, all peak in adolescence.

- Most mental illnesses, which often have significant physical repercussions have their roots in adolescence, depression and schizophrenia being the prime examples.

- For girls, the onset of menstruation regularly causes abdominal cramps, headaches, mood swings, and tiredness.

- For boys, the increase of growth hormones flooding the body can cause frustration, irritability, a feeling of being totally out of sorts, much of the time.

- In addition to these well-documented illnesses, vague aches and pains often rear their ugly heads in adolescence leaving puzzled doctors forced to give a diagnosis of "growing pains."

All in all, adolescence is not a time of robust good health. It is a period of physical vulnerability, due to the strain of rapid growth.

The average adolescent grows at an astonishing rate, often becoming taller than his own parents, in the space of a year or two.

This results in a host of maladies, which thankfully are almost all, non-life-threatening.

Perhaps, nature wants all of us, including the adolescent himself, to have a visual reminder of the physical vulnerability of adolescence.

Maybe, just maybe, that's why, they're "so spotty."

31

WHY IS SHE SO TOUCHY?

(Emotional Changes in Adolescence)

I can't remember where I saw this, but it was a few seconds clip from a film where a middle aged father is sitting at his kitchen table, only half awake, over breakfast. His teenage daughter walks into the kitchen, grabs a handful of dry cereal from the pack and starts to eat it like popcorn. Her hair is hanging over her face so you can't really see her expression. The father, absent-mindedly mutters.....'morning, how are you today?" The daughter flies into a rage, throws the cereal into the sink screaming,

"Always the third degree,
Why cant you mind your own business!
Just leave me alone!"

Then she storms back up to her room and slams the door.

It was a funny sketch, meant to be lighthearted, but, you know, I regret to say, that I remember behaving in a similar fashion on one occasion with my own father when I was 16, even though I was otherwise a very well-balanced, measured, peaceful type of person, and I remember being totally shocked at the intensity of my own outburst.

The fact that I can still remember the outburst, some 40 years later, is proof of its intensity. So, why is she so touchy? What's going on emotionally during the period 12 to 18 years? In her book, From Childhood to Adolescence, Montessori pointed out that the adolescent suffers: "doubts hesitations, violent emotions and discouragements." The adolescent is often emotional and sensitive to a degree that the non-adolescent human being finds hard to comprehend. I remember well that feeling of being "empty and aching" that suddenly descends on you out of nowhere during adolescence and the feeling of being powerless to get rid of it and unable to comprehend it.

So what's the cause of all this turmoil? For decades, the experts have told us that raging hormones are the cause of all this emotional stuff and indeed hormones do play a large part in adolescent development. But, we believe that the answer as to why the human being is so touchy during this period of life lies in nature.

Nature needs the human being to start thinking about some very serious issues during this period of his life. The issues are big ones. They concern the purpose of life on this planet and, in particular, the purpose of his life on this planet. And just as the human being during the period of the creation of the child, feels an unconscious urge to construct himself, we suggest that during this parallel period, the period of the creation of the adult, nature causes the human being to feel an unconscious urge to seek out the meaning of life in general and the meaning of his life in particular.

So, while the teacher goes on about the Franco-Prussian war, the adolescent is thinking "why am I here?" and he doesn't mean why am I here in this classroom, he means "why am I here in this world?" "why is anyone here?" "Is there any purpose to my existence?" "If there is, what is it and how can I find it?

During this period of life, academically inclined adolescents will often immerse themselves in poetry and literature in the search for answers. Creatively disposed adolescents will turn to literature, dance or drama in the search for answers. Philosophically disposed adolescents will turn to discussion, debate and talks well into the small hours about life, love, and the human predicament. Most adolescents will turn to music, both passively, through listening and actively through playing instruments in their search for answers and many will compose songs during this period of life. Indeed some of our most penetrating songs and pieces of music owe their origin to this period of life. Many adolescents will turn to relationships with the opposite sex, in an effort to find meaning and purpose.

Other adolescents will find different ways of dealing with the emotions that flood over them. They will immerse themselves in alcohol, drugs, promiscuous sexual relations, and illicit behaviours. For them perhaps the quest for the meaning and purpose of life seems too hard or too painful so they opt to shut out the voice of nature and they refuse to engage in the quest.

Some readers may react with scorn to all of this and say this is way too serious an interpretation of adolescent moods. We would put the statistics of self harm, alcohol abuse, drug abuse, sexual disease and suicide in this period of life in front of them and say, the figures don't lie. Adolescence is a dangerous period of life. The questions that human beings face at this period are huge and scary and that's "why she's so touchy."

32

WHY CAN'T HE CONCENTRATE ANYMORE?

(Intellectual Changes in Adolescence)

Keith was a terrific schoolchild. During the years 6 to 12 he had a voracious appetite for learning. He wanted to know the why and wherefore of everything. You couldn't keep up with him. His dad used to buy him science kits and techno magazines every Saturday, and he loved to go to astronomy clubs, zoos, museums and just about any place that opened up the world to him. He would be so engrossed in his reading and his computer games that an earthquake couldn't distract him. He had powerful concentration.

Now, he's 14. He is sitting at his desk in his bedroom trying to complete his homework assignment on algebraic equations. He's been at it for two hours. He's written his name and the date! So, why can't he concentrate any more?

We suggest that, once again, the answer lies in nature. During the period 12 to 18 years, we suggest that nature steers the human being's attention away from purely academic things and urges him to focus on other areas that involve a huge amount of hand and brain activity.

Once again the similarities between the period of life devoted to the creation of the child and this period which is devoted to the creation of the adult are remarkable. During that earlier period, Montessori discovered the crucial role of the hand in developing the brain especially during the first six years. The brain in the first six years is literally "handmade". We know this because children who have had very little opportunity to use their hands to manipulate objects during this period of life suffer huge cognitive deficits in later life and sometimes never catch up, leaving them mentally deficient for the rest of their lives. Now, during the creation of the adult, we suggest that something very similar is going on.

We suggest that nature is urging the adolescent to use his hands to develop his brain, because the brain development that needs to occur at this time, can only occur by the use of the hands, acting under the control of the brain, in the carrying out of activities that attract, engross, and challenge the brain at this period of life.

Let me tell you a true story of something I witnessed about 40 years ago that set me thinking about how nature directs the human being in adolescence.

In my locality, there was a particular family who suffered a succession of mis fortunes that could have devastated them. It was a large family with about six to seven young children. They were not very well off, as indeed was the case of most of the families in that locality.

The mother, in the family was diagnosed with a serious illness and within a very short time died, leaving the father to care for the seven children. The father very soon turned to drink and the children were deemed to be neglected. The social welfare department separated the children to have them cared for by different relatives. Only the two older boys were left in the house with the father. They were both school-aged boys probably about 10 and 12 years old. The legal age for leaving school was, I think, about 13 years .

The younger of the brothers attended school but the older one constantly failed to attend and school inspectors were forever coming out to the house to look for him. I often saw the older boy leaping over railings into the nearby field to escape the inspector.

I'm sure the inspectors wrote woeful notes in their journals about how this boy was wasting his life "mitching" school. But I know the other side of it. I daily saw what that boy spent his days doing, because I passed his house on the way to school each day.

This boy had an interest in car engines and obviously had discovered, through tinkering around with them that he had a flare for mechanics. He would spend his day, from dawn to dusk, tinkering with engines, obviously teaching himself, since no one ever seemed to be with him, how to fix engines.

As the years went by, I used to pass him every day as I walked by his house to and from my bus stop. I was now one of the one per cent from that locality in University, though I still lived at home and took the bus each day. I would often see him at nine in the morning and nine that same evening still working on a car.

How's that for concentration! I was too shy to talk to him and he was too engrossed to do any more than nod, but I often thought about how he had created his own university in his front driveway while I travelled in and out on the bus to mine. I also thought about how my choice of subject, Medieval English was so obscure, and his was so practical. I often wondered had I made the right choice.

Sometime soon after this, I heard that he had taken a car mechanics course and then done something remarkable. He opened a small garage and became a car mechanic. He then put a sign up on his house that I cannot quote here because it would identify him, but it reflected the fact that he was now old enough to reclaim his brothers and sisters back from their scattered homes and bring the family back home to be together again. Each time I passed his house now, I felt a lump in my throat, I felt the pride that he felt, I had watched it grow.

This boy had followed the promptings of nature telling him how to use his interest in engines to build his brain and as a consequence to create his future life's work.

What would have happened to this boy if the inspectors had caught him and forced him to attend the local school? Would he have been able to work on car engines and develop his brain and perfect his skills? I'm certain the answer is no. I would hazard a guess, from my knowledge of what happened to other boys in the locality, that school would have failed to interest him. He would probably have become delinquent, possibly violent from frustration and would probably have ended up in jail. Instead, he became a businessman.

The successful end to this story centres on the fact that this boy choose to listen to the voice of nature, not the voice of the school inspector.

Montessori, as we shall see, argued that schools can only be useful if they are tailor-made to meet the needs of the human beings they are supposed to cater for. If they don't do this, they are irrelevant and probably harmful.

School for this boy, on the traditional model would have been irrelevant, but a school that included substantial time doing car mechanics would have been very helpful.

So, in answer to the question why can't he concentrate any more, we would say-open your eyes, the adolescent can concentrate, but just not on the things you are offering him. We suggest that nature is telling him that he needs to work with his hands to help the construction of his brain at this period in his development. Remember the caterpillar with the irresistible urge to follow the light? Well, look around you, adolescents all over the world are showing, by their behaviour that they feel an irresistible urge to work with their hands.

Around this age, boys who previously never knew one end of a screwdriver from another suddenly become interested in car and motorbike engines. Homeschooled adolescent boys, who have much more free time than schooled adolescents, often build amazing kit cars, having taught themselves, through the use of manuals, how to fit motors in home-made engines and how to make axles and wheels. We witnessed this firsthand at the home-school conventions we used to attend years ago when we were homeschooling our three children.

Similarly, at around this stage, girls become very interested in activities that involve the hand and the brain working in unison. Fashion, dressmaking and design intrigue them. Jewellery making, pottery, quilting even shoe and boot making begin to absorb the minds of adolescents, particularly girls. Once again, this phenomenon is more easily seen in homeschooled or unschooled adolescent girls probably because they have more time to devote to these activities and more importantly because they are less concerned about looking "uncool" in front of their peers on account of doing "women's work" than high school adolescents would be. The phenomenon is so universal and seen in so many different cultures, nature has to be behind it. We have known young girls who worked their fingers to the bone, sewing costumes by hand at this stage of development, because of some passion that urges them on.

Similarly, at this period of time, adolescents become spontaneously interested in learning to play musical instruments. Boys, in particular, become interested in playing the guitar. Now, you see teenage boys, who previously seemed all fingers and thumbs , spending hours perfecting finger positions as they teach themselves several different types of guitars. This attraction to the guitar in particular is interesting because it necessitates using the fingers of both hands at the same time, which in turn means that both sides of the brain are being " fired up." We will come back to this in our section on "sensitive periods in adolescence".

Because these phenomena in adolescence are so universal, we are convinced that nature is still hovering diligently over the human being in adolescence making sure that he/she feels the urge to do the activities with his/her hands that will insure optimum brain construction at this "critical period" of development.

So the question should not be "Why can't he concentrate any more?" but rather, "Why don't we offer him the things he needs to concentrate on during this period of his development instead of the things he doesn't need?

33

WHY ARE THEY SO OBSESSED WITH HANGING OUT?

(Social Changes in Adolescence)

Some evening, take a stroll around your neighbourhood. Hail rain or shine, it will be hard to find a wall or railings that doesn't have a group of adolescents sitting on it.

You'll probably recognise a few familiar faces (though the adolescents will do their level best not to make eye contact with you).

You'll spot young Susie, who used to come into the library with her mom every week and young Tommy who used to mow everyone's lawns.

They look very different now. Perhaps it's that Gothic look that has altered them, or the weird looking clothes that they wear now. Whatever it is, they look different and they certainly behave differently.

Only a year ago Susie would have run a mile rather than hang out with these spotty boys and Tommy wouldn't have been caught dead in this perfumed, nail-varnished company.

So what's going on now? Why are they so obsessed with hanging out?

Once again the answer lies in nature. During the period 12 to 18 years, nature directs the human being to focus his attention on something that up until now he never really thought about, and that is, human relationships.

Up until this point, the child enjoyed friends and acquaintances but something very different happens now.

During the period 12 to 18 years, nature needs the human being to prepare for something very serious in the years ahead....something that is necessary for the survival of the species.

What is it? It is finding a long-term mate, procreation and the raising of a new generation of human beings.

Now, when it comes to animal life, all nature needs is for the animals to be physically formed enough to reproduce. But in the case of the human being, it is a different story. Nature needs him to have more than just the physical capability to reproduce.

The fact is, human beings do not do well without stability. They need stable family units, stable homes, stable social and emotional environments.

If they don't have these in place during childhood and adolescence, they run a very high risk of becoming dysfunctional.

They very soon begin to manifest deviant behaviour which, if it occurs on a large scale, ultimately poses a threat to the very survival of the species.

So, nature needs human beings to create secure environments to raise their future offspring in. This security demands a long-term mate.

So, how does nature push the human being towards finding a long-term mate and the creation of a stable family unit?

Well, nature is practical. It starts early. The preparations begin in the period 12 to 18 years, so that in the plane 18 to 24 years and beyond the human being will be ready to choose a long-term mate and create a stable family home and raise a new generation of human beings.

Remember the caterpillar and its irresistible attraction to the light which leads to the food it needs to stay alive? Well, something very similar is going on here .

The human being ultimately needs to find a long-term mate, so that, in the years ahead, new offspring will be produced and raised in a secure environment to perpetuate a healthy new generation of the human species.

Think of the long-term mate as the equivalent of the delicate leaves that the caterpillar needed to get to.

The caterpillar was unaware that he needed the delicate leaves, he just felt an unconscious urge to follow the light which ultimately lead to the delicate leaves that he needed for his survival.

Similarly, the human being, during the period 12 to 18 years, does not wake up each day thinking, "I need to find a long-term mate, create a secure family unit and reproduce so as to perpetuate the species."

Far from it, he simply responds to an unconscious urge he now feels to start mixing with people, especially those his own age.

He feels a new sensitivity to form emotional attachments with new people. Friends, pals, buddies become vitally important now.

The urge to be part of a social group is so strong, he goes out in rain, hail or snow just to be in the company that now so attracts him.

Often the urge to be in the company of this social group is so strong that it overrides all other considerations. The human being is now willing to take risks if it means being in the company that he so desperately desires.

I remember a very conservative friend telling me how years ago she did the unthinkable and rode as a pillion passenger on a motorbike with no helmet or protective clothing on a very dark wet night, just because she felt a huge attraction to the driver of the motorbike and couldn't say no to the opportunity of putting her arms around his waist .

The boy had no interest in her and was very surprised that she asked for a lift. She was even more surprised at herself for asking. She found the ride terrifying and wouldn't want to do it again but in a strange way she also noted - "It was worth it, I felt elated."

This is the strange atmosphere the adolescent human being finds himself in. It is a dangerous, heady time. His thoughts are constantly on human relationships.

During this period, the human being falls in and out of love many times. This is no accident, it is also part of nature's plan to help the human being to learn to search for the most suitable partner, the one who will become "long-term".

Why? because the survival of the next generation depends on it. Remember, human beings do not do well in unstable environments.

Nature needs the adolescent to start learning how to select from the large range of possibilities the partner who will be best for him/her.

Nature does not want the human being 12 to 18 years to choose a partner now, it is much too soon. Nature needs the human being to have some time of preparation before entering into a long-term relationship. That time of preparation is now, the years 12 to 18.

This doesn't mean that the human being 12 to 18 years should be involved in a string of romantic relationships, far from it.

What nature wants is for the human being to explore a variety of human relationships during this period of life.

What is needed is simply that the human being uses this period of time to learn to recognise the particular qualities he will need in a future partner. The human being can only learn from experience. So nature plants in the human being, during this period of time, an unusual sensitivity to and interest in human relationships.

After all, he has spent twelve years building his own unique self. Soon he will enter a new phase of life where he needs to be able to blend his unique self with that of another person who has also spent twelve years building his/her unique self. Harmony and happiness will only come if the blend is right.

Experience in human relationships is vital and that's why, at this period of life, the human being is "so obsessed with hanging out ".

34

ARE THEY LOSING THEIR MINDS?

(Neurological Changes in Adolescence)

The short answer is "yes" and it's not by accident but by design.

Facts:

- Neuroscience (the study of the brain) has now proven by the use of functional magnetic resonance imaging (fMRI) brains scans, that the human brain is undergoing major reconstruction during the teen years.

- At around age 13, a major pruning process begins and continues throughout adolescence. During this time, brain cells and neural connections that are not actively being used get the chop! This process is called "synaptic pruning".

- During the same period, the brain simultaneously goes through a process of strengthening and "hard wiring" the brain cells and neural connections that are actively being used. This process is called "myelination".

- This is a "use it or lose it" period of life.

- It is a period of huge opportunity and also of huge risk.

- To make matters even more precarious, neuroscience has also shown that the Prefrontal Cortex, i.e. the part of the brain that gives us:

> Good judgement
> Impulse control over our actions
> Impulse control over our emotions

is still under construction in adolescence. In fact, it is not until the mid twenties that it finally becomes "finished".

So, "yes," adolescents are "losing" their minds even as we speak but, (and this is the exciting bit), at this "critical" time in development nature is literally giving all adolescents an opportunity to build a "new" brain, a stronger, faster, more sophisticated brain, i.e an adult brain.

That is why Montessori called this plane "a period of creation" because it is the period when the human being is literally "creating" the new brain of the adult he is going to be. What an extraordinary period of life! It is paralleled only by the period, birth to six years, when the human being is literally "creating" the brain of the child.

Now, the crucial question is why? Why is this neurological pruning going on? Couldn't nature create an adult brain by using the "exuberance" of brain cells it has just created? Wouldn't this make more sense?

Answer: because the human being is entering a period of life in which "less is more," the sculpted figurine will be better than the block of stone it came from. The "pruned" brain will be superior to the unpruned brain it came from. So, how does nature go about pruning the brain?

Answer, through "specialisation". In fact, we would suggest that "specialisation" is nature's way of helping the human being to build his brain at this period in his development. We suggest that, the human being is "primed" to "specialise" at this particular period of life. This does not mean that he will never again "un-specialise," i.e. apply himself to other things.

But, the fact is, that somewhere during this period 12 to 18 years, most human beings feel a very strong impulse to specialise, i.e. to zoom in on one thing or one area. This is not an aberration, it is nature at work. Let me tell you my story.

In primary school, (5 to 12 years), I was always what was called a "good pupil". Learning came easily to me. I was interested in every subject. I always read way ahead of my class. While others were still struggling with the beginnings of some subject, I had quietly mastered it to the end.

No one knew this except me, because, in my day, in primary school, you weren't allowed to read ahead, you could get into big trouble for even reading a few extra pages in your, "English Book," (as my best friend found out to her detriment).

When I went to secondary school, I was very excited about the prospect of learning lots of "new subjects". I immersed myself in French grammar and devoted myself to Latin parsing like nothing on earth. However, after three years of doing really well at every subject offered to me, something changed.

In Ireland, at this time, you studied for three years, usually from 13 to 16, for the Intermediate Certificate, and then studied for two more years for the Leaving Certificate, which was the final exam in secondary school. When I returned to school after the summer holidays, aged fifteen and a half, I began my studies for the Leaving Certificate. The only problem now was that I found I could only focus on the two subjects I was passionate about, English and French.

I actually found it impossible to study anything else. Our maths teacher, who was a very good teacher, would speak and draw formulae on the blackboard, but it was as if she was speaking Chinese, I couldn't comprehend a word. Our history teacher spoke, and I felt as though I was in a coma and couldn't make out the fuzzy words in the background. Our geography teacher was there somewhere in the room, but I was on another planet where verses from Shakespeare, W.B. Yeats, John Milton, T.S. Eliot and Marcel Proust floated by. For the English and French teacher I was a dream pupil, able to make connections and comparisons that were more akin to a final year university student than to a secondary school pupil. But, I couldn't learn anything else! I was so obsessed with English and French literature and so single-minded in my studies, that there was a real danger that I wouldn't pass enough "other" subjects in my Leaving Certificate to allow me entry into the University to study English and French, which was the only thing I wanted to do!

Finally, by the "skin of my teeth," I passed my Leaving Certificate with accolades in English and French and fairly mediocre results in everything else, but at least I got into university. Once there, I spent five glorious years immersed in "Pure English," i.e English literature from Anglo-Saxon times to the present.

But, the strange thing was this. When I reached age 22 or 23, I suddenly became interested in a whole range of subjects that had nothing to do with English literature. I found I wanted to study nutrition, law, motor mechanics, ancient languages, archaeology, bricklaying, early civilisations, even history! I didn't know what was happening to me, but I felt an amazing confidence that I would be able to conquer any of these areas and that it really wouldn't be such a big deal. I suppose I had, without realising it, learned "how to learn." I also, developed a deep understanding of what "lifelong learning" really means. From that time on, my ability to teach myself new subjects has never ceased.

In fact, shortly afterwards, I began the study of Montessori education, and that became my vocation and passion for the next 30 years, and shows no sign of abating. But my years of applying myself, heart and soul to the area I was passionate about, taught me discipline, application to a task and dogged persistence. Most importantly, I had, without knowing it, learned how to learn.

We suggest that the human being, during the period 12 to 18 years, and in particular during the period 16 to 18 years, experiences a need to "specialise" in some area. Usually, this is an area he feels passionate about. This does not mean that he has found the area he will spend his life working at, but it is an area that will, in some way, attract him so much that he will feel the need to focus on it and in the course of this intense application of his mind he will "learn how to learn," thus priming himself for lifelong learning. This application to his passion, will "sculpt" his brain and prepare him to undertake the "vocation," which he will, hopefully, find during his twenties, or even thirties. It is nature's plan that when he finds that "vocation," he will be able to "hack it," because of the "indirect preparation," he has just had in his youth by devoting himself to his passion.

This, we believe is what lies behind the neurological "pruning" that takes place in adolescence. The prepubescent brain, which is "exuberant" with possibilities, becomes pruned in adolescence, to allow for the "creation" of the adult brain, the "sculptured" brain, which can learn anything because it has been primed for life-long learning, in order that it can adapt to whatever world it finds itself in.

Now, some people will immediately react to this proposition with fear, thinking, "if my child does not study science in her teens, when she reaches 19 she won't be able to become a nurse or go to medical school and so on.

Our reply is, "why can't she?' The period between 12 and 16 , provides four good years, when the brain has an "exuberance" of brain cells, allowing it to take in vast amounts of knowledge. But the period between 16 and 18, should be a period of specialisation, when the human being can devote himself to the subject he is passionate about. If the human being discovers at 19 years of age, that he wants to become a nurse or enter medical school, what stops him from applying himself exclusively to the study of the subjects he needs to enter medical school? (especially now since he's learned "how to learn," by applying himself to his passion for the last two years.)

The answer is nothing except the arbitrary rules of the medical schools which demand that a prospective student must have a specific number of points to get in. That, then, is the area that we should have the foresight to change if we decide to radically change the way we educate to make education a better fit for the neurological characteristics of the adolescent brain.

So, in answer to our question, "Are they losing their minds?" The answer is yes, especially during the period 16 to 18 years, but on the plus side, they are "sculpting their brains," trimming off what is superfluous to requirements, and they do this by the act of "specialisation," by focusing in on a particular area, which is usually the area they are passionate about.

"Passion" is to the adolescent what "Imagination" is to the child. It is the key that opens the door into real learning, the type of learning that "sculpts" the brain and enables it to "learn how to learn" thus equipping the human being for the rest of his life, with the skills to learn to live successfully in whatever world he finds himself in. This is nature's amazing plan to aid the survival of the species.

Does Nature Help The Human Being To Find His Passion?

The short answer is yes. When nature gives the human being an "exuberance" of brain cells just before the teen years begin, we suggest that this is nature's way of giving the human being the chance to find his passion, the chance to select what he wants to do and the ability (i.e the brain power) to do it. We suggest that nature gives the human being the ability to decide whether to paint graffiti on walls or paint a masterpiece on canvas, whether to play the spoons on his knees or play the grand piano in concerts. This is not a value judgement, all of these activities have merit and we are all limited to some extent by our genetics and the environments we are born into, but even so, many of us have choices.

Will They Lose It If They Don't Use It?

Once again, the short answer is yes. Let me give you a recent example of this principle at work in real life. Recently, our teenage daughter took me to a production of Shakespeare's "As You Like It," performed by the Upstage Youth Theatre in York. Our daughter had choreographed the dance scene at the end of the play. This production was one of the "play in a fortnight" performances that the theatre puts on every summer, where the actors, all teenagers, have only two weeks to learn their lines, perfect their acting and learn their dances if needed.

Two years ago, our daughter played Prospero in a production of Shakespeare's The Tempest with the same youth theatre. This was her first Shakespearean acting part, and by all accounts, she was breathtaking. The passion she put into the role was palpable. To cut a long story short, the performance last night was brilliant. Shakespeare was brought to life once again. The Bard's masterful use of the English language was wonderfully portrayed. But here's the astonishing thing. These teenagers had literally put this performance together, not in a year, not in a month, but in a fortnight. (Under the very able direction of a member of the Royal Shakespeare Company).

Now, I studied English literature for five years in University, and I can recite a few poems, but I could never, ever, learn a whole Shakespeare play in a fortnight. I still can't fathom how our daughter learned all Prospero's lines in a week.(She didn't get the script till late). My point? There has to be something extraordinary about teenage brains to allow them to accomplish these feats. And this is exactly what neurology confirms.

The teenage brain starts out with an "exuberance" of brain cells which reached their peak in late childhood, (around 11 or 12 years of age.) But, and this is the scary part, the clock is ticking, the process of "synaptic pruning" has already begun, so the " use it or lose it" principle applies. On stage, last night, those kids were "using it" to the fullest extent.

Now, switch over. Recently, I was on a bus in a different country. The bus was full of teenagers, most of them were texting or talking on their phones. Most of the phone calls started and continued like this: "Yo, Waz-up?' So, how come some teenagers can recite Shakespearean dialogue with passion, while others limit themselves to "Yo, Waz-up"? The answer is simple, you either use it or you lose it. The teens doing Shakespeare were using it, the kids who limited themselves to "Yo, Waz-up" were losing it.

Now, what makes some teenagers sign up for the intense hard work of putting on a Shakespeare play in a fortnight, while others limit themselves to "Yo,waz up"? The answer has to do with Role-Models.

Role-Models:
What's the ingredient that turns that drive towards passion into a reality rather than just a floating thought in the adolescent's head? Answer: good role-models, coaches and guides. The adolescent needs good role-models and mentors at this time of life, people who can help him to turn his drive toward passion into something tangible like this production of a Shakespeare play.

The role-model the adolescent needs must be a person of passion, of charisma, not a boring person. Teenagers need great role-models. Great role-models can bring out the very best in teenagers. They can take a teenager from "Yo, waz up?"

to "To Be Or Not To Be" in a fortnight. These kinds of role-models don't follow a school curriculum. They don't dish out rewards or punishments. They don't drill the kids for tests. They "just do it". These are people of passion and they share that passion with the teens. They are lovers of drama, lovers of dance, lovers of music, lovers of sport, lovers of life and culture and they are in touch with the human spirit, with what it means to be human.

The role-model behind the excellent play I watched understood intuitively that Shakespeare did not write his plays to be part of exams. He wrote because of his passion for dramatising the comedy and tragedy of the human condition. He wrote because of his love of language and what he could make it do. And the teenagers responded to this whole-heartedly. How different from what happens in school where Shakespeare is treated as an exam subject to be tested and graded. The difference between the ordinary English teacher and the director of this group of teenage actors who put on the "play in a fortnight" is her passion and love for drama in general and Shakespeare in particular. She has the gift of being able to share that passion and that's what attracted the teenagers, fired them up and got them through their self imposed, gruelling rehearsals. Now, passion is neurological. It has a lot to do with levels of dopamine in the brain.

Passion and the Role of Dopamine in the Teenage Brain:

Ever since 2005, when the National Geographic magazine alerted the world to Dr. Jay Giedd's very important discoveries about the teenage brain, the internet has been flooded with articles on teenage behaviour and its possible neurological causes. In particular, there has been a plethora of articles on the link between teenage risk-taking and levels of dopamine in the brain.

We would like to suggest that instead of focusing on "risk-taking" and the role of dopamine in the adolescent brain, we should instead be focusing on "passion," and the role of dopamine in the adolescent brain. We would also like to suggest that passion is what the adolescent is looking for, not risk. Risk is the side-effect not the goal. The goal is passion, and it doesn't have to have negative side effects. With a bit of adult help the focus could be placed squarely on the goal, and the negative side effects could be significantly reduced. Let us explain.

- What makes teenage girls scream themselves into hysteria at concerts featuring their favourite pop-stars?

- What makes teenage boys roar themselves hoarse at football matches featuring their favourite teams?

The answer is passion. During the period 12 to 18 years, nature urges the adolescent to seek passion. Passion is to the adolescent what imagination is to the child. It is a driving force. It is the invisible force which energises the adolescent, puts a light in his eyes and a feeling of hope in his heart. Passion puts a voice in the adolescent's head saying "What a piece of work is man."

The adolescent is attracted to passion in the same way that the caterpillar was attracted to the light. It is an irresistible force, placed in the adolescent by nature and its purpose is this: - exposure to passion through music, sport, drama, literature, art, love, or anything else, makes the adolescent feel the greatness of being a human being. In so doing, it changes the brain, it re-structures it, creates new pathways in it, and then, through frequent use, myelinates these pathways, to make them hardwired and strengthened for adulthood.

This is why nature causes the adolescent to be so attracted to passion, because passion is vital for the creation of the adult brain, and by extension, the adult human being.

Now, the point is, this has all the hallmarks of a sensitive period. So, we would suggest that that's exactly what this is.

The Sensitive Period for Passion.

- During the period of adolescence, the teenager has a heightened sensitivity to passion. He feels things more intensely than at any other time of his life. Everything for him is more intense, e.g. love, music, drama, art, literature.

- This sensitive period has a clear purpose and that is the re-shaping of the brain from a child's brain to an adult's brain.

- This period is short lived. It is confined to the years of adolescence. The human being does not seek passion with this intensity all through his life. Emotionally, he would not be able to sustain it.

I remember very well, in my teenage years, reading Walter Pater's book "The Renaissance: Studies in Art and Poetry". I can still remember where I was when I read the part which said "To burn always with this hard gemlike flame, to maintain this ecstasy, is success in life." I remember thinking how wonderful it would be to live always in a heightened state of passion, never having to live with the mundane and mediocre. Once out of my teens, I found myself discounting

Pater, realising that no normal human being could live with that intensity of passion all his life, nor was he ever meant to. Adolescent passion is something that is there for a season, to be replaced by something less intense in the following season. Such is nature's plan.

Now, how does nature attract the adolescent towards passion? Answer, by playing around with his dopamine levels. So far, we have seen nature loosening the six year old's front teeth, putting hair on the fifteen year old's chin and now nature causes chemical changes in the adolescent's brain. So, the next question has to be :

What Is Dopamine?
Ten years ago, most of us had never come across the word dopamine, and if we had, we probably wouldn't even have known how to pronounce it. Nowadays, everyone is talking about dopamine. But, a word of caution, a little knowledge is still a dangerous thing. Dopamine is a very complex chemical. It doesn't just do this or that, it is involved in a large and varied number of processes in the brain. Basically, dopamine is a hormone that plays a number of important roles in the human body and especially in the brain.

In adolescence, fluctuations in dopamine levels in various parts of the brain start to occur. In early adolescence, the prefrontal cortex has higher than adult levels of dopamine circulating in it because of its increased number of nerve cells, brought about by the exuberance of nerve cell growth during the years 10 to 13.

However, also in adolescence, dopamine levels in the reward centre of the brain, (the nucleus accumbens) are declining. These decreasing levels of dopamine in the reward centre of the brain cause the adolescent to require more excitement and stimulation to achieve the same level of pleasure as an adult. So the teenager will need to engage in activities that are "out of the ordinary" to reach what would be an "ordinary" level of pleasure, by adult standards.
Research suggests that although in adolescence, the baseline levels of dopamine in the brain's reward centre is the lower to start with than it is in adults, its release in response to thrilling experiences is higher. This goes a long way towards explaining why teenagers show lethargy and boredom and regularly lie slumped across school desks, half unconscious, unless someone breaks through this stupor and engages them in some stimulating activity. If someone does that, the enhanced natural dopamine released in the brain of the adolescent, gives him an exhilarating sense of being fully alive and engaged in life.
The downside is that this good feeling caused by increased levels of dopamine in the brain at the expectancy of something exciting about to take place, can lead an

adolescent to focus so much on the positive reward that he feels sure he is about to experience that he ignores the potential risks and dangers associated with the experience.

Now, how does all this relate to "passion and the role of dopamine in the adolescent brain"? We suggest that, in adolescence, as nature goes about its restructuring of the human brain, in its attempt to turn the child brain into an adult brain, it must protect the human being from losing valuable brain cells as the necessary pruning process is carried out. We have talked about the "use it or lose it" principle. Well, here it is an action.

Nature cannot trust that the growing human being will "use it", nor can nature risk that the growing human being will "lose it," so nature dangles a carrot in front of the human being. That carrot is dopamine. If he will get up and engage in activities of his own selection, sport, drama, music, literature, art, craft, whatever, nature will make sure he is rewarded with pleasurable feelings. Dopamine surges in his brain will thrill him to the core. But he must take the first step. He must engage in some activity.

Once he does this, nature will take care of the rest. If he selects something from that pool of possibilities that the "exuberance" of brain cells in the years 10 to 13 have just put before him, nature will flood his reward centre with dopamine making his choice of activity his passion. And a loop begins. The more he engages in the activity, be it sport or drama, music, art or whatever, the more passionate he will become about it as dopamine levels in the brain are produced to go hand-in-hand with his engagement in a self selected activity.

At this period of time, role models who exude passion for their area of interest are vital for the adolescent. We suggest that the adolescent does not need teachers at this period of life, he needs passionate role-models, people who can attract the adolescent to a possible area of interest and then just leave him free to explore it giving him every possible help if asked for.

We suggest then that it is passion that the adolescent is seeking, not risk. Risk-taking is what happens when the adolescent cannot find the role models to lead him to find the area of activity that he could potentially develop a passion for.

So, at this period of time, dopamine sits ready waiting to do its job. The adolescent also sits waiting. All that is needed are the passionate role-models, the links, the catalysts who can turn "waz-up" into "what piece of work is man". Then the adolescent can safely lose his mind as nature helps him sculpture a new one.

35

WHY ARE THEY ALL PLAYING GUITARS, DANCING AND SINGING LOVE SONGS?

(More Sensitive Periods in Adolescence)

I remember many years ago, asking the question "why are they all playing guitars, dancing and singing love songs?" I was about 10 years old and much more interested in the adventures of "Huckleberry Finn" than in love songs.

But no one would answer my question. The funny thing is, when I reached my teens and everyone was "playing guitars, dancing and singing love songs," I don't remember thinking it was odd. It seemed to be the natural thing to do.

So, back to the question, during the period twelve to eighteen years, "why are they all playing guitars, dancing and singing love songs?"

We believe the answer has a lot to do with neurology and sensitive periods.

During the period twelve to eighteen years, adolescents become spontaneously interested in learning to play musical instruments.

Boys in particular, become interested in playing the guitar. Some of the world's best guitar players taught themselves how to play the guitar during this period of life.

But why this interest all of a sudden? Playing the guitar is not easy. It involves tricky finger work with both hands simultaneously.

It involves concentration, hours of practice, patience and hard work. So why the attraction?

We suggest the answer lies in neurology and sensitive periods. It's another "caterpillar" story.

Neurology has proven that the adolescent is "losing" brain cells that are not actively being used during this period.

At the same time, nature is hard wiring brain cells and neural connections that are being used during this period.

We believe that nature causes the human being, especially the male of the species, to feel a powerful attraction to music at this period of life.

Why? because, that attraction will cause him to want to teach himself how to play musical instruments such as the guitar, which, in turn, will cause him to train both hands simultaneously.

In doing this, he is developing both sides of his brain and consequently ensuring optimum brain development at this "critical period" in the construction of the "adult brain".

Nature is astonishingly clever. She doesn't rely on boring homework to get the human being to "create" his brain. She uses the interests she currently gives him.

In this period of life, the interests she gives him are music, dance and love songs.

So, nature, we believe, gives the adolescent, especially the male of the species, an irresistible urge towards music making, in order to get him to train his two hands simultaneously, for the purpose of helping him to develop the brain cells and neural connections he will need in the "adult" brain that he is in the process of "creating".

We believe, that a very similar natural urge, causes the adolescent to become interested in dance, which involves, concentration, diligent practice, hard work and the use of both feet simultaneously. All of this, necessarily "fires up" neural connections on both sides of the brain.

Some years ago, I signed up for a salsa evening dance class. It looked so easy, thirty people all moving in unison...... until I tried it.

I found it totally impossible to concentrate on my right foot while trying to do something else with my left foot. I eventually gave up in defeat.

But, the point is, adolescents, all over the world, spontaneously, teach themselves all sorts of extremely difficult dance moves.

Why? We believe it is because nature urges the adolescent to dance, because dancing, more than any other physical activity, builds neural connections and therefore can help the adolescent to "build" the new adult brain he is in the process of creating.

Does any kind of dancing do this? No, but the kind that adolescents engage in does. The best kind of dance to increase neural connectivity is the kind that involves the integration of several brain functions at once, the kind of dance that involves split second, rapid-fire decision-making.

This is the kind of dance that adolescents devise for themselves (often on the streets) when they are given the time and the freedom to dance.

In a nutshell, the benefits of dancing are:

- Dancing dramatically increases the levels of serotonin in the brain. Serotonin is the neurotransmitter responsible for enhancing many of the brain's functions. So serotonin helps the brain to learn better.

- Dancing reduces stress, which helps the brain to function better.

- Dancing promotes a general sense of well-being which helps to make the brain function better and therefore make better decisions.

- Dancing improves the memory because it increases serotonin levels.

- Dancing makes us eat and sleep better which has a positive knock-on effect on brain development.

- Dancing builds neural connections because it necessitates a significant amount of decision making as we follow our partner's moves. In dance, this decision making is usually split-second, rapid-fire, decision-making which causes our brains to constantly develop new neurological pathways. The result of this is that we become more intelligent because we have created more neurological pathways in our brains to use for problem-solving.

- Dancing, more than any other physical activity, affords significant protection against brain decline, according to a long term study on dementia.

What could be better for a human being in the process of creating a "new" adult brain? The Bee Gees were right when they told us "You should be dancing yeah."

Now, what is it that encourages the adolescent to get up and dance? Answer: the irresistible urge towards relationships and social life.

Although there are many serious young dancers who practice alone for hours just to perfect their moves (our youngest daughter being one of them), for most adolescents, the irresistible attraction to dance is inseparable from their overriding attraction to social life and relationships.

Once again, nature holds the carrot of relationships before them in order to lead them towards dance, so that the real purpose, brain development will take place. This is the nature of a sensitive period. The person is led indirectly to the thing it needs for optimum growth.

So, if guitar playing and dancing are sensitive periods which have to do with nature's way of ensuring brain development, what is "singing love songs" all about?

We suggest that the adolescent's sensitivity towards "romantic love" represents a true "sensitive period" in this stage of development, designed by nature to enable the adolescent to learn an essential skill and that skill is, how to live in harmony with a member of the opposite sex.

Think of it this way.

One of the biggest problems affecting the survival of each new generation is parental conflict. Young human beings do not do well in a war zone of parental conflict. Yet in each generation, divorce, separation, parental discord, custody battles, all cause huge damage to the new generation of the human species.

But, was it meant to be avoided? Did nature put some "invisible" plan in place to prevent all these problems from happening in the first place?

We believe the answer is "yes".

We suggest that nature has always had a plan in place to ensure that the children of each new generation had the optimum opportunity of having stability and security in their lives. This involves having a mother and a father who can actually live together in harmony, under the same roof.

What is this plan? It is the sensitive period for human relationships, especially relationships between members of the opposite sex which kicks in during the period of adolescence 12 to 18 years.

We suggest that nature gives the human being a "prolonged adolescence" in order to allow the human being time to learn how to get on with members of the opposite sex so that, eventually, they can live together, create a home, have children, giving the next generation the benefit of a stable life.

We suggest that adolescence is most definitely a "critical period" in human development and that Dr Montessori recognised it as such.

Think of it this way:

- Women spend much of their adult lives saying that men don't understand them resulting in conflict in their relationships.

- Men spend much of their adult lives saying that women don't understand them resulting in conflict in their relationships.

The result? - affairs, separations, divorce and a damaged new generation. If you don't believe this have a talk with a family law Judge, your eyes may be opened.

Yet, here in adolescence, we have a brief window, when boys actually want to understand girls and vice versa.

Many experts will tell us that it's only about sex at this period, and that is all that is on the adolescent's mind, especially the boy's mind. This is simply not true. Sure enough, the sexual attraction is what makes the sensitive period happen but having made the connection happen, nature now causes the human adolescent to want to learn more about what makes their "opposite number" tick.

When is there ever going to be another period in human development when a male will give so much time to thinking about a female and vice versa? It is truly a sensitive period in development.

Now, the purpose of a sensitive period is to master some skill at a specific period in time. During that period of time, the learning of that skill will come easier to the human being than at any other time in his life precisely because nature gives him an irresistible attraction towards the area which incorporates the skill to be mastered, causing him to focus intently on it.

When that sensitive period comes to an end, the human being should have mastered some skill that he didn't have at the beginning of that sensitive period, and he should be ready to move on to the next plane where he will refine that skill, perfect it and ultimately put it to good use.

We believe that this is precisely the plan nature has made for adolescence.

We agree with Montessori that nature gives the adolescent a sensitive period towards human relationships during this critical period, but, we would go a step further and suggest that this sensitive period particularly targets opposite sex relationships.

It is nature's plan that at the end of this sensitive period the human being will emerge with a specific skill and that skill is a "foundational" understanding of human relationships, especially relationships with the opposite sex.

This "skill" is vital for the human being, so that during the next plane, the human being, can build on this skill and perfect it, so that, at the end of the fourth and final plane, the human being will have mastered the skills needed to-

a) commit to a long-term relationship, build a new family unit, mate and reproduce in order to perpetuate a new generation of the human species.

b) become a contributing member of society by using the knowledge and understanding of human relationships that he has gained in the preceding plane.

So, to answer our original question, we believe that this is why, during the period 12 to 18 years, they are all "playing guitars, dancing and singing love songs."

36

RUNNING INTO TROUBLE (AGAIN)

(Obstacles to Normal Development in Adolescence)

True Story:
Thomas and Billy are brothers. They have grown up in a fairly average middle class home and they have both lead fairly non-eventful lives..........until recently.

Billy, who is now 14 started secondary school a year ago. Thomas, who is now 16 started three years ago. Sadly, for Billy, the last 12 months will be hard to forget.

Billy seemed to make a smooth transition into to secondary school. Thinking back, his parents realise, he never really said much at all about school. He always seemed to be dashing off somewhere, to meet "the gang". His parents were actually delighted that he seemed to have found new friends so quickly. His brother Thomas, had stayed friends with the two boys he knew since he was six, and although he played football with some of the new kids from secondary school, he spent most of his free time with his two long time friends.

Billy was different. He liked novelty, and making new friends was part and parcel of that novelty. Although the parents tried not to compare the boys, they now admit that they felt that Billy had probably adjusted better to secondary school than Thomas had.

Now, after just one year in secondary school Billy's parents have been called in to hear the shocking news that Billy has been caught on CCTV camera, along with four other students, smoking an illegal substance on school grounds and participating in worrying behaviour with two of the female students, who are only 14 years old.

Billy's parents are speechless and heartbroken.

Thomas has been in the same school for three years and has never, not even once been in trouble for anything. How could Billy have done this? How could this sweet, polite boy, engage in such activities? His parents have no answers.

How is it, that even within the same family some teenagers will fall prey to one or many of the familiar adolescent excesses, alcohol, drugs, risky behaviour, promiscuity, etc. yet their siblings, brought up in the same home with the same parents, keep a steady course and get through the teenage years with little more than a few cheeky outbursts?

Another True Story:
Anne and Susan are teenagers. They live next door to Liz and Chloe. They are all in their late teens now. They have very similar socio-economic backgrounds. Both sets of parents are lower middle class and working.

The major difference between the girls is that, while Liz and Chloe have always attended the local schools, Anne and Susan are "unschooled" i.e. they have never been to a traditional school.

They follow a fairly informal course of instruction, organised by themselves following their present interests and their parents help them along by bringing them to wherever they need to go, or to whomever they need to meet, to pursue their present interests.

For years, both of their parents have been involved in helping them daily with their homeschooling. This has resulted in a close bond between Anne and Susan and their parents.

For all their lives these four kids have been best pals, always hanging out together, sharing birthdays etc. Now, since Liz and Chloe have reached their late teens, (Liz is 16 and Chloe is 17), a change is occurring.

Liz and Chloe have started to go out on Friday and Saturday nights with "the crowd". "The crowd" appears to mean other teens from their school and their friends and associates. "The crowd" can be quite large, often numbering 12 or more teenagers, some of them teenagers Liz and Chloe would know well, others they have never met before and may never meet again.

When "the crowd" meet up, they tend to spend the evening in pubs with a few more hours spent back in someone's "pad".

Liz and Chloe, always invite Anne and Susan to join them, but after the first one or two evenings out with "the crowd," Anne and Susan have declined further invitations.

Anne and Susan have revealed to their parents that they feel very uncomfortable in the company of Liz and Chloe when they're out with "the crowd".

They say that Liz and Chloe behave like different people when they're out on the town. Partly, this is due to the amount of alcohol they consume when out and partly it is due to "the face" they seem to put on when they're with "the crowd".

Anne and Susan don't understand this behaviour. They don't behave this way themselves. They've been mixing with plenty of kids of all ages, at home school conventions, for years. Here all the families spend a weekend or a mid week together either camping or boarding. They've had lots of fun filled gatherings and barbecues, but they never felt the need to put on "a face" or drink themselves into oblivion.

Anne and Susan always felt very comfortable with the easy-going way all the kids, of varying ages at these conventions, would always help to mind the younger children, spontaneously organising football and other games for them, without having to be asked or persuaded.

Anne and Susan don't want to be part of "the crowd". They think it's false and they can't understand why Liz and Chloe, who are always talking about "being an individual," would want to be part of a "crowd" that demands that everyone dresses the same, talks the same, drinks the same, laughs at the same stuff and generally behave like "clones". Anne and Susan can't understand why Liz and Chloe find this enjoyable. They find it weird and a bit threatening. That's why they decline the invitations to join in.

How is it that among "unschooled" adolescents there is a distinct lack of desire to spend free time out drinking, smoking, engaging in risky behaviour, or promiscuity? Indeed, there is, among "un-schoolers" a large amount of evidence of just the opposite, i.e. positive behaviour in adolescence.

Is there something different about the brains of "un-schoolers" which makes their behaviour different?

Similarly, was there something different about Billy's brain which made him behave differently to his brother Tommy?

The answer, we believe, is no. We suggest that the difference in their behaviour has more to do with OBSTACLES to the adolescent's normal development, than to neurology.

Let me tell you a story about sausages.

Many years ago, I sat in a cafe and had a grilled meal with a friend. The meal contained, among other things, pork sausages. After the meal, I said goodbye to my friend and went home.

About two hours later, I was in A+E, doubled up in pain, with a doctor who thought I had appendicitis. Many hours later, after much throwing up, I was better, still very sore in the stomach area, but better. The diagnosis was "food poisoning".

I kept telling the doctor that it couldn't be food poisoning because, my friend had eaten the same meal and my family had checked with her and she was fine. The doctor replied: "she didn't have your sausage."

While it seems logical for us to ask how come two brothers brought up in the same family, with the same life experiences could behave so differently, it is actually not logical at all. Every human being is different and unique, (just like the sausages).

If Tommy had met "the gang" that Billy became so involved with and influenced by, he probably would have rejected them, he probably would have had nothing to do with them, preferring the safe company of his life-long friends. This is not a failure in him, it is his personality, his preference for "not playing with fire". And this human uniqueness is probably what explains why one adolescent goes one way and his brother goes another way.

We suggest that, even taking into account the neurological discoveries recently made about the adolescent's "unfinished" brain, the fact that not all adolescents go "off course" is proof that certain "external factors" (i.e. obstacles) merging with certain "unique personality dispositions," rather than "brain deficits" are at the root of why some adolescents go "off course" and others don't.

In other words, OBSTACLES merging with particular unique personality dispositions rather than neurological factors cause some adolescents to go "off course" and others not to.

But, neurology explains why certain adolescents are more vulnerable to the dangers that these "external factors," i.e. obstacles pose than, for example, an older human being would be.

What we're saying is, it's not that "his brain made him do it," but rather, some "external factor," some "obstacle," merging with his particular unique personality disposition, tempted him to do it, but his brain, because it was not fully finished, didn't have the capacity to "put the reins" on him and hold him back from doing it.

So the big question is: what kinds of "external factors" could prove to be real obstacles to the normal development of some adolescents?

Rounding up the Usual Suspects (Again).

Once more, it may seem unfair, even unjust, but we suggest that the greatest obstacle to the adolescent's normal development usually comes from:

The place he spends his days in, i.e.   SCHOOL.

Secondary Schools:

In the western world, we are so familiar with the concept of secondary schools that we act as though they have been there since the beginning of time, but they haven't. Secondary schools are a fairly recent invention in human history, and, in our opinion, not one of our best ones. Montessori observed that, "schools, such as they are today, are not adapted to the needs of the adolescent or to the age in which we live."   (From Childhood to Adolescence page 95)

She invited us to think about what happens to an adolescent in the secondary school. She pointed out that first of all, he changes teacher and subject every hour and this happens without logical continuity. The adolescent is expected to adapt his thoughts to a new subject every 60 minutes. He must move from dealing with the details of mathematics to matters of religion and on to the details of literature and then on to the complexities of science.

She pointed out that, it is in the midst of this state of "mental agitation" that the human being must get through adolescence, with all of its own difficulties. She pointed out that the adolescent is forced to deal with a multitude of unrelated facts and details at a period of life when he is least equipped to deal with them. Added to this is the burden of exams.

As a consequence of all this, she says, studies, instead of being a privilege become a "crushing burden" on the adolescent. The emphasis on exams and what we now call "teaching to the test" cause "the young adults, the men of the future," to be, "formed in a narrow and artificial mould". Montessori writes:

> "What a miserable life is offered them, what a penitence without end, what a futile renunciation of their dearest aspirations."
>
> (From Childhood to Adolescence page 100)

Montessori made these statements many years ago, yet sadly they have been echoed by many people in more recent times, especially by John Taylor Gatto, a prize-winning teacher in New York state schools. He said,

> "The first lesson I teach is confusion.
> Everything I teach is out of context.
> I teach the unrelating of everything.
> I teach disconnections."
>
> Dumbing Us Down p.2

While writing this book, we talked with a number of adolescents who attend secondary schools to see if anything has changed. We learned the following:

A large number of adolescents feel that:

- secondary schools feel like prisons.
- secondary schools look like prisons.
- secondary schools lock out all that is beautiful in the world,-
- the sight of life: flowers, trees, the sky, sunshine.
- the sound of life: families, the mixture of ages.
- the smell of life: food cooking, coffee brewing.
- the taste of life: home-made meals.
- the feel of life:the freedom to move around.
- secondary schools make you feel like a criminal.
- secondary schools make you act like a criminal.

Not everyone was so bleak.

Other secondary school pupils told us things that we have written in our own words:

Our teachers are trying to do their best but they seem to be caught up in a no-win situation. They know the exam targets actually prevent us from really engaging with any subject, yet they can't do anything about it or they'll lose their jobs. The teachers are just cogs in the wheel. They are pawns, just as much as we are, in this huge "crazy" industry, which actually makes kids either sad, bad or mad.

They suggested that:

Kids seem to be divided into three groups:

1) Those who just grit their teeth and, with amazing fortitude, just get through it, somehow knowing instinctively that they will get their life back at the end of it, (like a prisoner getting his belongings back on release day) and then they will begin the real education of themselves, usually through life experiences. These are often, but not always, "sad" students.

2) Those who turn to alcohol, and drugs, risky behaviour, etc. in order to numb their minds and get them through it. Some adolescents, with these behaviours, don't actually make it to the end of the school years. These are often thought of as the "bad" students.

3) Those who turn inwards, developing various problems of a psychological nature. These students often suffer from secret problems like anorexia, bulimia, self harm, depression, even schizophrenia. These are often thought of as the "mad" students.

We asked every secondary school pupil we interviewed one last question. It was:

"Do you feel that secondary schools meet the social, physical, cognitive, emotional, spiritual and psychological needs of most adolescents?"

The universal answer is summed up in one adolescent's reply"

"No, secondary schools are not there to meet those needs, their function is to get you through exams so that you can either go out and get a job, or go on to University, so that, in another three or four years, you can go out and get a job, either way, that's what secondary schools are for, getting you through exams."

(Statement by a 16 year old UK student in April 2014)

It is interesting to compare this contemporary comment with Montessori's comment of many years ago:

"The secondary school, such as it is at present, has no other aim than to prepare the pupils for a career......"

(From Childhood to Adolescence p99)

Now, back to our discussion, how exactly do secondary schools pose an obstacle to the normal development of the adolescent?

We suggest that the majority of secondary schools, inadvertently pose obstacles to the normal development of the adolescent because their very structure mitigates against the adolescent's needs socially, physically, emotionally and spiritually.

Let's examine this.

Socially:

Firstly, secondary schools pull the human being out of the real world, at the very point in his development when the social man is being created and the human being has the greatest need of being in society. Montessori pointed out that the world of education, "is like an island, where people cut off from the world, are prepared for life by exclusion from it".................(The Absorbent Mind page 11.) Moreover, the secondary school, such as it is today, is an obstacle to the adolescent's normal social development because it places him in an unnatural environment where all the people he is forced to spend his days with are: the same age, at the same level of development, have the same neurological deficits and are suffering from the same "hangups". Schools call these his peers, but spending all day with peers can have very negative results.

Recently, we spoke to a thirty-something woman, who said that her life had really been defined by the fact that she became a single parent in her early teens. She said she had experienced years of difficulties in bringing up her child, which had caused her to have limited job opportunities which in turn led to her never being able to purchase her own home etc. She said, "looking back, I know, that if I'd never hung around with X and Y, whom I met in school, and been influenced by their ways of behaving, I would never have become a single mother in my teens and my life would have been very different."

All over the world, responsible parents are worried about who their teens are hanging out with and they have every reason to be, their teenager's whole life can be helped or harmed by who they spend time with during this "critical period" in development. Yet, the adolescent, in a secondary school is forced to spend hours every day in the company of peers who may very well be a very bad influence on him, but he cannot escape their company.

What the adolescent needs socially, is to be in a mixed age group, with people who have different life experiences, and are at different levels of neurological development, and have different "hangups".

Physically:

Secondly, secondary schools, such as they are today, involve far too much time sitting down and not enough time spent in movement. Who was it who came up with the idea that we have to sit down to learn? Many academics walk up and down as they lecture. Why? because they have to move to think. Montessori wrote a lot about the importance of movement and brain function. She emphasised the importance of "synthetic movement," that is, movement where the mind directs the body to an intelligent purpose. It is the kind of movement that we witness in the dancer's feet, the pianist's fingers, the surgeon's hands. But we also witness it in the young child, polishing brass objects, in the older child, pumping up his bike before going out on a long cycle, in the adolescent carefully stringing his guitar, in the young adult painting the walls of his first home. "Synthetic movement" is a biological need in humans at every period of life, lack of it causes the personality to warp and "deviate". "Synthetic movement" always involves work with the hands. Today's secondary schools do not know how vital this activity is for the normal development of the human being. Montessori pointed out that "Manual work, having a practical aim, aids in the acquisition of an inner discipline. When a skill is perfected in a freely chosen field, and it creates the will to succeed and to overcome obstacles, something more than a simple accomplishment has occurred; a feeling of one's own worth has developed." (From Childhood to Adolescence p134). Montessori also pointed out repeatedly that the human being should not be either an intellectual or a manual worker, he should be both. She wrote: "Men who have hands and no head and men who have a head and no hands are equally out of place in the modern community." Montessori pointed out that "society builds itself by means of various kinds of activities not only by purely intellectual ones". We would also submit that the worldwide obesity problem is due in no small part to the secondary school's misguided idea that we have to sit down to learn and that all learning involves "headwork" rather than "whole-body" work. Montessori stated that the secondary schools of her day, were "an obstacle to the physical development of adolescents". (From Childhood To Adolescence Page 100.) We believe, sadly, that the same could be said of the secondary schools of our day.

The simple fact is this: Life means movement. Things that don't move are usually dead.

Emotionally:

Thirdly, this is the time of life when the human being feels very self-conscious. He becomes aware of every little defect in himself and magnifies it one hundred per cent. We have known many teenagers who were in fact, utterly beautiful, yet they considered themselves to have all sorts of flaws.

The adolescent is not just self-conscious about his/her looks, he is self-conscious about everything, clothes, money, economic background etc. all loom large in his consciousness.

Now, during this period of extreme self-consciousness, adolescents are forced into a giant "goldfish bowl" called secondary school, where they have no escape from the glaring eyes of their peers and teachers. Some kids grow their hair so that it hangs their eyes, at this period of life. Others develop mannerisms like putting their hands up to their face when they talk. Interviews with adolescents, individually, revealed that even the adolescents who looked comfortable, happy, at ease in the secondary school setting, often feel quite the opposite on the inside. It is often not until late adulthood or even middle age that people begin to open up about how they really felt behind those smiles and confident strides.

Not every adolescent feels self-conscious in secondary school, but many, many do. We would submit that the secondary school, such as it is today is an obstacle to the adolescent's emotional development because it places him in the equivalent of a giant "fishbowl," at the very period in this life when he wants to hide from the glare of others, because he is so self-conscious about himself.

Intellectually:

Fourthly, the secondary school, such as it is today, poses an obstacle to the normal intellectual development of the adolescent because it places too much emphasis on exams and academic work, ignoring the fact that, as Montessori put it, "there occurs at this time, a diminution of the intellectual capacity."

She pointed out that this reduction in the adolescent's ability to concentrate on school subjects is not his fault. She wrote, "it is not due to a lack of will that there is difficulty in concentration, it is due to the psychological characteristics of this age." Had she lived longer, she would have been able to prove her theories about the adolescent's particular cognitive problems by the use of f MRI scans, just as neurologists are doing today.

She did however emphasise the adolescent's preference for works of creation and she pointed out the need for work with the hands as well as work with the head. Remember, she said, "men who have hands and no head and men who have a head and no hands are equally out of place in the modern community."

We would like to go a step further and suggest that work with the hands in adolescence is vital for the proper development of the brain. We suggest that secondary schools, which do not allow the adolescent to devote substantial time to work with his hands, are actually posing a serious obstacle to the normal development of the adolescent's brain.

Spiritually:

Fifthly, the secondary school, such as it is today, poses the cruelest of obstacles to the adolescent's spiritual development. We use the word spiritual here, not to refer to religion but to refer to the human spirit, the mysterious ingredient that makes us a unique species. How does it do this? By failing to feed the adolescent's hunger to experience human greatness. The adolescent has spent the whole of his childhood sensing that man has the potential for greatness.

He remembers the thrill of telling everyone,

> See how high I can jump
> See how fast I can run

He remembers some years later discovering,

> How vast our universe is
> How amazing man's achievements are
> How much men have transformed the world
> How amazing is their capacity for greatness

Now, in adolescence, he wants to join in. He wants to be able to say,

> See how amazing my generation's achievements are
> See how much we are transforming the world
> Look at us, look at our capacity for greatness

But, the school is not interested in anyone's capacity for greatness, it is only interested in its own puny agenda, its points systems, its exams, its attempts to quantify everything. Powerful, passionate literature is turned into graded homework. Earth moving music and art are turned into exam subjects. Exhilarating scientific discoveries become a "crushing burden" of things to be remembered by rote. At the end of it all, everything that was great is destroyed by the academic police, the examiners who have lost the plot and forgotten why Shakespeare wrote his sonnets, why Michelangelo painted the Sistine chapel, why Mozart composed the concertos. They have forgotten, or perhaps they never really knew, that all of these great works came about because of the human passion to achieve greatness.

And so, within a few months of secondary school, the adolescent feels cheated, hoodwinked, betrayed by the adults who work there and the adults who sent him there. He asks himself, "Is this it?" "Is this what I worked for all through childhood?" "Was it all just to arrive at this, a factory, a conveyor belt of heads all rattling off the correct answers to the correct questions? Where is the room for the unique human being they told me I was? Was it all just a lie? Am I to become a cog in a wheel in this great machine called school? Will I ever escape? If I do escape will I still be me or will this huge machine rob me of everything that is me?"

Shortly afterwards, for many adolescents, panic sets in, mind numbing panic, the kind that freezes the brain and stops it from learning anything. When this happens all is lost. The once vibrant, inquisitive child slips further and further into a downward spiral, into an inferno of Dante'esq proportions. The obstacle has done its job, deviations will now follow with a terrifying inevitability.

37

GOING OFF COURSE (AGAIN)

(Deviations from Normal Development in Adolescence)

When an adolescent starts to spend his time drinking excessively, taking drugs, engaging in risky behaviour, crime, self harm, promiscuity etc, he is showing signs that he has deviated from the road of normality.

These behaviours should not be accepted as normal adolescent behaviours any more than the two year old's screams should be seen as the terrible twos. They are all signs of abnormality, of deviation.

They occur when the human being encounters obstacles to his normal development, that he does not have the capacity to overcome. Consequently he is forced off the main road of normality and pushed down side roads of deviation.

Montessori wrote, "all psychic deviation sets man on the road to death and makes him active in destroying his own life". (The Secret of Childhood p 192.)

Some Saturday night, in the inner cities, have a look at the teenage girls vomiting on the pavement, from excessive consumption of alcohol. Look at the teenage boys slashing each other with broken bottles in violent drug or alcohol induced rages. Can you say, with your hand in your heart that this is normal?

No. There is nothing normal about it. This is a classic example of human beings who have deviated from the road of normality and are now set "on the road to death" and are "active in destroying" their own lives.

What, you may well ask would cause a human being to set out on a course that could destroy his own life?

The answer is stated clearly by Montessori. She writes, "does not all of this indicate precisely the loss of a vital inner sensibility, which should work for the preservation of the individual?"

This is precisely what's going on in the human psyche when deviations take over. There is "a loss of a vital inner sensibility which should work for the preservation of the individual."

That protecting instinct, which nature, hovering diligently over the human being, so carefully placed in his psyche, is lost, and once it is lost, there is no guiding instinct, no "vital inner sensibility" to get him back on the road to normality. The human being is lost, he is like a ship at sea without a compass.

Montessori pointed out that "psychoanalysis indirectly supports our theory of a loss of the guiding instinct or preserving sensibility. To this however, psychoanalysis gives a different interpretation, and speaks of the "death instinct".

She points out that psychoanalysis "recognises in man a natural tendency to assist the inevitable advent of death, facilitating it and hastening it, and even running to meet it by suicide".

Psychoanalysis further proposes that "Man becomes attached to poisons like alcohol, opium, cocaine, by an irresistible urge, that is, he attaches himself to death and summons it, instead of attaching himself to life and salvation".

Montessori recognises all of this but disagrees on the cause of it. She says, "If such a tendency were due to the inevitability of death, it should exist in all creatures".

Montessori could see clearly that it is not a "death instinct" but the loss of the guiding instinct or preserving sensibility which nature placed in man from birth which is the cause of these deviations which set the human being on the road to death and make him active in "destroying his own life".

Deviations represent the antithesis of everything the human being was meant to be. They are vile and degrading and they try to rob the human being of his true self.

Dr. Montessori stated that the human being was "a new creature" with a "new destiny". Shakespeare marvelled saying "What a piece of work is Man," but deviations reveal man at his lowest level, when he is, his most "in-human" self.

It is interesting to note that when Montessori, using a medical metaphor, described deviations as "maladies" or "illnesses", the psychological equivalent in the mind, of physical illnesses in the body, she had many critics as well as supporters. Yet nowadays, we hear constantly of celebrities going into "rehab" for alcohol and drug abuse, anger management or sexual addiction. And what is rehab? It is a medical facility for people with illnesses.

So wasn't Montessori right? These behaviours are deviations from normality. They are aberrations, the very opposite of normal human development.

Just at the period of life, when the human being should be focusing on what his contribution is going to be, what role he will play in the drama of human life, he is cruelly side-tracked into a spiral of self destroying behaviour.

If you "interviewed" the gangs of youths hanging around streets causing trouble, you might be surprised to find that some of them, just a few years ago, were intelligent people, full of questions, ideas, good intentions, yet a short time into adolescence and they became "louts", spending their weekends in drunken oblivion. This is not normality. This is deviation.

Different Personalities / Different Deviations.

We saw in early childhood that different personalities manifest different deviations. Well, exactly the same thing happens in adolescence.

Montessori used the terms "week" and "strong" when describing the two types of child and their associated deviations. We used the terms "submissive" and "dominant" as rough equivalents to Montessori's terms. For the adolescent, we will use the terms "introverted" and "extroverted".

Adolescents who have encountered obstacles to their normal development and have "deviated" off the main road onto side-roads often display the following deviations:

The "extroverted" adolescent may:

- abuse alcohol
- use drugs
- become promiscuous
- engage in risky behaviour

The "introverted" adolescent may:

- become anorexic
- become bulimic
- become addicted to painkillers or sleeping pills
- become engaged in abusive relationships
- engage in self harm
- attempt suicide

The behaviours may look different, but they are all the same under the skin. They are all deviations from normality.

38

GETTING BACK ON TRACK (AGAIN)

(A Return To Normal Development In Adolescence)

When an adolescent has encountered obstacles causing him to "deviate" off the main road of normal development and go down side roads leading to deviations in behaviour and personality, the big question is, can he be helped to get "back on track" again and if so, how?

The short answer is "yes" he can be helped to get "back on track" but our efforts, will only be successful if two things happen:

- The obstacle which sent him "off course" in the first place, must be removed.

- We must normalise the conditions under which he lives.

Removing the Obstacle which sent the Adolescent "off course".

We don't need to be great detectives to find the "obstacle" which sent the adolescent off course in the first place. Montessori has already done the detective work for us. She told us clearly what the cause of all deviation is. She said:

"Does not all of this (i.e attachment to poisons instead of to life) indicate precisely the loss of a vital inner sensibility, which should work for the preservation of the individual?"

This is the central obstacle, "the loss of a vital inner sensibility, which should work for the preservation of the individual."

Peers, schools, society etc are all peripheral things surrounding this one central obstacle, "the loss of a vital inner sensibility which should work for the preservation of the individual."

We cannot get away from it, this is the central obstacle. And what is this "vital inner sensibility" which has been lost?

Answer. It is the force that urges the tiny infant to drag himself up to a sitting position so that he can be involved in the world that he finds himself in.

It is the force that urges the baby to keep pulling himself up, no matter how many times he falls as he tries to teach himself to stand unaided and take those first amazing steps which lead to walking, running and climbing.

It is the force that urges the toddler to poke, prod, lick, sniff, and stare intently at everything in an effort to understand what the world is made of.

It is the force that urges the young child to set challenges for himself, to say, "see how fast I can run," "see how high I can jump".

It is the force that urges the older child to "ask so many questions" and to seek out the answers to them. It is the voice that tells the human being "what a piece of work is man".

It is the force that urges the adolescent to seek to relate to other human beings, to philosophise with them, laugh with them, cry with them, struggle with them, celebrate with them, and share a common humanity with them.

And where does this "vital inner sensibility" come from? Answer, the human being is born with it. It is a gift he arrives with. It is essentially what makes him different from all other creatures. It is the essence of what it means to be a human being. It cannot be purchased or manufactured. But it can be stolen or lost.

It is our belief that secondary schools as they are today "rob" many adolescents of their "vital inner sensibility". They don't do this intentionally, but they do it all the same. It's like taking the heart out of a person and then wondering why their legs and arms won't work. If you take the central, life-giving force out of the human being, nothing will work, you are wasting your time even trying.

Well, if the obstacle is the "loss" of that "vital inner sensibility," then to remove that obstacle we must find a way to help the human being to "regain" it.

This is very hard, because we cannot manufacture or purchase it. It came from nature or God. So, what can we do to help the human being to regain it and therefore remove the obstacle that caused him to go off course in the first place?

There is no easy answer to this question, everyone is an individual. But one thing must happen in all cases. We must normalise the conditions under which the adolescence lives to enable him to try to regain this lost sensibility. For some adolescents, this vital inner sensibility can be regained through involvement with art, music, spirituality, literature, drama or dance.

For others it can be regained through hard physical work that has some primal significance like farm work, forestry work, or some other outdoor work that involves a closeness to mother earth.

We cannot make this "vital inner sensibility" return. For some people, it never returns making their life a "living death" or resulting in their suicide. But although we cannot make this "vital inner sensibility" return, we can do a lot to try to revive it.

So, what can we do? The answer is, we must normalise the conditions under which the adolescence lives.

Normalising the Conditions under which the Adolescent Lives.

In the western world, most adolescents spend eight hours a day in school. For most of these eight hours they are expected to sit, immobile, listening to an adult speak. If they lose concentration, they are reprimanded.

After these eight hours are over, they then go home where they are expected to do another 2 to 4 hours of sitting immobile doing homework. This madness goes on for six years, 12 to 18.

Let's come straight to the point - THIS IS NOT NORMAL. The human being is not a head on a stick. Human life should not be about cramming knowledge into heads. It should be about experience. Experience cannot be gained by sitting on a chair. Immobility is not normal. Life is about movement. Things that don't move are usually dead.

To make matters worse, there is the whole insanity of exams. I remember as an adolescent realising how ridiculous the exam system was, how it could never assess anyone's ability, yet here it still is, some 40 years later.

Many years ago, Dr Maria Montessori wrote:

"My vision of the future is no longer of people taking exams and proceeding on that certification from the secondary school to the university, but of individuals, passing from one stage of independence to a higher, by means of their own activity, through their own effort of will, which constitutes the inner evolution of the individual." (From Childhood To Adolescence)

This statement came from a woman who held a professorship at the University of Rome and the Chair of Hygiene Science at the women's college. She knew all about exams. She was an examiner herself. So she knew both sides of the story, and yet she believed exams should be abolished and replaced by real achievement in the form of the growing, tangible, evident, independence of the human being, not a lot of rote learning regurgitated on exam day.

Over the years, we attended several homeschooling conventions with our three children who were "unschooled". It was extraordinary to find that a large number of the homeschooling parents were actually teachers, and university lecturers. All of them knew about schools and exams from the inside because it was their "work". Yet they had made up their minds not to subject their own children to any of it. When I asked some of them the obvious question- "do you not feel hypocritical working as a teacher yet keeping your own child out of the system?," they all, without exception said, "we're just counting the days to get out of it." Secondary schools, like cigarettes should carry a health warning-

"Attendance Here Can Cause Harm".

Why? Because it can. Again, these are hard things to state and to swallow, but they are true. Some of our best friends are secondary school teachers, so that makes it even harder for us to write these things, but these things are true nevertheless. People can learn how to become plumbers, doctors, electricians, nurses, bakers, hairdressers, lawyers, without spending years locked up in concrete buildings looking at the back of someone's head followed by a trip home to write endless essays about it.

There are ways to grow, develop and blossom but the secondary school way is not one of them. It's been tried. It's failed. Now, it's time to move on, and in so doing we will be taking the first step in the process of normalising the conditions under which the adolescent lives.

39

SUMMARY OF THE CHARACTERISTICS OF THE ADOLESCENT
12 - 18 YEARS.

The period of adolescence
A period of creation
The creation of the adult

Duration: 12 to 18 years
Subdivision: 12 to 15 years
              15 to 18 years

General Description:

A period of huge transformation, both physically and mentally, the child is becoming an adult.

Physical Characteristics:

At the age of 12 or thereabouts, nature sends a sign that a change is coming, the child is entering a new plane, a new stage of life. This sign is what we call puberty, i.e the physical changes that happen to every boy and girl around 12 years of age. All over the world, people know that the physical changes in boys and girls at age 12 or thereabouts, signal the end of childhood and the beginning of adulthood. Physically there are huge hormonal changes in the child and a return to a more fragile physical state. Gone are the years of robust good health. Now adolescent complaints are common. Acne on the skin, pains and aches in the limbs, and all sorts of vague maladies are common.

Often people are not sympathetic with adolescents, thinking that they are just moaning and groaning at this age, but Montessori, as a doctor, knew that the vague illnesses of adolescents are very real, you only have to look at their skin, their spots and rashes to be convinced.

Mental Characteristics:

Remember the great mental powers of the second plane of development? Well now there's a significant change. There is an unexpected decrease in the ability to concentrate on school subjects. The adolescent is easily distracted, which makes study difficult.
Yet, the adolescent wants to discuss complex ideas, philosophy, the meaning of life, and spirituality. He wants to debate the big issues. He is very honest and he deplores hypocrisy.

Neurological Characteristics:

Neurologically, a major reconstruction of the brain is taking place. A process called "synaptic pruning" begins whereby brain cells and neural connections which are not actively being used are pruned away and they die off while brain cells and neural connections that are actively being used are strengthened and hard-wired.

Social Characteristics:

The overriding desire of the adolescent is to fit in socially.
Often the adolescent becomes introverted, self-conscious and lacks confidence.
He becomes sensitive to even the mildest criticism.
He feels he is being observed, judged, even ridiculed.
He becomes very conscious of his social status.
He has a desperate desire to fit in socially.
He becomes very concerned about social standing, so that, things like clothes, pocket money, and appearance take on huge importance to him.
He may challenge authority during this period especially if he feels it lacks sympathy and understanding.
Yet, the adolescent has a great interest in humanity and a very genuine desire to help others. He feels concerned about world issues such as poverty, war and injustice. He wants to do his bit to change things for the better.

In many ways, the adolescence, in the sub-period 12 to 15 years shares many of the characteristics of the young child in the first plane, in the sub-period 0 to 3 years. There the human being is vulnerable, fragile and goes through a huge period of transformation both physically and mentally in the space of three years. Now the adolescent feels that same fragility again, that same vulnerability. Interestingly, these are both periods of creation. The period 0 to 3 years is all about the creation of the child and the period 12 to 15 years is all about the creation of the adult.

Emotional Characteristics:

New psychological characteristics appear in the adolescent from 12 to 18 years. The adolescent often becomes confused about life. In her book, From Childhood To Adolescence, Montessori points out that the average adolescent sufferers from "doubts, hesitations, violent emotions and discouragements." He is often very emotional and very sensitive .

Needs:

The dominant need of the adolescent is to achieve the right "social adjustment". This is the thing he is striving towards but it is also the thing that is so hard to achieve.

Because he is constantly evaluating his life and thinking about things, the adolescent needs solitude and calm. He has a need for quiet reflection. He has a great need also for the strengthening of his self-confidence. He has a great need of close, one to one adult attention, just as he did in the first three years of life. Only now he needs this one-to-one attention from people who are not his parents. He needs mentors, coaches and guides that come from outside of his immediate family, people who will listen to his questions and take him seriously, people who will discuss the big issues with him. At the same time, he needs the comfort and companionship of his peers, because he is vulnerable and may suffer loneliness and a sense of isolation.

He has a need at this period for creative expression. The creative urge is a means for self-expression and self discovery. That is why so many teenagers learn to play the guitar, write songs and poetry and often make crafts or paintings to express their feelings. There is also a need for financial independence which brings dignity and increased self-esteem.

Sensitive Periods:

Nature gives the adolescent three very clear sensitivities during this plane.

- A sensitivity to everything that relates to life as a social being.

- An intense interest in forming new emotional attachments in his life.

- An irresistible urge to work with his hands.

We would further suggest that the adolescent experiences three other sensitive periods. These are:

- A sensitive period for music.

- A sensitive period for dance.

- A sensitive period specifically designed by nature, to help the human being to learn to relate to, and eventually share a life with, a member of the opposite sex.

40

HOW CAN WE HELP THE HUMAN BEING DURING THE PERIOD 12 - 18 YEARS?

"Schools, such as they are today, are not adapted to the needs of the adolescent or to the age in which we live."

(From Childhood to Adolescence).

Not long ago in human history, young children were pushed up chimneys with brooms in their hands. Why? - Because adults decided they would make good chimney sweeps. Most of us in Western society are horrified to hear of this. We ask what did they do to deserve this?

Sometime in the future, we believe that society will be equally horrified to hear that there was a period in human history when young people, between 12 and 18 years were forced to spend their entire days sitting in a giant, locked, concrete building, looking at the back of someone's head, having to ask permission to go to the toilet, and then, following a brief escape to go home, had to sit again for hours, often still in the same government issue clothing, doing homework, the submission of which further exposed them to humiliation, detention or bad grades. Why? - Because adults decided this was good for them. We ask again- "what did they do to deserve this?"

Many years ago, Dr Maria Montessori could see plainly that the institutions i.e. schools that we have invented for the human being during the period of life from 12 to 18 years, are totally unsuited to their neurological, physical, social, emotional, intellectual, psychological and spiritual needs.

Over the last hundred years, adolescents have been forced to spend most of their days in institutions that were built on a 19th century factory model.

Dr. Montessori realised that no amount of tinkering could make this model a good fit for the human being in this period of life.

She was certain that a totally new approach was needed. She suggested a new model based on the characteristics, needs, drives and sensitive periods of the human being during the period 12 to 18 years.

Firstly, she divided this period of life into two subdivisions 12 to 15 years and 15 to 18 years because her observations of adolescents showed her that the needs of younger adolescents differ substantially from those of older adolescents.

Physical Considerations:

Montessori recognised that the period of adolescence between the years 12 to 18 and most particularly between the years 12 to 15 is one of huge physical transformation. She highlighted the fact that during this period, physical growth occurs at an extraordinary rate. She also noted that, as a result of this rapid growth, physical illnesses are common.

Taking into account this physical vulnerability, Montessori recognised that the human being, during this period of life has a great need for-

- Fresh air
- Sunshine
- A diet rich in vitamins and minerals
- Organic food
- Sleep
- A calm environment
- Silence
- Exposure to the rhythms of nature

Intellectual Considerations:

Montessori highlighted the fact that the period of adolescence between 12 to 18 years is a period in which the human being experiences an unexpected decrease in the ability to concentrate on school "subjects."

Taking into account this change in intellectual capacity, Montessori recognised that the human being during this period of life needs-

- Less exams.
- Less homework.
- Less purely academic subjects to study.
- More practical courses offering real life skills.
- More creative subjects.
- More courses that arise from a "need to know" basis.

Social Considerations:

Montessori recognised that the period of adolescence between 12 and 18 years is a period in which the human being experiences a profound urge to come out of his own individual world and become a member of society.

Taking into account this newfound need for social life, Montessori recognised that the human being, during this period 12 to 18 years needs-

- Opportunities to develop meaningful relationships with persons of his/her own age.

- Opportunities to develop meaningful relationships with older persons who act as coaches, mentors and guides.

- Opportunities to develop meaningful relationships with his/her own parents.

Emotional Considerations:

Montessori highlighted the fact that during this period of adolescence 12 to 18 years, the human being often suffers swings of emotions that are frequently violent, turbulent and discouraging. Depression and anxiety are common. In the worst cases, suicidal ideations emerge.

Taking into account this emotional instability which emerges in the human being during the period 12 to 18 years to a lesser or greater degree, Montessori recognised that during this period the human being needs-

- A calm environment.
- Therapeutic activities.
- Opportunities to be alone.
- Opportunities to distance himself a little from parents and draw near to mentors and guides as well as peers.

Economic Considerations:

Montessori recognised that the period of adolescence between 12 and 18 years is a period in which the human being feels a great need to earn his own money. He feels embarrassed by having to rely on his parents for money, so he seeks ways of supporting himself.

Taking this newfound need to earn his own money, into account, Montessori recognised that the human being between 12 and 18 years, needs:

- Opportunities to start small businesses which will give him an income.

- Opportunities to use some of his skills to tutor others, also providing financial return.

- Opportunities to learn how the world of economics works, starting with his own small world.

Spiritual Considerations:

Montessori pointed out that during the period of adolescence, 12 to 18 years, the human being spontaneously starts to think about spiritual matters.

Taking into account this human tendency at this period of life, Montessori recognised that the human being during the years 12 to 18, needs-

- Opportunities to discuss spiritual issues.

- Information on spiritual issues and religions.

- Tranquil environments in which to meditate or pray.

**Montessori's suggestions for a suitable environment
for the human being during the period 12 to 18 years.**

Taking the physical, intellectual, social, emotional, economic and spiritual needs of the human being in the period 12 to 18 into consideration, Dr Montessori came up with a plan for a suitable environment for the human being during this time. She called it Erdkinder.

Erdkinder is a German word meaning earth children. The Erdkinder is a place, usually a farm setting where adolescents between 12 to 15 years or 12 to 18 years can:

- Live close to nature.
- Eat fresh organic farm foods grown by themselves.
- Discover first hand how the world works by working with other young people in a mini society, learning how to provide shelter, food, clothing, transport etc. for themselves and their group.
- Earn money by selling farm produce or by starting small businesses.
- Continue with intellectual study but tailor it around their interests.
- Have a period with no exams/no academic stress.
- Learn practical skills such as cooking, woodwork, and the skills needed for farm work.
- Learn about mechanics and machinery.
- Have a museum of machinery that could include machines from the typewriter to the iPad.
- Experience being away from home, fending for themselves, knowing that their parents are not too far away and can visit the farm school at weekends and even stay in the hotel run by the adolescents in the grounds of the school.

Yes, it is radically different from a traditional school. The question is - does it work?

Is it successful at "aiding" the development of the human being during this critical period of life?

To answer that question we should first listen to the reports of adolescents who have experienced life in a farm school and ask them for their feedback and opinions. One of the best ways of doing this is to view the videos made by the adolescents at the Hershey farm school in Ohio USA.

245

The Hershey Montessori Farm school in Ohio offers one of the most well-known adolescent programs in the world. It offers both boarding and day school facilities. The school is housed on a large working farm, and it has a main house which is run by both the adolescents and the adults. The students are actively involved in every aspect of the school from its finances and yearly budget to its daily activities which include cooking, cleaning, planting and growing crops as well as harvesting and processing the foods that come from them.

The main house is the hub, the centre of all the social activities going on. It is also the place where creative activities are pursued and where chats, debates and friendly discourse goes on among the students and the adult mentors and guides who also run the farm.

The house is surrounded by numerous barns and workshops which are used by the students in the care of the animals, and in the teaching of crafts such as woodwork and in the practising of dramatic arts and so on.

The farm is also surrounded by acres of forest which students explore by hiking and tracking. Students also swim and ride on horseback in the beautiful countryside.

The students also run a type of hostel or bed-and-breakfast for the public, which helps to bring in much needed finances and follows Montessori's suggestion that a hostel or bed and breakfast type of arrangement would aid the economic needs of the adolescents at this period of life and teach them business and economic good sense.

While all this outdoor life of action and indoor life of creativity is going on, the mental development of the adolescent is not neglected. From their hands on, "real life" experiences running the farm, the adolescents are learning-

- Mathematics.
- Environmental sciences.
- Animal husbandry.
- Land management.
- Food science.
- Domestic sciences.
- Biology.
- Ecology.
- Business skills.
- Accounting

- Economics.
- Humanities.
- Conflict resolution.

all in a day's farm work! How many schools could compete with this?

But the difference is, all of these important subjects will not be taught as in a traditional school, the student will learn them on a need to know basis as he grapples with real life situations while helping to run a farm.

It's an exhilarating experience, especially when you're only in your teens. As the adolescents get older, 15 to 18 year olds, spontaneously begin to pursue more academic studies without being badgered by anyone.

Dr Montessori only wrote guidelines for the creation of Farm Schools. Had she lived longer she would, no doubt, have made more specific suggestions. Therefore, it comes down to her followers to take her outline guidelines for an environment suitable for a human being from 12 to 18 years and build on them. It is generally believed by people involved in Montessori education that the most successful Farm Schools will be those where the students have previously attended Montessori schools and so already have a structure, a well founded platform on which to build. This does not exclude participation by students who have no previous experience in a Montessori school, but we know from first-hand experience that adolescents who have never had the benefit of a Montessori education prior to the farm school experience can take a little longer to settle in and take responsibility for the running of the school. But in time, it usually works out very well for all .

We believe that society is spontaneously moving closer to the idea of Erdkinder type schools. Parents are exploring Forest Schools and alternative schools or simply no schools.

Home schooling or un-schooling is becoming more and more popular. Perhaps more and more parents are coming to see what John Holt meant when he stated that schools "create their own pathologies."

The concrete prisons that we call schools are making many of our adolescents ill. The time has come to revolutionise education and set our children free to become all that they have the potential to be.

Surely that is how we can help the human being during the period 12 to 18 years.

PART SIX

HOW DOES THE YOUNG ADULT COMPLETE HIMSELF?

(The Years 18 to 24) (The Age of Commitment)

41

FROM UGLY DUCKLINGS TO BEAUTIFUL SWANS

(Physical Changes in Early Adulthood)

Every now and then, our eldest daughter says "hey mom, do you want to see the photos of xxxx's wedding?

Then, I find myself once more, staring, with my mouth wide open, at the crowds of photogenic "beautiful people" on the Facebook pages.

To my mind, they all look like film stars. The young men all seem to be tall and handsome and the young women all look extraordinarily poised and beautiful.

But, I know these kids. Some of them came to our Montessori school when they were little. I knew them when they were three, six, nine, and seventeen years old.

I saw their spots, their braces, their lanky limbs, what seems like, just a short while ago.

So what's happened to all of these "ordinary people"? Have they all had "work done"?

Happily no. What's happened is they've entered into their twenties. They are "twenty somethings" now and during the twenties, everyone seems to become beautiful.

Did you ever look at photograph albums of your parents back in the "old days"?

Well I did and I couldn't believe how handsome my father looked and how beautiful my mother looked linking his arm.

It wasn't just the black-and-white photography that made them look so good, it was something about their age, that "twenty-something" glow.

The physical changes that occur in early adulthood are subtle ones.

There is no huge change in height or body shape. Usually the human being has reached his/her maximum height by the end of adolescence i.e. eighteen years approximately. But changes are visible all the same.

The spots and pimples have usually cleared up. The greasy hair has become normal again. The puppy fat has disappeared. The lanky limbs have somehow "grown into" the rest of the body and everything seems to be a good fit now.

The physical ailments of adolescence have eased off and good health becomes the norm.

The "ugly ducklings" have indeed turned into "beautiful swans."

42

WHERE HAS ALL THE "ANGST" GONE TO?

(Emotional Changes in Early Adulthood)

Recently, we were talking to a friend who was lamenting "the awful few days" she had recently gone through.

She said that on Friday she was supposed to be taking her 20 year old daughter over to her best friend's new house on the other side of town, but half an hour before they were due to go, her car broke down and leaked oil all over the driveway, forcing them to abandon the trip.

The next day, Saturday, she had promised to accept a parcel from the postman which her younger daughter was eagerly awaiting.

Unfortunately, as she was out back talking to the car mechanic, she didn't hear the doorbell ringing, so she didn't sign for the parcel, so the postman left a note saying, he'd called but no one had answered, so he had taken the parcel back to the sorting office, and, as it was a bank holiday weekend, it couldn't be collected for three days!

The next day, Sunday she took her eldest daughter over to her friend's house in her "fixed" car, but halfway there, her daughter realised that she had left the "Welcome to your New Home" card that she had so carefully handmade, alongside the beautiful bouquet of flowers that were to accompany the card, on the kitchen table, all because her mother, (our friend), had asked her to go back into the house to make sure that the oven was "switched off".

Monday came and went with no problems (possibly because they all stayed indoors!), but Tuesday brought another headache.

How To Build a Human Being

On Tuesday evening, when she set out to collect her daughter from her friend's new home, (she had stayed over for a few days), the car broke down again. This time it had to be towed and she had no phone to contact her daughter to tell her what was happening, because her phone somehow got damaged by the rain while she was trying to contact the tow truck company.

Her daughter ended up standing for over an hour outside a closed mall waiting for her.

Fast forward to the following Saturday afternoon. Our friend and her two daughters, who are aged 19 and 20, are sipping Mocha Lattes together in a cafe, and laughing, yes laughing at the events of the last week.

Our friend said philosophically, "Thank goodness they're older now, because if this had happened just a year or two ago, Jenny would have accused me of trying to ruin her few days with her friend, and Becky would have been convinced that I was somehow in cahoots with the post office to stop her receiving the "questionable outfit" that unbeknownst to me, the parcel contained, and that she (also unbeknownst to me) intended to wear to a teenage party the next evening.

"Ah," she said, "isn't time a wonderful thing."

When it comes to teenage "angst," time certainly is "a wonderful thing."

Why? Because we now know from neurology that the most likely reason that these two young ladies were able to restrain themselves from blowing up in anger at their mother and hurling hurtful accusations at her is that they are no longer just using the "gut-reaction," instinctual, amygdala section of their brain in their responses to events, but are using their now more mature and more finely tuned, reason oriented, prefrontal cortex.

A mature and finely tuned prefrontal cortex cannot be bought, nor can it be borrowed, it can only come about through the passage of time.

The old proverb, "you can't put an old head on young shoulders," turns out to be true.

Let us explain.

Some years ago, a group of scientists at the McLean Hospital in Massachusetts, carried out a very interesting and significant experiment.

They hooked up a group of adults and a group of adolescents to functional MRI scanning machines. They then presented each person with a series of specially selected photographs.

Then they asked each person to identify the expressions on the photographs which were snapshots of adult faces.

When the adults were shown the photographs, they correctly identified the expressions. For example, all of the adults correctly identified the photograph representing 'fear' as 'fear'.

However, the adolescents, in contrast, misinterpreted the photograph of fear. They interpreted the face as showing anger, surprise or shock. Not only that, but the MRI scans showed that the adults were responding with a different part of the brain to the part that the adolescents were using.

In the case of adults, the part of the brain which 'lit up' was the prefrontal cortex, i.e the part of the brain which is associated with reason.

In the case of the adolescents, the part of the brain which 'lit up' was the amygdala, the part of the brain which is associated with 'gut' reactions, and emotional responses.

Experiments like these may well explain why adolescents react differently from adults to the same set of events.

Firstly, this experiment suggests that adolescents react quickly from the emotional part of their brain without running those reactions by the more rational frontal cortex, (because the frontal cortex is still under construction in adolescence).

Secondly, this experiment suggests that adolescents may have a tendency to 'misread' expressions and consequently the intentions behind them.

A mature and finely tuned prefrontal cortex helps a person to relate to and understand another person.

So, if an adolescent does not yet have a finely tuned prefrontal cortex, he may not be able to relate to or understand the real intentions of others and he may misjudge a parent's genuine worry as criticism, or more commonly, a parent's genuine concern as anger.

To put it simply, what the experiment suggests is that, adults, respond to experiences with the frontal cortex, the part of the brain that helps them to restrain impulses, to apply emotional brakes and reason out the why's and how's before delivering judgement, while adolescents, on the other hand, response to experiences with the amygdala, the part of the brain that is one of the key areas for instinctual reactions such as fight or flight. It is a primal emotional centre located further back in the brain.

These experiments and their results suggest very strongly that the adolescent may very well just see the world differently from adults, and therefore respond differently.

So, to answer our question, where has all the "angst" gone to, we would suggest it has moved locations.

Now that the human being is older, the "angst" is now being dealt with by the rational pre-frontal cortex and not the emotional amygdala.

This probably explains why our friend's two daughters, who are now young adults and not adolescents, are sipping mocha lattes with her in a cafe, rather than throwing the mocha lattes over her in her kitchen!

43

HE ACTUALLY WANTS TO STUDY NOW!

(Intellectual Changes in Early Adulthood)

Remember that fog, I described, that hung over me in maths class, history class and geography class, during the period 12 to 18 years, well during the period 18 to 24 years, it started to lift.

It took a while. I was 21 before I could apply myself to any other subject except English literature, but at 22, I had a part-time job, as a, (who'd have guessed it), mathematics tutor! As I prepared for my classes, I literally had to learn the actual stuff I was scheduled to teach the next week and I remember exclaiming to myself on more than one occasion, "Wow, so that's what it was all about!" Suddenly, maths seemed so easy, and there was nothing Chinese about it!

Well, it turns out that I was not unusual. Research shows that somewhere, during the period 18 to 24 years, something "neurological" happens in the brain that makes it a lot easier for us to focus and learn.

We become able to study things that we do not particularly have a passion for, but we need to learn anyway, and it's no longer a "big deal" to have to do it. We take it in our stride. We make a commitment.

So what's going on in the brain? Answer, all sorts of things, but the most significant of all is the completion of the pre-frontal cortex.

In our 20s, we may have to learn about mundane things like car loans, lease agreements, budgets, how to fix a leaky tap or a squeaky floorboard. We may also have to learn about how to run a grocery store, how to be a hairdresser, how to sell advertising space, how to drive a bus, how to make kitchen cabinets, how to fix televisions etc., because these may be our jobs. And the funny thing is, we suddenly find we can apply ourselves to these things.

We have no illusions about them. We don't pretend to be passionate about fixing televisions or driving buses, but we appreciate that they are jobs that have to be done, and we willingly study to develop the expertise necessary to do them.

In our 20s, we find that we are clear-headed about this. We learn fast. Things we knew nothing about before, we find we can become expert in, in a relatively short period of time.

It seems like one minute we are a foggy headed student and the next, we are a be-suited or be-uniformed 20-year-old, able to "do inventory," "administrate" from behind a desk, "assist" customers, "usher" crowds, "advise" clients, and do other high sounding, adult type things.

It is usually during this period that the human being begins to get a clearer idea of what he wants to do in life and he often declares: "I want to study to become a nurse, pilot, surveyor, chef, teacher, manager, hairdresser, translator, or whatever".

This is the key to this period of life. The young adult discovers what he wants to study. He may only discover this at the end of his three-year, very expensive college course, and the "thing" he wants to become may be very unrelated to the three year very expensive college course he has just completed or dropped out of.

This happens every year to thousands of young people worldwide. In fact, the dropout rates in third level institutions are frighteningly high in many countries and the reasons behind the dropout rates should be studied and not ignored.

We believe that the high dropout rate in college courses is mostly caused by the fact that, because of his neurological make-up, it is not until the mid 20s that the young adult actually begins to get a clear picture of what he wants to work at, as opposed to what he has been streamlined to work at. If the two don't match, he often drops out.

When he discovers what he wants to work at, it naturally follows that he discovers what he wants to study.

That's why during this period, 18 to 24 years, incredulous parents and other onlookers can be heard to exclaim with astonishment, "He actually wants to study now!"

44

THE QUEST FOR "MR. AND MRS. RIGHT"

(Social Changes in Early Adulthood)

"Don't say you love me, unless forever."

So go the words of that beautiful song by those multi-talented artists, The Corrs.

While it's true to say that the adolescent, 12 to 18 years does not wake up in the mornings thinking "I need to find a long-term mate, build a home and start reproducing the species," it would be untrue to say that the young adult doesn't have these thoughts.

Young adults don't like to say this out loud, but most of them are looking for long-term relationships. "Don't say you love me, unless forever," is the kind of relationship most young adults are longing for, but they can only admit it in song.

True, there are many young adults, of both sexes, who will say that they are not looking for "anything serious," but, the truth is, the vast majority of young adults are, they just feel very uncomfortable about saying it.

So, what's going on?

Well, during the period 18 to 24 years, nature ups the ante. Nature needs the human being to select a long-term mate somewhere in the next few years (the childbearing years) in order to propagate the human species.

As we've discussed earlier, it is not nature's plan for the human being to mate casually. As Montessori pointed out, man is not like the animals. He is a new creature with a new destiny and he has specific human needs that animals don't have and the most important of these is the need for security and stability of lifestyle.

Nature needs to ensure that the offspring of each new human generation will have the optimal conditions necessary for healthy growth and development. As we've pointed out earlier, human beings do not do well when they are born into unstable conditions.

So nature, watching vigilantly over the young adult determines to help him to provide this stability and security for his future offspring. How? By encouraging the young adult to seek a long-term, stable relationship. Now how does nature do this? Answer, by activating the strange phenomenon called "falling in love".

When young adults "fall in love" they become exclusive. They want to spend all their time together. They cut down on their socialising with other friends. They start to build a nest.

This can be very irritating to their "single" friends who accuse them of being too engrossed in each other. The problem usually corrects itself when the "single" friends fall deeply in love themselves and the same thing happens to them. Nature is powerful, it can even override the views of our peers!

So, the social change we witness in early adulthood is this: the human being meets someone special, falls in love, becomes exclusive, starts to cut down on socialising with other friends because he/she feels a stronger desire to be with "the beloved" than with his/her previous friends. This is not a betrayal of those friends, it is just a natural part of life.

Sometimes these relationships work out and the young adult realises that he/she has found "the one". More often, it takes a bit of trial and error before Mr and Mrs right are found. The search can and often does preoccupy young adults for most of their 20s and even early 30s. But, for the vast majority of young adults, the quest for Mr and Mrs Right is successful. They meet, they merge and nature takes a bow.

45

WE WANT TO FEED THE WORLD, WE WANT TO SAVE THE PLANET

(Spiritual and Moral Changes in Early Adulthood)

"Man is that superior being who is........ destined to do a great task on earth."
(The Formation of Man p96)

If you want to know why terrorist organisations have no problem recruiting young adults willing to die for a cause, this is it.

If you want to know why religious cults attract young adults rather than older people, this is it.

If you want to know why our psychiatric services are at breakdown point dealing with the increasing numbers of young adults suffering from the effects of depression, self harm, etc. this is it.

If you want to know why intelligent, talented, beautiful young adults, spend their weekends drinking themselves into oblivion, or drugging themselves into unconsciousness, this is it.

If you want to know why suicide among young adults is rising at such an alarming rate, this is it.

The bottom line is, human beings seem to know instinctively that they were made for something bigger and greater than a humdrum existence, but they also know that that's all they are being offered and they are looking for someone who can point them to something better.

The young adult doesn't need anyone to tell him that he is a "new creature" with a "new destiny," because he has sensed this all through his life. Nature, hovering vigilantly over him, has been relentlessly whispering in his ear that he was made to do something significant with his life.

But now, he is getting older, and he's beginning to panic. Where's the outlet for his particular talents? What is his role? What is he meant to do for the world? Everywhere he goes now, people ask him "what are you doing with yourself these days?" "are you in college?" "are you working?"

Some young adults are made to feel so uncomfortable by these questions that they avoid being in company. Others often make up stuff and just tell people what they want to hear.

No one wants to say "I'm doing a boring, soul destroying job, or, my university course didn't turn out to be what I thought it would be and I'm afraid to drop out because my parents would be either furious or devastated.

So the young adult often carries a burden that he dare not reveal to anyone. He desperately wants to have a life of significance, but nothing, in his education, has ever really addressed this deep human need. His years of schooling have always emphasised the need to get a good job, earn money, have possessions, but they never really addressed this deep human need to live a meaningful life, making our mark on the planet.

Now there is nothing wrong with getting a good job, earning money, and having possessions, but, and this is the bit that the young adult has a problem with, if you only do this so that your future children can get a good job, earn money and have possessions, so that their future children can get a good job, earn money and have possessions, so that their future children.......etc. etc, the significance of your life becomes questionable.

During the period 18 to 24 years, nature gives the human being a new sensitivity designed to urge him to "take action" to help his world. It is described by Montessori as a "spiritual" and "moral" sensitivity.

It whispers in everyone's ears at this period of life. Some people block it out, others listen hard.

I remember years ago, seeing a bunch of scruffy, hairy bikers collecting money in a pub for orphans in some foreign war torn country. I remember, (to my shame) thinking - I wonder how many motorbike parts will be bought with that money?

I later found out, that, not only did these guys collect the money, they travelled in person to the country in need to deliver the money directly to the agency distributing the aid, risking their lives in the process.

Nature does not discriminate, she whispers to all. It was a scruffy, foul-mouthed, rock star named Bob Geldof, who listened to nature's whispers and, Band Aid, the greatest charity event, the world had ever seen, came about as a result.

During the period 6 to 12, the keyword is Imagination, during the period 12 to 18, the keyword is Passion, and now during the period 18 to 24, the keyword is Commitment.

This is the age when nature urges the human being to make a commitment to something. For some, this commitment will be to a marriage, for others it will be to a particular profession or course of study. For others, it will be to "a cause".

But those, who fail to find something to commit to will feel a sense of being -"ill at ease", unhappy, unfulfilled.

This is the period of life when many young adults turn to politics, hoping they can change things for the better.

This is the period of life when many young adults give up their comfortable life for a year or more and go out to third world countries offering their services as teachers, nurses or aid workers.

This is the period of life when those in caring professions such as childcare, social work, nursing, try to bring about change, try to improve standards, try to make things better for the next generation.

But, the biggest problem in this period 18 to 24 years is, that those who cannot find something to "commit" to, fall between the cracks. They feel lost. They feel that there is no place for them. They feel as though they are the forgotten ones.

So, what happens to them? Well, without a doubt, some of these young people, will be recruited by extremist groups or cults, who will offer them "a cause".

The human need for "a cause" is so strong at this period of life that the young person can easily be "hood-winked," "brainwashed," or "indoctrinated."

All thought of reason, familial loyalty and upbringing, goes "out the window" at this point, because the attraction to "a cause" is so powerful.

The leaders of these extremist groups understand this need to have "a cause" to work for, much better than anyone, certainly they understand it much better than the "clever" teachers in our schools and universities.

Those who are not lured into cults or extremist groups and have still not found something of significance to do, are usually the ones who spend their time out drinking and drug-taking, because the human being cannot have a fulfilled existence when he is unable to respond to the voice of nature telling him that he is meant to do something significant with his life.

So, we must ask the question. Is there a shortage of meaningful jobs in the world? Has every meaningful job been taken? Is there nothing left but the hum-drum?

The truth is, there are many, many meaningful jobs that need to be done in this world, many of them have not even been invented yet, and many young adults, in the period 18 to 24, have the spiritual and the moral capacity to do them. But they need direction.

This is the period of life when the human being is most in need of adult help to aid him to find meaningful work. Yet it is the period of life when the young adult is most abandoned by adults. He is told to "go and find a job" or "find a course to study".

No one understands his desperate need to find work that is meaningful, that will make a contribution to humanity.

No one really knows his heart. No one really knows that he wants to "feed the world" and he wants to "save the planet."

46

ONLY THE CAR RENTAL COMPANIES GOT IT RIGHT

(Neurological Changes in Early Adulthood)

"In terms of brain anatomy, the only ones who have it right are the car rental people."

So says Dr. Jay Giedd, referring to the fact that, in most states in America, a person must be over 25 to rent a car.

Dr. Giedd, who is Chief of Brain Imaging at the National Institute of Mental Health, points out that it's not until age 25 that the prefrontal cortex, the part of the brain that helps us to make good judgements, control our behaviour, reign in our emotions, plan, weigh alternatives, finally reaches maturity.

In other words, before age 25, we have adult capabilities, i.e we can fall in love, make babies, build homes, have adult passions, energies and emotions but the executive part of the brain, the part that helps us to control all of this, is not fully formed yet.

It's a bit like having a turbo powered Lamborghini at our disposal, without the brakes.

For some reason, only the car rental companies seem to have cottoned on to this.

So, what exactly are these neurological changes which occur in early adulthood?

Dr. Giedd's research shows that, in early adulthood, around age 25, the physical development of the prefrontal cortex finally reaches completion.

So, what's the significance of that?

Well, a fully completed prefrontal cortex gives the human being the following abilities:

- The ability to make mature judgements

- The ability to look ahead

- The ability to predict how actions taken now could affect the future

- The ability to see cause-and-effect

- The ability to use moral intelligence

- The ability to think abstractly

- The ability to see beyond the immediate set of circumstances

- The ability to plan and make important decisions

- The ability to act rationally i.e. to follow the head, not just the heart

- The ability to understand the rules of social conduct

- The ability to follow the rules of social conduct

So, basically, the physical completion of the prefrontal cortex is what makes us officially "mature", i.e. adult, and we now know, from neurology that this does not happen until the mid-twenties.

For that reason, Dr. Giedd is right on the nail when he says that "only the car rental people got it right."

47

SUMMARY OF THE CHARACTERISTICS OF THE YOUNG ADULT 18- 24 YEARS.

A Period of Maturity
A Period of Consolidation
The Consolidation of the Adult

Duration: 18- 24 years
Subdivision: 18 -21 years
                       21-24 years

General Description:
This is a period of stability.

Physical Characteristics:
Once again, the human being is strong and robust. The acne and adolescent problems settle down and the young adult feels physically healthy and well.

Mental Characteristics:
The mind becomes stable. There are fewer turbulent emotions. This is a stage of relative peace after the turbulent years of adolescence. The young adult can study and concentrate better now than he could in the previous period, 12 to 18 years.

Neurological Characteristics:
During these years, the prefrontal cortex, the part of the brain that gives us good judgement, impulse control over our actions and emotions is nearing completion though it will not be completely "finished" until the mid twenties or later.

Social Characteristics:
Socially here is a real change in the young adult in this period. He usually becomes less shy, less introverted, less self-conscious, less embarrassed, less sensitive to everything. He doesn't feel that everything is a criticism of him. He doesn't feel so judged. His interest in humanity continues and even strengthens. He becomes more conscious of the possibility that he can play a role in life, and make a meaningful contribution to society. The human being in this period of life yearns for a life that will have meaning both personally and socially. He doesn't just want a "job" he wants to find the work that will give his life meaning and significance and that usually means work that affects others in society.

Emotional Characteristics:
During this period (18 to 24) years, there is a calming down of the emotions. The "doubts, hesitations, violent emotions and discouragements" of the previous six years, calm down.

Needs:
Because this is a period of relative stability and peace, after the turbulent years of adolescence, there is a tendency for parents and society to ignore the true needs of the young person at this time. Often we sit back as parents at this time and think, "our job is done now, our child is becoming an adult. He's very independent, he's handling everything very well, we're not needed now with our old-fashioned advice". But nothing could be further from the truth. This is the adult's last chance to significantly influence the young person while he is still in a formative stage. He may look like a fully formed adult, but he is not a fully formed adult yet. And this is the time when the young person can make serious mistakes, mistakes that he may spend the rest of his life paying for. So there is a real need for parents to stay close to their young offspring during the years 18 to 24, and help them to become part of their society.

Sensitive Periods:
During this period of life, nature provides the young adult with:

> A specific sensitivity to the spiritual side of life.
> A specific sensitivity to what is just and what is unjust.

Nature does this to help the human being to reach the goal of this period of life, which is - spiritual and moral independence.

48

HOW CAN WE HELP THE HUMAN BEING DURING THE PERIOD 18 - 24 YRS?

If we want to help the human being during the period 18 to 24 years, we must first of all keep at the forefront of our minds a summary of his characteristics. Top of the list has to come his neurological status. The fact is, his brain is still unfinished.

Physically, he may look like an adult. Emotionally, he maybe calmer and more adult-like in his handling of situations. Socially, he may be more confident and adult-like in company. Intellectually, he may have less of a fog about him and seem more alert and focused. Spiritually and morally he may show an awareness and concern for world events that may bring a lump to our throats and perhaps some guilt to our consciences, but, and this is the crucial reality, he is not fully mature yet, and he won't be until his mid twenties or possibly thirties.

So, taking all of this into account, what can we do to help him? There is an abundance of research, ideas and suggestions out there, but at the end of the day, the studies show that the single most effective, protective and supportive infrastructure for the developing human being during the period 18 to 24 years is family, especially parents who are prepared, from time to time, to step in and offer "executive function" when it is most needed.

The Role of the Family.

Human beings are first and foremost social creatures. We are wired to create and preserve family bonds. Parents need to be pro-active in preserving (or building) their bond with their young adult offspring. Even taking into account the hectic schedules that many young adults keep, parents should strive to set up a regular arrangement to spend time with their nearly grown-up kids.

The easiest way to do this is to make sure to pencil in some family dinners to suit the young adult's schedule. Arranging a movie night is also a good way to stay close to your young adult offspring, or plan a bowling event or some similar social activity.

Don't exclude the young adult's boyfriend or girlfriend, but, if possible, try to arrange to see him/her sometimes without their romantic partner because, often he/she is experiencing problems, problems that have a lot to do with their romantic partner, and these problems will never be aired if the partner is present.

A word of warning.

Parents should be careful not to use these events to pry into their young adult's private affairs. Nothing will alienate him/her more. Parents should use this time together to preserve or build their bond with their child who is now becoming a fully fledged adult.

But, parents should be open to clues that might indicate that something is not quite right, e.g. if your young adult appears to have money problems, yet you know she/he has a reasonably paid job, be alert to the fact that he/she may have fallen into debt.

This can happen easily to young adults who, as we know do not have a fully finished executive function to help them to make good decisions, yet they are old enough to get loans. Credit card companies make fortunes on the young adult who is old enough to have a credit card but not mature enough to resist maxing it out.

During this period of life, a young adult, who appears to be doing all the right things can suddenly do something "crazy" because of poor judgement. Some of these actions can affect them for the rest of their lives.

Some years ago, a lecturer in education told us, how, thirty years ago, she and her fiancee were saving up to get a deposit on a house so they could get married. They were doing very well, but, out of the blue, because she felt slighted by something her father said, and she wanted to show she was independent, she went out and splashed half of the house deposit money on a sofa, thus seriously sabotaging her own future prospects. She said her action was completely out of character because she was regarded by everyone as being mature for her age.

Looking back, it is clear to her that it was a lack of a fully developed "executive function" which lay behind her reckless action.

A sofa, can be returned, but something like a baby can't be. Many young single women in this period of life find themselves with an unplanned pregnancy. Depending on their circumstances, their family supports, and their attitude towards children, this can be something that they can turn around for good or it can be something that devastates them, closing doors to their future educational and employment dreams.

Once again, it is the family bond and its accompanying supports that will be most beneficial in helping a single young adult to get through an unplanned pregnancy. These things happen in life, and though not ideal, the young person needs help not criticism.

Similarly, during this period of life, single young men, who seemed mature and reliable can suddenly, get up, leave the job that they only just started, and seemed to be doing very well in, and announce that they are off to some foreign country, with no plans, no financial provisions and no idea what they want to do with their lives. Once again, family bonds are crucial here. Parents will have to stand in for the missing executive function and try to help the young man to plan ahead, to see that actions have consequences, and that poor judgement in some countries can land you in prison or even cause your death.

A parent in this situation, walks a fine line between alienating the young adult who doesn't want to hear that anything can go wrong and helping the young adult by giving him planning, strategising and organisational advice.

The Role of the University:

"At the University men live as children even though they are men".
(From Childhood To Adolescence p130)

Nowadays, a very significant number of people between the ages of 18 to 24 go to university. Why? Because they have been told that university is the pinnacle of education, something we should all aspire to. Many years ago, I went to university. I was and still am very grateful for that experience. Although, it was more than 30 years ago, I can still remember my first impressions clearly. They were:

Time Wasting:
Talking Nonsense
Losing Altruism:

The students were guilty of these things also.

Montessori's Views on University Education:

Maria Montessori knew a lot about universities. She attended university for several years while she was studying to become a doctor. She then went back to university and enrolled in another faculty to research everything related to education. She then accepted an appointment as professor of pedagogical anthropology at the same university and lectured to students for several years thereafter. Hence, she experienced university life from both vantage points, as a student and as a professor.

Her comments on the effectiveness of a university education are insightful and despite the passage of time, still have a ring of contemporaneousness about them. She said that the university is a place where young adults, "ought to become conscious of their responsibilities,........Instead, they generally, show a lack of conscientiousness. They form erroneous ideas of life". She wisely observed that-
"One cannot hope that such men will contribute to the betterment of society."
She said that many "young people leave the university with their minds so shackled and sacrificed that they have lost all power of individuation and can no longer judge the problems of the age in which they live." (Absorbent Mind p11)
She said many graduates, when they, "pass out into the world", are "useless to themselves, and a burden to their families and friends".   (Absorbent Mind p12)

Dr. Montessori questioned the effectiveness of traditional undergraduate programmes in meeting the needs of the human being between 18 and 24 years. She pointed out that......."study, even in its broadest terms, and even when assimilated, does not satisfy the human personality". She said, "...other needs remain", which if not met lead to "inner conflicts" which have a negative influence on the "mental state" of the human being.
What are these "other needs" we may well ask? Montessori describes them clearly. "Joy, the sensibility of one's just value, feeling appreciated and loved by others, feeling useful and able to produce - these are factors of immense interest to the human spirit."

Can these come from inside the four walls of the University? Montessori says no. She says, "Life must be the focal point, and education the means". (Ch-A. p134) "All the points noted put the finger on the impossibility of enclosing education within the limits of a room where the individual at work is inert, perpetually dependent on the teacher, separated from the rest of mankind." (Ch-A. p135)

She said that since a child's education "cannot be carried out in the confines of four walls, that of adults is still less capable of being carried out satisfactorily there."

She advocated that university education be combined with a job, and the emphasis should be on lifelong learning. She recommended that the student be able "to achieve financial independence during his university studies". She pointed out that:

"Many young people are already teachers in private schools, journalists, artists, working in business etc." She pointed out that such people "have greater chances of working for the love of study, with a view to human progress, and not just to achieve immediate aims." She said, if it takes them a longer period to complete their studies, "it matters little," because, "their studies are never to finish."

She suggested that since every human being needs lifelong learning, it is disingenuous to dispatch the young adult off to the University between 18 and 24 years to get his quota of university education.

She argued that the "function of the university is teaching to study". She said, "The diploma is nothing more than the proof that one knows how to study, that one knows how to acquire culture by oneself, that one has been shown the way to do scientific research."

Then she asks quite logically, "If the diploma is nothing else than a certificate of ability to learn, why must university studies take from 3 to 6 years?"

She points out that, " A man who studies at university knows that it is necessary to study all his life or study will lose all its value". She then asks, "Why must he endure these several years of harassment to acquire a body of knowledge which will never be complete?"

She says there must be another way to aid the education of the young adult, a way that would allow him to be part of society.

The approach she suggests is a combination of work and study. She stresses that the human being needs economic independence while studying. He can achieve this by having a job and a place in society, while studying.

So, once again we see that Montessori's views on education even education at the fourth plane of development go against the tide but they are based on the needs of the human being, not on the arbitrary demands of the University.

The White-Collar versus The Blue-Collar:

" Men who have hands and no head and men who have a head and no hands are equally out of place in the modern community."

(From Childhood To Adolescence p98)

When I was growing up I was very aware of the huge distinction that existed between white-collar workers and blue-collar workers. The snobbery was so pronounced that I even felt self-conscious standing in front of the post office clerk. He wore a white shirt and tie, that meant he was better than me.

Although we consider ourselves more advanced, I would argue that this snobbery is still there, ingrained in all of us, and unconsciously, we pass it on to the next generation. I also remember, in my late teens and early twenties, becoming more aware that the notion I had grown up with, that white-collar work was more important and more lucrative than blue-collar work was utterly misplaced. It was downright untrue. I began to meet plumbers, electricians, oil-rig workers, arctic truck drivers, even factory workers, who made a lot more money than most ordinary white-collar office workers, and to be honest, I felt we were all being duped about the realities of life.

I also noticed that many people working at manual jobs were very happy and, if they chose to, they could feed their intellects by reading books or attending night school. Contrariwise, I noticed that people working at intellectual jobs often found it harder to feed their need for manual work because they either didn't know how to do anything (many young adults don't even know how to wire a plug) or because they thought it was beneath them to do manual work, after all, they were "white-collar."

This snobbery which surrounds work with the hands versus work with the head is still deeply ingrained in all cultures. It seems to go back to some primal urge to have masters and slaves.

Montessori was adamant that the human being, to grow normally needs to use his hands as well as his head. She said, "intellectuals will remain crippled as long as their hands remain untrained". She also said, "Labourers today need education. They need to understand the complex problems of our times."

So, what's the solution to all this? Answer, it's very simple, man should be allowed to function as a whole man, body and mind. Education should not be something where our head is placed on a desk and put to work, while the rest of our body must sit inert. Such a plan is ridiculous and dangerous. The human being was never intended to be treated like that. He cannot grow normally under these conditions.

What a human being, during the period 18 to 24 needs, is adult education which is not designated as white collar or blue-collar. It should simply be education which is active, using both the hands and the head. For some this may be training in the army or navy as pilots, engineers, chefs or soldiers. For others, it may mean training as doctors, nurses, teachers, care assistants, plumbers, electricians, truck-drivers, bakers, shopkeepers, street sweepers. Apprenticeships are an excellent path to a career.

But, here's the point, even within these professions, we must stop the white collar versus blue colour prejudice from creeping in. For example, many years ago, the shopkeeper was a family man, he opened a shop where he did everything from stacking shelves to doing inventory to doing the accounts. And he derived purpose and satisfaction from the "wholeness" of this work. But now, if a young person takes up work in a store he will be designated either to the "till" which is "head" work or "stacking shelves" which is "hand" work. He will rarely be allowed to do several aspects of the job which would give him an understanding of the whole job (and a great feeling of satisfaction and subsequently self-worth). Instead, he is relegated, probably from the time of his interview, to either "head" work or "hand" work. Then, the store management wonders why he becomes apathetic, bored and eventually leaves the job. If they would allow him to use his head as well as his hands he would become a happy as well as a more productive worker.

The solutions to problems are in our hands literally. People need to work with the hand and the head. Descartes with his splitting of hand versus head, did us a huge disservice. This is something which we need to take account of if we really want to help the human being during the period 18 to 24 years.

Arbitrary Rules Versus Fairness For All:

When I was in my very early teens, starting to think about possible careers, I remember making the sad discovery that the rules which totally controlled my future educational and career prospects were based on arbitrary and completely nonsensical adult decisions. For example, I remember, in my early teens thinking that I would like to become a speech therapist. I read a little about it, and learned that in the country where I lived, there was a great shortage of speech therapists. So, excitedly, I thought I would study to become one. I approached a teacher who had some training in the new area called "career guidance." She immediately told me to forget about it, as the intake into the training college for speech therapy was very small, and subsequently the qualifications needed to get in were astronomically high, so it wasn't worth thinking about. I later learned that it was much the same for most of the higher professions. So what I learned, in my early teens, was that, we had a shortage of doctors, nurses, teachers, speech therapists, etc. Common sense told me that there was a simple solution to this shortage,— train more. However, I then learned that the institutions which had a monopoly on training for these professions, wouldn't let the people who wanted to train for these professions into their colleges. They prevented entry by limiting intake.

What a crazy situation! What seemed to me even more crazy, was the fact that everyone passively accepted this madness, and to my knowledge, they still do. No one, seemed to think that it was insane to have a shortage of speech therapists in a country and yet limit the intake to a ridiculously small number, thus ensuring that this shortage would continue. I know the answer given is that it costs huge amounts of money to train a speech therapist, but again we have to ask why? Why can't people be trained at a reasonable cost? Everything is arbitrary. It costs huge amounts of money to get dental treatment in some countries, but the same work can be done in other countries for a fraction of the price. Perhaps the same is true for the training of speech therapists and other professionals. But what I found to be really unjust was the fact that these rules were made by nameless and faceless adults, and the young people whose future education and careers hung in the balance were not allowed to have any input into the decision-making on what criteria were necessary for entrance into these professions.

To my knowledge, the young adult still has no say in the rules about how many "points" are needed to study certain professions. Adults make the hoops for the young person to jump through and the same adults can move that hoop higher or lower whenever they want to, leaving the young person, like a desperate poodle, pathetically leaping up and down, trying to jump through the hoop.
Does this start to adult education fill the young adult with a sense that he is valued, respected and wanted? I think not. I think it breeds cynicism. The young adult sees things for what they are. Rules are arbitrary.
Proof of this was seen in recent years when the global recession affected the numbers of students enrolling for science degrees in a particular country that I am familiar with. After three of four years in succession of low enrolments, the central applications office lowered the number of points needed to do a science degree. So what happened? Do you no longer have to be very, very smart to study science? Is it okay to be just "smart"? Apparently yes. The hypocrisy of it all is not lost on the young adult, it hardens him, its leads to cynicism.

So, to answer to our original question, what can we do to help the human being in the period 18 to 24 years, we would say the following. Firstly, rethink education and make it something that helps the human being, not something that harms him. Make it possible for college students to work at jobs in the day and do their studies part-time. Secondly, bury the notion that white collars are better than blue and allow the human being to function with his hands as well as his head. Transform education so that it meets the human need to be a whole person, not a head on a desk. Thirdly, end the arbitrary points system for entrance into colleges and universities. End the obsession with exams and focus on proven ability. Take note of Montessori's "vision of the future," where people move from one "stage of independence to a higher," not through sitting exams but "by means of their own activity," which she rightly points out "constitutes the inner evolution of the individual". (From Childhood to Adolescence Preface)

PART SEVEN

CAN WE RECONSTRUCT A HUMAN BEING?

(The Later Years)

49

CAN WE CHANGE OUR MINDS?

(The Question of Neuroplasticity)

"Neuroscience," "Neurology," "Neurobiology," "Neuroplasticity," is it all just a load of neurobabble? Well, some of it is.

A little knowledge is still a dangerous thing. Nowadays, people from all walks of life are making statements about neuro-this and neuro-that, but we need to separate the facts from the fiction. So what are the facts?

Firstly, let's get a definition of neuroplasticity. Dr. Norman Doidge, author of the best selling book "The Brain That Changes Itself," gives a very straightforward definition. He states: "Neuro is for neuron, the nerve cells in our brains and nervous systems. Plastic is for "changeable, malleable, modifiable."

So, "neuroplasticity" refers to that property of the brain that allows it to change its structure and its function.

Dr. Doidge's book gives fascinating accounts of cases where brains have literally changed themselves. He tells the story of Michelle Mack, a woman who, it turned out, was living her life with only half a brain. It appears that she only had one hemisphere, the right one. Yet she was leading a fairly normal life. No one, not even her doctor ever guessed that she had only half a brain, though her doctor knew that something was not quite right.

The fact is, her left hemisphere had never developed and no one really knows why. It's possible there may have been a blood clot or some other fault preventing its development.

What is clear is that her right hemisphere managed to take over the functions of her "missing" left hemisphere. How do we know this? Well, the left hemisphere normally processes speech, so a person with no left hemisphere would not be expected to have speech, but Michelle has speech. She also has a sense of humour. She lives, she loves and she laughs just like everyone else. So clearly, her right hemisphere has stepped in for her missing left one.

Dr. Doidge tells of people who had been blind since birth whose brains were trained to see as a result of neuroplastic techniques.

He tells of deaf people whose brains were trained to hear using neuroplastic techniques.

He tells of people who had strokes decades ago and were told they were incurable, learning to retrain their brains by means of neuroplastic techniques so that they were actually "cured" years after the stroke.

He tells of people with learning disorders whose IQs were dramatically raised by retraining the brain through neuroplastic techniques.

He saw "evidence" that eighty-year olds "can sharpen their memories to function the way they did when they were fifty-five".

He says he "saw people rewire their brains with their thoughts, to cure previously incurable obsessions and traumas".

So, what does all of this mean? Basically it means that the long held notion that the brain was a hard-wired machine that couldn't change was wrong.

The brain can change, not just at critical periods such as early childhood and adolescence, but throughout our lives, from the cradle to the grave. It is, however still likely that some changes may be restricted to critical periods such as early childhood.

Obviously, this discovery may have great relevance to our approach to age-related problems, especially the problem of dementia. So let's have a close up look at dementia.

50

WHY IS EVERYONE TALKING ABOUT DEMENTIA?

(Some Dementia Facts)

Less than twenty years ago, the ordinary man on the street hardly ever heard the word "dementia". "Senile Dementia," was a term used by doctors in whispered tones to denote mental decline in an individual. It was incorrectly believed that serious mental decline was a normal part of ageing, yet it had a very real stigma attached to it.

Nowadays, it's hard to get away from the word "dementia". Everyday, in the media, there's a reference of some kind to "dementia". Recently, our young grandson heard an advert on T.V. about "dementia friends" and asked "can I get one of those?"

Well, it's a step in the right direction to de-stigmatise dementia but there's still a great need to explain to the ordinary man on the street, what dementia is, what causes it, how widespread it is, and what, if any, treatments are available for it. So, let's get straight to the facts.

What Is Dementia?

"Dementia" is an umbrella term used to describe symptoms that may include:

- memory loss
- confused thinking
- difficulty paying attention/concentrating
- difficulty with planning, organising and problem solving
- problems with language and communication
- disorientation
- visual perception problems

In addition to these problems which come under the heading of "cognitive symptoms," people living with dementia will often have problems associated with mood changes. They may become anxious, irritable, withdrawn, frustrated, easily upset or unnaturally sad and depressed.

Some people living with dementia may experience other symptoms as the illness progresses. These include: pacing up and down, asking repetitive questions and disturbed sleep. Physically, people living with dementia may experience weight loss as a result of lack of appetite and muscle weakness as a result of lack of movement, especially as they get older and are less mobile.

Are All Dementias The Same?

No, there are several different types of dementia. The most documented types are:

• Alzheimer's Disease:
This is the most common type of dementia. It accounts for about 50 to 80 % of dementia cases.

• Vascular Dementia:
This is the second most common type of dementia after Alzheimer's disease. It accounts for about 20% of dementia cases.

• Dementia with Lewy Bodies:
This is the third most common type of dementia after Alzheimer's disease and vascular dementia. It shares some of the symptoms of Alzheimer's disease and some of the symptoms of Parkinson's disease. It probably accounts for about 10% of all cases of dementia.

• Fronto-temporal Dementia.
This is one of the less common types of dementia, however it is a significant cause of early onset dementia i.e dementia in people between 45 and 65 years of age.

• Mixed Dementia:
The prevalence of this type of dementia is difficult to quantify as it can only be verified with certainty by autopsy. Mixed dementia refers to a situation in which a person has more than one type of dementia simultaneously. It is now believed by many experts in dementia that the prevalence of mixed dementia is probably significantly more common than was previously realised.

• Other Types of Dementia:
Any condition that causes damage to the brain or nerve cells can cause dementia. Some of these conditions are:

> Parkinson's Disease
> Huntington's Disease
> Creutzfield-Jacob Disease

• Pseudo-Dementias or Reversible Dementias:
Certain physical illnesses mimic the symptoms of dementia, but when treated with the appropriate medications the symptoms of dementia lessen and sometimes disappear completely. Some of these conditions are:

> vit B12 deficiency
> hypothyroidism
> adverse drug effects
> alcohol abuse
> normal pressure hydrocephalus

Certain mental illnesses, in particular certain types of depression, can mimic the symptoms of dementia. Persons with these conditions, may exhibit symptoms such as sleep disturbance, confusion, memory loss and other cognitive problems. However, when careful testing is carried out it is found that the person's memory and cognitive functioning are in fact intact. Persons diagnosed with these conditions often respond positively to antidepressants.

What Causes Dementia?

The causes of dementia vary according to the type of dementia. The main causes are as follows:

• Alzheimer's disease is thought to be caused by not one but a number of factors, which include age, genetic inheritance, environment, lifestyle, and overall general health.
Although the causes of Alzheimer's disease are not yet fully understood, the damage it does to the brain is clear. Alzheimer's disease kills brain cells. The brain of a person with Alzheimer's disease has fewer cells and fewer connections among surviving cells than a healthy brain has. As more and more brain cells die, the brain of a person with Alzheimer's disease starts to shrink.

The disease was named after Dr. Aloise Alzheimer, a German physician, who, in 1906, first identified the brain cell abnormalities that are now collectively referred to as Alzheimer's disease. While performing an autopsy on one of his former patients, who had died after years of suffering from confusion, severe memory problems and difficulties with language and comprehension, he noted particular brain abnormalities. These were; firstly, dense deposits surrounding the nerve cells (neuritic plaques) and secondly, inside the nerve cells, he observed twisted bands of fibers (neurofibrillary tangles). Even today, over 100 years since this discovery, Alzheimer's disease can only be physically diagnosed by autopsy.

• Vascular dementia is caused by problems with the blood supply to the brain. It may occur suddenly especially after a major stroke, or it may progress slowly over a period of time, usually after a number of "mini-strokes". A major stroke causes sudden restriction of blood flow to the brain resulting in brain cell death. Mini strokes cause tiny but cumulative damage. Over time, mini strokes or transient ischaemic attacks (TIAs) cause widespread damage to the brain.

• Dementia with Lewy bodies is caused by the build-up of tiny clumps, called Lewy bodies, which are protein deposits, inside brain cells. These clumps build up in areas of the brain which control muscle movement and memory. Why this occurs is still not fully understood.

• Fronto-Temporal Dementias are caused by the build-up of abnormal proteins in the part of the brain behind the forehead (the frontal area) and above and behind the ears (the temporal area). These abnormal proteins clump together and become toxic to the brain cells, causing them to die. Over time, the brain tissue in the affected lobes (frontal and temporal) shrinks. Why these abnormal proteins build up is not yet fully understood, but there is often a strong genetic link to their appearance.

• Other Types of Dementia are usually caused by specific medical conditions.

Who Gets Dementia?

Dementia mainly affects people over the age of 65. Some figures suggest that dementia affects one in 20 people over 65 and one in five people over the age of eighty. However, a significant number of people have early onset dementia, i.e. dementia which occurs long before the 65th year. Some dementias have a generic cause and these types of dementia usually appear before age 65. Dementia affects both men and women. International research shows that dementia occurs in every country of the world. A recent world Alzheimer's Report, estimates that worldwide there are over 35 million people living with dementia. This number is expected to double by 2030 and to more than triple by 2050 to 115 million people.

How is Dementia Diagnosed?

Dementia is usually diagnosed by either a geriatrician, a neurologist or a psychiatrist. The diagnosis has to be based on a combination of factors because as yet, there is no single test for diagnosing dementia. These factors usually involve:

Firstly, taking a detailed medical history of the person's problems.
Secondly, cognitive testing, i.e. tests of the person's memory, his/her problem-solving skills, and general thinking patterns.
Thirdly, physical examination and tests to rule out other possible causes of the symptoms such as a specific vitamin or hormone deficiency.
Fourthly, a brain scan, this is usually how vascular dementia is diagnosed. The usual progression is for a person to be referred by their GP on to a specialist doctor or team who have expertise in dementia and so can carry out more specific tests and/or brain scans. The diagnosis is then explained to the person and their closest relative if possible.

How Is Dementia Treated?

As yet, there is no cure for dementia. All we can do is try to alleviate the symptoms. Treatments to alleviate the symptoms fall into two categories: drug treatments and non-drug treatments.

Drug Treatments.
There are a number of drug treatments which, especially if administered early on in the course of the disease, can not only help to ease the symptoms but also halt the progress of the disease for some time.

Some of these drugs may temporarily relieve memory loss and improve concentration and general interest in life for some persons with mild to moderate levels of dementia. Other drugs may be given to persons with later stage dementia to relieve symptoms of agitation, anxiety and delusion. People with vascular dementia will need to take drugs to control their blood pressure, cholesterol, heart or diabetic symptoms.

Non-Drug Treatments.
Many non-pharmacological therapies are used by care workers in the treatment of people living with dementia. These include:

- Aromatherapy and massage
- Music therapy and white noise
- Bright light therapy
- Psychological therapies.

Can We Prevent Dementia?

Since there is still a great deal of uncertainty about what actually causes dementia, it is difficult to know exactly how to prevent it.

However, since the causes of some dementias such as vascular dementia, are clear, there are steps we should take to try to avoid their development.

To help to prevent vascular dementia we should do what we can to help people to avoid strokes and mini-strokes. This involves controlling blood pressure, cholesterol, diabetes, and heart problems.

To help to prevent pseudo-dementias, we should help people to get early treatment for depression, vitamin and hormonal deficiencies.

To help to prevent Alzheimer's disease, we should encourage people to: eat a healthy diet, exercise, control weight, be socially active, exercise their brains through doing puzzles, crosswords etc. People should also be encouraged to avoid tobacco and excess alcohol.

51

WHY IS EVERYDAY LIKE GROUNDHOG DAY?

(Short-term Memory Problems In People Living With Dementia)

Several years ago I had my first visit to a "dementia" ward. A striking looking lady in her late 70s walked up to me, shook hands and introduced herself. She told me her name was Rebecca Wilcox, (not her real name) and that she was from "the Brontë country". She said her husband's name was Reginald P. Wilcox and her daughter Charlotte, her only child, was a university lecturer in London.

She chatted about her love of music, literature and art for about twenty minutes. Then she said she had to go off to have a rest. I was left thinking, what a lovely lady, but why on earth is she in here? She's so lucid and such an interesting person to talk to. She should be working here, not spending time as a resident!

About fifteen minutes later, I noticed at the end of the long corridor which led to the bedrooms, the same lady walking cheerfully in my direction. I smiled and waved and she waved back at me. She walked right up to me, shook hands, and introduced herself. She told me her name was Rebecca Wilcox and that she was from the Brontë country. She said her husband's name was Reginald P. Wilcox and her daughter Charlotte, her only child was a university lecturer in London. I said, yes, I remember you telling me this a short time ago. She stared at me with a puzzled expression and said, "Were you here a short time ago? I don't remember meeting you, but it's nice to meet you now?"

I was there for a long time that day and I had a third encounter with this lovely lady which went pretty much the same as the first two. That was my first direct encounter with short term memory problems in people living with dementia.

This lady had so many "strengths". She could walk unaided. She had no mobility problems, indeed she had the stride of a ballet dancer. She could chat, joke and laugh at any amusing incident which took place. She could wash and dress herself unaided and braid her still beautiful white hair. She could choose from a

287

menu what she wanted for breakfast, dinner and tea and she liked to read, do cross-word puzzles and listen to music. It appeared her only deficit was memory. She couldn't remember events that had just recently occurred.

Yet, to my shame, I now found myself focusing on her very obvious deficit. I was no longer thinking that she should be "employed" at the care-home instead of being a resident there. I started seeing only her problems. That, I now realise, is one of the biggest obstacles facing people who have been diagnosed with dementia. We start to focus on their deficits rather than their strengths. We, the onlookers, start to become anxious, nervous, terrified of what this condition could develop into. We start to see problems of all kinds ahead, and often, like a self-fulfilling prophecy, the problems start to appear. Yet the person living with dementia is often blissfully unaware that there is a problem, just like Rebecca Wilcox, who happily introduced herself to me three times, totally unaware that she was repeating herself, while I became tense and anxious.

I was like the Bill Murray character in the film Groundhog Day, who is exasperated by the insanity of having to live the same day over and over while the people around him are blissfully unaware that they are stuck in a time-loop.

This is a key problem in dementia, our unease. When we become agitated by the irrationality of it all, we send out signals that "all is not well," something is very wrong. In fact people living with dementia will often keep asking the persons caring for them "what's wrong?," "you're acting strange," "what's wrong?"

The person living with dementia is usually not aware that he/she is living in Groundhog Day, but we, the carers, are. And it is often we who unintentionally create a tense atmosphere. The person living with dementia is very sensitive to the atmosphere. Once they sense our tension, they become tense and a cycle of negative emotions arises, from which it is difficult for both the carer and the person living with dementia, to escape.

Now, we're not suggesting that anyone should be in denial about the very real problems facing people living with dementia, but we need to stop focusing on the problems as if that's all there is to the person. The person is "still in there", behind the problems.

So, what's the solution? Well, as yet, there is no cure for short term memory loss. So, until there is, perhaps we have to be like the Bill Murray character in the film, and put our time to good use while we are stuck for another day, another week, or another year, in "Groundhog Day".

52

WHY CAN'T MY MUM REMEMBER HOW TO MAKE A CUP OF TEA?

(Executive Function Problems In People Living With Dementia)

Someone very close to us is living with dementia. In fact, she is living with us while she's living with dementia. Let's call her Betty. Betty never drank alcohol, she never even tasted coffee and she only rarely drank fizzy drinks. But, she had a weakness for one drink......tea. Betty is an Irish person and Irish people love tea. The famous poet T. S. Eliot wrote about measuring out your life in coffee spoons. He wrote this to imply a note of sadness, a wasted life, but Betty, measured out her life in teaspoons and it wasn't sad or wasted. She loved her cups of tea and loved to put the kettle on the minute anyone came to visit her. She could have given "Mrs. Doyle", the housekeeper/tea-lady from the "Father Ted" comedy series, a run for her money!

Betty has vascular dementia, probably brought on by a series of mini strokes, which occurred over the years and could have gone undetected but for an MRI scan she had while in hospital getting treatment for a bout of pneumonia. Vascular dementia affects the front part of the brain, the part that controls what's known as "executive function". "Executive function," is a fancy name to describe the ability to perform important tasks such as: planning, making decisions, seeing consequences. But it also controls more down-to-earth things like remembering the sequence of steps for doing everyday tasks such as, putting your shoes on, getting dressed, and most importantly, making a cup of tea.

Now, hindsight is a great thing, but when life is actually happening, we don't have the benefit of hindsight. With hindsight, we now realise that some time ago, when Betty gave you a cup of tea and you found it was actually hot water with milk in it and no trace of a teabag, something was going wrong. And when Betty laughed and said "I must be losing my mind, imagine forgetting the teabag!" she actually was losing her mind. She was losing executive function which is part of the declarative memory system.

Memory is a fascinating phenomenon. We talk of "memory" as if it is just one mental ability, but memory is actually made up of a number of different types of mental abilities. Basically, we have two types of memory, short term memory, where we store memories of things which have recently occurred and long term memory where we store memories of things that have occurred in the past.

Long-term memory can be further divided into declarative memory i.e. ("knowing what") and procedural memory i.e. ("knowing how").

To put it simply, declarative memory is memory of facts or events that we consciously recall and bring to the forefront of our minds. For example, when we tell someone, "my name is X and my date of birth is XXXX and my telephone number is XXXX," we are using declarative memory. Specifically, in this example, because we are recalling information of a factual nature, we are using semantic memory which is a subcategory of declarative memory. If we said, "Hi, I'm Mary, remember we met at the grocery store last weekend," we would also be using declarative memory, but it would be another sub-category of declarative memory known as episodic memory, i.e. the type of memory which recalls specific things we have experienced, it is information of an autobiographical nature.

Another part of the declarative memory system is called "executive function." As we stated above, "executive function" is a term denoting the ability to plan, organise and make decisions. It also gives us the ability to understand the sequence of steps needed to perform many routine activities such as getting dressed in the mornings.

When a person is living with dementia, declarative memory is usually the part of memory that is most adversely affected. For this reason persons living with dementia may start to forget things of a factual nature like names, phone numbers, dates, even meanings of words, as their semantic memory becomes impaired. Similarly, persons living with dementia may begin to have difficulty recollecting specific events they have experienced as their episodic memory becomes impaired. And, if the executive function of a person living with the dementia is damaged, they may have trouble remembering the sequence of steps that are needed to carry out routine activities, and that probably explains why my mother, "can't remember how to make a cup of tea."

NOTE

EVERY PERSON WITH MEMORY LOSS IS UNIQUE AND
WILL RESPOND DIFFERENTLY, AND EACH PERSON
CHANGES OVER THE COURSE OF THE CONDITION.

53

WHY CAN'T MY DAD REMEMBER THAT I VISITED HIM LAST SUNDAY?

(Episodic Memory Problems In People Living With Dementia)

Marsha's dad, Tom, is 79. He was diagnosed with Alzheimer's disease six years ago. One of the first signs that something was wrong was his gradual inability to remember events that had happened either recently or in the past. For example, over the past year when Marsha came to visit her dad and asked him "did you have lunch yet?", Tom couldn't remember. In fact he usually couldn't remember whether he had eaten breakfast either. He couldn't remember if he had taken his pills and he couldn't remember if he had received any phone calls from relatives.

Over the last year, he started to forget more significant events, such as Marsha's wedding which took place five years ago, the birth of Marsha's baby three years ago and the passing away of his own wife, Marsha's mother, one year ago. Tom also can't remember the fact that Marsha comes to visit him every Sunday.

These events, which Tom is unable to remember, are all part of his episodic memory and regrettably, episodic memory is often the first part of our memory system to become damaged by dementia.

What is Episodic Memory?
The term "episodic memory" was first coined by Dr. Endel Tulving in 1972. He defined episodic memory as "memory for personal experiences and their temporal relations.."
Episodic memory has to do with the, who, why, what, where and when of information storage. Examples of episodic memory include:

- Knowing who came to visit you in your home this morning.
- Knowing why you had to go to the A&E last week.
- Knowing what you had for lunch today in the cafe.
- Knowing when you first started to wear hearing aids.

291

Tulving proposed that episodic memory is a unique type of memory in that it involves "mental time travel" i.e. the feeling that we are going back in time in our mind's eye to revisit the scene of the event.

Not only that, but with episodic memories, we are consciously aware that we are recollecting something that is now past. We experience the "feeling" of remembering. Whether that recollection is a revisiting of the kitchen where we had a bowl of porridge this morning or the church we got married in five years ago or the hospital ward we spent time in last year, the recollection involves "mental time travel".

Episodic memory is also unique in our memory system in that it allows us to remember personal past events, entirely from our own perspective. For example, 50 people may attend a wedding and each of those 50 people will create an entirely personal episodic memory of that event.

One person may remember the smell of the fresh air and the apple blossoms on the walk up to the church door. Another may remember the sound of the church bells. Another may remember the shimmer of sunlight on the sequins of the bride's dress. Another may remember the tears in the eyes of the bride's mother. Another may remember the softness of the bride's skin as she kissed the guests after the wedding service. Episodic memory therefore is closely related to "autobiographical" memory.

Episodic memory also gives the human being the power of "episodic future thinking" i.e. the ability to mentally envisage the future. It makes possible "mental time travel" into the future as well as into the past. No other memory system has this same capacity. Tulving calls it, "a marvel of nature".

The fact that episodic memory involves not just the recollection of cold hard facts, but the personal, sensorial, recollection of an event, may provide us with an insight into how to try to retrieve these lost memories, even when a person is living with dementia and has suffered damage to his/her episodic memory.

Marcel Proust, the famous French novelist was the first person to coin the term "involuntary memory". This is the type of memory that "explodes" on us "out of the blue" when "cues" encountered in everyday life evoke recollections of the past without conscious effort.

In Proust's novel, A La Recherche du Temps Perdu, translated in English as, "In Search of Times Past," he describes how the taste of a little piece madeline cake dipped in tea inspired an "involuntary memory," which took him back years into the past, to his childhood when his aunt used to give him a madeline cake that she had first dipped into her own cup of tea.

He noted that the sight of the little madelines in the cake shop window had not brought back anything to his mind. It was the taste of the cake dipped in the tea that did it, having a powerful emotive effect on him making him feel intense happiness.

These "involuntary" recollections can be pleasant or unpleasant depending on what events they bring to the surface.

In my own experience, the sight and smell of a wide-brimmed cup of coffee takes me straight back to the street in Paris where I once spent a summer as an au-pair and floods my mind with the memory of the smells, tastes and sounds of the outdoor cafes in that specific street in Paris.

These memories usually trigger more "involuntary" memories, often bringing a flood of very specific episodes which I had long forgotten about, up to the surface.

Perhaps neurological research into "involuntary memory" holds a key to helping people living with dementia to retrieve episodic memories from their past.

However, until such breakthroughs occur, Marsha will just have to accept that it is damage to her father's episodic memory that continually prevents him from remembering that she visits him every Sunday.

NOTE

EVERY PERSON WITH MEMORY LOSS IS UNIQUE AND WILL RESPOND DIFFERENTLY, AND EACH PERSON CHANGES OVER THE COURSE OF THE CONDITION

54

WHY DOES GRANDMA KEEP FORGETTING MY NAME?

(Semantic Memory Problems In People Living With Dementia)

Josh is eight years old. He lives with his mum, his dad and his grandma. Josh has a very close relationship with his grandma. Since he was a baby, she played a big part in his life. She was the one who taught him how to ride a bike, how to splash in puddles, how to blow bubbles with his own saliva, how to get chewing gum off his shoes with ice cubes, and lots of other cool stuff. (Some stuff mum doesn't know about because she might get "grossed out".) Yes, Josh and grandma are as close as thieves. They go bug hunting together in the summer and they like to sip cocoa and marshmallows together, all cosy under the duvet in winter.

But, in the last two years something has changed in grandma. She can't seem to remember the names of things. She calls the remote control the "highery-lowery" thing. She calls Josh's bike his "wheely thing" and sometimes she can't remember Josh's name. She says it's "on the tip of my tongue" but she often can't remember it at all. But grandma is still a very cool granny and Josh just "fills in" the missing words for her.

So, what's going on with grandma? Well, last year she was diagnosed with Alzheimer's disease. She is in the very early stages and the only noticeable difference is her memory. What's happening is, the disease is affecting her semantic memory.

What is Semantic Memory?
Semantic memory refers to a part of long-term memory that acts as a database for the storage of memories of facts, concepts and names of objects, people and places that are not personal but are part of common knowledge. Semantic memory includes the memory of what the functions of things are. Examples of semantic memory would be:
- Knowing that snow is white.
- Knowing that London is the capital of England.

- Knowing that scissors are used for cutting things.
- Knowing that fridges are used for keeping things cold.
- Knowing that grass is green.
- Knowing that there are 12 months in a year.
- Knowing that kettles are for heating water.
- Knowing that Christmas falls on the 25th of December each year.
- Knowing that Josh's name is "Josh".

The concept of semantic memory was introduced in 1972 by Dr Endel Tulving. Dr. Tulving defined semantic memory as "a system for receiving, retaining, and transmitting information about the meaning of words, concepts, and the classification of concepts."

Semantic memory has been the subject of much research in recent years and the big question is: have the semantic memories been wiped out in the brains of people living with dementia or are they still there but the brain can't make the right connections to retrieve them?

The answer is not 100% clear yet. But one thing is clear. Most persons living with dementia have difficulties with semantic memory. They can no longer access facts and concepts that they had accumulated over their lifetime, either because they are wiped out or because they cannot be retrieved from their database. These facts involve everything from their knowledge of the capital cities of the world, their knowledge of the political parties of their country, their knowledge of the basic laws of their society, to the functions of ordinary, everyday objects, such as refrigerators, hairdryers, ovens, kettles, telephones, knives, forks and spoons.

The list is endless because it involves thousands of objects which their healthy brain had named and categorised over a lifetime. It also involves concepts such as what things are used for. Most importantly, it also involves remembering the names of your relatives.

The level of impairment in semantic memory differs from person to person living with dementia. For some people it presents very real problems and causes very real life changes. For others, it's just another annoyance and they just accept it and get on with life.

Grandma is one of those persons who just accepts it and gets on with life. So, until there is a cure for semantic memory problems, young Josh will just have to be on hand again to give his beloved grandma the "highery-lowery" thing when the TV channel needs changing.

NOTE

EVERY PERSON WITH MEMORY LOSS IS UNIQUE AND WILL RESPOND DIFFERENTLY, AND EACH PERSON CHANGES OVER THE COURSE OF THE CONDITION

55

HOW COME WE NEVER FORGET HOW TO RIDE A BICYCLE?

(Procedural Memory Strengths In People Living with Dementia)

We've been living in York, UK for a few years now. It's a beautiful city steeped in history going back to Roman times. One thing that stands out about York is the number of people riding bicycles. Bicycles are everywhere. Babies ride them, toddlers ride them, school children race along on them, and generally people from eight to eighty (and possibly beyond), cycle everywhere. Sometimes, when we've just waved to the third or fourth octogenarian cycling by, we find ourselves pondering the question - how come no matter how old we are, we never forget how to ride a bicycle? After all, we weren't born with the ability to cycle, it's not built in. Well, the answer lies in "muscle memory," or "procedural memory".

What is Procedural Memory?
Procedural memory, or "muscle memory," as it's sometimes called, is a type of long-term memory that involves the performance of actions that are so hardwired into the brain that they have become automatic. We've all heard the term "driving on automatic pilot," what is implied here is that an action is being carried out by someone who does not have to consciously think about the action, he just does it automatically.

Examples of actions carried out by the power of procedural memory would be:
• walking, without having to consciously think about it.
• talking, without having to consciously think about it.
• combing your hair, without having to consciously think about it.
• shaving without having to consciously think about it.
• riding a bicycle, without having to consciously think about it.
• driving a car, without having to consciously think about it.
• playing a musical instrument, without having to consciously think about it.
• singing a song, without having to consciously think about.
• reciting a poem, without having to consciously think about it.
• swimming a few strokes, without having to consciously think about it.

- typing on a keyboard, without having to consciously think about it.
- reading a book or magazine, without having to consciously think about it.

Now, the good news is, that because memory is located in various parts of the brain rather than in one part only, when dementia strikes, it doesn't immediately damage all of our memory systems. Neurology shows that the part of the brain which controls procedural memory is often "spared," that is, left undamaged in people living with dementia, despite the damage done to other parts of the brain which control other types of memory, such as episodic and semantic memory.

This is huge. This is where the potential for helping the person with dementia lies. If the person with dementia still has a fairly intact procedural memory then there is a window of opportunity available to us. Our job then, is to discover how we can use this remaining "strength" to allow the person living with dementia, to show us "who" they were and who they are now, especially if there is no relative there to tell us. We may be very surprised at what we discover.

This fascinating phenomenon has become a theme in films in recent years. A quiet unassuming man presents with amnesia. He doesn't remember his occupation or his name, yet he can sign his signature. Suddenly he is crossed by someone on the street and all of a sudden all hell breaks loose. The amnesiac floors the person, using trained assassin "moves" on him, suggesting that he is not "a quiet unassuming man" at all, but rather a secret agent of some kind. But how does he remember all those "defence moves" when he has amnesia?

The answer is they are stored in his procedural memory, his muscle memory, a part of the brain not affected by his amnesia. It's as if the memories are literally stored in his muscles or his very cells. That's really what procedural memory is all about. The memory has become part of our bodies, it is not just something stored in our heads. It is as if the memory has gotten into us at a cellular level.

Now most of the elderly persons we meet who are living with dementia will not have been "secret agents" in the past, but, in many ways they are "secret agents" now, in the present, because we don't know much about them and they may not be able to communicate with us. So, that's where procedural memory comes in.

It is through procedural memory that we will learn all about Dom and Henry and Betty and Cedric and Marie-Therese. Through procedural memory they will reveal to us "who" they really are. So, let's have a look at how the Montessori approach can "jog" the procedural memory and help people living with dementia to reveal to us who they were in the past and who they still are.

56

HOW CAN WE HELP THE HUMAN BEING IN THE LATER YEARS?

(Montessori-Based Programmes For People Living With Dementia)

> "An aged man is but a paltry thing,
> A tattered coat upon a stick, unless
> Soul clap its hands and sing, and louder sing
> For every tatter in its mortal dress."
> W.B. Yeats.
> Sailing to Byzantium.

The key word here is "unless".

In the early 1900s, Dr. Maria Montessori worked with mentally deficient children and she revealed to the world the heart-breaking conditions in which these human beings would be forced to live out their lives UNLESS there was a programme of carefully thought out interventions.

When she started to take mentally retarded children out of the asylums and through the painstaking application of her "brain science" taught them to hold a knife and fork, to dress themselves, to play, to write, to read, to pass the state exams, people of discernment could see that what Dr Montessori had discovered about the human brain was revolutionary. She had discovered that the human brain could be reorganised, reshaped, possibly even reconstructed, resulting in the transformation of people's lives.

Dr. Montessori went on to apply her "brain science" to the education of young children with normal brain function, older children, adolescents and university students. Had she lived longer, there is no doubt that she would have conducted experiments with the middle aged mind as well as the elderly mind. Sadly, she didn't get that chance.

History of Montessori Based Programmes For People Living With Dementia.

In the nineteen nineties, Dr. Cameron J. Camp, Director of the Centre for Applied Research in Dementia, Ohio USA, found that he was "beginning to see linkages between Montessori's approach and the translation of concepts in neuroscience into practical interventions for persons with dementia."

In 1999, he edited a book entitled "Montessori-Based Activities for Persons with Dementia" Volume 1.

This was a manual based on Dr. Camp's original idea of using Montessori-based programmes for people with dementia. The manual was made possible through the efforts of many individuals.

A second volume was published in 2006, again involving the talents of a large number of people who supported Dr Camp's original idea.

Since then, certain gerontologists in the United States, Canada, Australia and parts of Europe have begun to use Montessori's ideas in their approach to the care of people living with dementia, both within care home settings and without, and the results are very encouraging.

Here then is a summary of what Montessori programmes for people living with dementia are all about.

The Term:
"Montessori - Based Programmes for People living with Dementia" is a term now used to describe an infinite number of individually planned programmes of activities which are designed to meet the needs of an individual or individuals living with dementia, through the use of the unique, "brain-based" approach known as the "Montessori Method."

The Aim:

The aim is to focus on the surviving "strengths" of the individual living with dementia rather than his deficits, and to create activities which will protect these "strengths" for as long as possible and even build on them.

The Approach:

The approach is exact and scientific. It involves:

- A very detailed assessment of the individual living with dementia, including details of his/her past likes, dislikes, interests and abilities.

- The creation of "a prepared environment."

- The creation of "tailor-made" activities which :

  - are heavily based on the procedural memory system, i.e. "muscle memory," rather than the declarative memory system, as procedural memory is the memory system most "spared" i.e. left undamaged, in dementia.

  - make use of established rehabilitation principles and techniques such as:
    - Task breakdown.
    - Repetition.
    - Progression from the simple to the complex.
    - Progression from the concrete to the abstract.

- The use of few or no words in the presentation of the activity. Verbal instructions, if they are needed should be short, simple and pleasant.

- The use of a much reduced "tempo" in the presentation of activities. We need to learn to slow down to the pace which suits the person living with dementia rather than the pace which most suits ourselves.

- The use of materials which:

  - are self correcting. i.e. have a built in control of error.

- isolate the area of difficulty, i.e. if the activity is about matching colours, the pieces of the activity should be identical in every respect except colour, so they draw the person's attention to the "area of difficulty," i.e. "colour."

- The use of positive reinforcement if looked for, i.e, if the person looks for confirmation that he/she is doing the activity correctly, positive feedback and encouragement should be given to enhance the person's feelings of self-esteem because it is the process that is important not the end result.

- The use of repetition of an activity to promote positive engagement and the possibility of new learning.

- The use of indirect activities as a means of "priming the pump" of procedural memory in order to help the person to move towards carrying out the "target skill," e.g. getting the person to use dressing frames in order to "prime the pump" of muscle memory so that he/she will start dressing himself/herself again.

- The use of materials that do not offend the dignity of the person, i.e are not childish.

- The use of a no-correction approach. The purpose of the activities is to help the person to retain and possibly strengthen their remaining skills, it does not matter very much if the person makes mistakes. The emphasis should be on encouraging the person to do things for themselves again. Correction, of any sort could discourage the person and dissuade them from even trying any activities.

The Principles:

Montessori-Based Programmes for people living with dementia are based on a number of key principles that form the essence of Dr Montessori's discoveries about the human being. These principles are:

KEY MONTESSORI PRINCIPLES

"Independence"
The human being cannot feel fully human unless he/
she is independent, i.e. able to do things for himself.
Independence is a law of life.

"Work"
The human being cannot feel fully human unless he/she
has opportunities to do work i.e. meaningful activities.
Work is a law of life.

"Respect for human dignity"
The human being cannot feel fully human unless he/she is treated
with respect, and his dignity as a human being, is recognised.
Respect for one's dignity is a vital human need.

"Self esteem"
The human being cannot feel fully human unless he/she
has a sense of self esteem. Self esteem cannot be purchased,
or given as a gift. The human being attains self esteem by
accomplishing tasks.
Self esteem is a vital human need.

"Contribution"
The human being cannot feel fully human unless he/she is given
opportunities to contribute to the world he finds himself in.
Contribution to the world we live in is a vital human need.

"Intergenerational Living"
The human being needs to live in the midst of a wide
variety of age groups. This is a vital human need.

Many people are not aware of Dr. Montessori's views on the need for
intergenerational living. Montessori wrote: "Nothing is duller than a home for
the aged. To segregate by age is one of the cruellest and most inhuman things
one can do." "The charm of social life is the number of different types that one
meets."

(The Absorbent Mind p226).

Examples of Montessori Activities For People Living With Dementia.

• Using dressing frames to stimulate the "muscle" memory of fastening buttons, zips and buckles so as to aid persons with dementia to dress themselves again thereby giving the persons a sense of independence and self-esteem.

• Scooping small objects hidden in a bowl of rice with a sieve spoon, in order to stimulate the "muscle" memory of spooning so as to aid persons with dementia to feed themselves again thereby restoring dignity to those persons.

• Pouring liquids from one jug to another in order to stimulate the "muscle" memory of pouring so as to aid persons with dementia to carry out real tasks such as serving drinks to others, thereby helping the persons to feel a sense of usefulness in the community.

• Using a light hammer and a peg board with wooden pegs to stimulate the memory of hammering in a person who used to do handiwork so as to evoke memories from the past and also to enable the person to carry out light handiwork again thereby helping the person to feel useful once more.

• Using play-dough and cookie cutters to stimulate the memory of rolling out pastry so as to aid the person to start baking again and thereby feel a sense of being useful and of contributing to community or family life.

The Evaluations:
Statistical evaluations have been collated over the past few years and all of them are positive showing higher levels of engagement and happiness in persons who are participating in Montessori Based Programmes for people living with Dementia. However, instead of listing statistics, let's look at some real people.

• Shirley:
In one centre for people living with dementia we read about Shirley, aged 73, a former school teacher, who is offered the job of grading the maths work of 5 and 6 year olds from a local Montessori school. This "job" addresses the cognitive part of the Montessori for dementia programme at the centre. The therapist working with Shirley says: "There is a misconception that patients who have been diagnosed with dementia can no longer learn or be productive....That's simply not true. This approach helps stimulate their minds while also helping them maintain their current abilities."

304

This particular job was designed specifically for Shirley to evoke memories and experiences from her past.

• **Harry:**
Harry, a former GP, spends hours writing out "prescriptions" on a note-pad, thereby evoking pleasant memories of a career he pursued for a life-time. Out of this activity, he derives a feeling of self-worth and usefulness.

• **Matt:**
Matt, a former plumber works with plastic piping, thereby bringing back memories of the trade he pursued for a lifetime, helping him to feel useful and productive.

• **Lucy:**
Lucy, a former waitress, spends hours setting tables with placemats, small vases of flowers and serviettes which she folds herself.

All of these activities are planned out and "prepared" earlier by Montessori trained carers who make sure that each activity is offered in carefully prepared stages. There is a progression from simple to complex in the activities and there is minimum chance of failure built into these activities. For example, Lucy's placemats have been carefully designed with a silhouette of a knife, fork, spoon and plate on them so that they act as a template for Lucy as she lays out cutlery and plates on the table.

Activities are a mixture of the practical, sensorial, mathematical literary and cultural. Cultural activities especially those involving music have been shown to have great success in "awakening" a person living with dementia from states of apathy and inactivity to states of liveliness, smiles, laughter, song and even dance. Let's look at some real people.

• **Dom: (Rediscovering your "joy," through the power of music).**

In their beautiful book, "You say Goodbye and We say Hello," Tom and Karen Brenner two experts in dementia, give a vivid example of procedural memory in action.

They tell the story of Dom, a person living with dementia in a locked dementia unit in a care home. They explain that "Dom had been a pianist and a choral teacher all of his adult life." When they met him he had "become withdrawn, belligerent and difficult to deal with". But, they witnessed first-hand how "when he sat down at the piano in the gathering room of the long term care home, he could play tunes from memory for hours!" Tom and Karen describe how;-

"He was a wonderful musician who played with flourishes, panache and with great joy. His whole face would light up and he would become lost in the music. People would spontaneously gather around the piano and join in the singing as Dom played." Tom and Karen write;-

" Dom was a happy man when he sat down to play the piano. That was the only time we ever saw him being gregarious, relaxed and happy. Music was the one thing that seemed to reach him. Through the music Dom gave himself and many others hours of unadulterated joy." p134

Tom and Karen then go on to talk about drum circles and how they use them to connect with people living with dementia. Tom and Karen's book is a must read for anyone interested in understanding dementia and how "we can" reach into the souls of the human beings trapped inside this cruel illness through their procedural memory which is still intact enough to be able to respond to the rhythms of music.

- **Henry: (Becoming animated again, through the power of music).**

Recently, a clip on the internet "went viral" showing the astonishing effects of music on an elderly man named "Henry" in a nursing home. Henry rarely spoke and often looked apathetic and lethargic just sitting in his chair. Yet when a care worker put a set of headphones on him and played his favourite music on an iPod, he started to sing along and move to the music. He became revitalised and communicative. He gave coherent and lively answers to the carer's questions. He talked about his favourite music. Neurologist Dr Oliver Sacks, commenting on the video said: "In some sense Henry is restored to himself. He has remembered who he is and has re-acquired his identity for a while through the power of music."

- **Betty: ("Staying Alive," through the power of music).**

I'm sitting at home watching an old Bee Gees concert on DVD with my 84 year old mother who is living with dementia. The brothers are singing songs from the films "Saturday Night Fever" and "Grease" and in the background they are showing clips from the films on a giant screen. My mother, who had been showing no interest in anything today, is suddenly very animated. She is starting to move to the music and has begun to tap her hands on her knees to the rhythm of "Grease is the word, is the time, is the moment, grease is the way we are feeling."

She is smiling and laughing at the video clips and clapping along at some of the disco-dance songs. We end up watching the entire concert twice! At the end of the second showing, and after about twenty cups of tea, she comments, "I hope they show that again tomorrow, the singing is really lovely, it's just one good song after another." Then she says, "it makes you feel alive."

I find myself unable to reply. All I can think of is why do we spend so much of our time writing about all the negatives in dementia, instead of snatching the positives and working with them and milking them for all they are worth? Why are we so limited in our vision? Well, I know the answer. It's because we get so tired and weary just dealing, day after day, with the realities of the negatives. But let's take heart. Let's see what we can do with "the power of music in dementia."

- **Marie-Therese: (Remembering your heritage through the power of music).**

A few years ago, I was asked by a young carer in a nursing home to come up to a locked unit to see a lady with severe dementia. The lady was originally French although she had lived in England for many years. The dementia had robbed her of language, and although she had been in the care home for several years, no one had ever heard her speak any language. She just grunted or screamed. The care worker had heard somewhere that I spoke French and hence my invitation.

I came along as asked, but before entering the lady's room, the care worker warned me to be very careful. She warned me that the lady who was bed ridden and had to be hoisted to be washed was usually very aggressive and if she grabbed hold of my hand, would probably bite me, with her few remaining sharp teeth.

I was a little nervous, but entered the room. I didn't speak or even look directly at the lady, I just started to hum the lyrics of a French mediaeval song that I had learned in my teens. It had a very soft, rhythmical sound to it and very repetitive words. I just kept singing it very quietly. The young care worker with me looked dumbfounded but thankfully she said nothing, she just stood silently beside me. Within a few minutes, the lady, who had started screaming when we entered the room, quietened down to a complete silence. All you could now hear in the room was the sound of my voice repeating the chorus of French words over and over. I was almost in a trance. I didn't know where the words were coming from. I was not even consciously aware that I still remembered this song from over 30 years ago, but I just kept on singing. The lady was staring at me now. Something had obviously been triggered in her brain. It was as if she'd had an electric shock.

She focused on me like a hawk on a mouse. I looked at her directly now and moved closer to her. I could see that she must have been a very beautiful woman in her youth, she still had high cheekbones and piercing green eyes. She started to move her mouth into a kind of smile, revealing a few very even front teeth. I just kept singing. My companion, the young care worker, stood still as if at a performance, and then slowly, as if in slow motion, began the work of washing and dressing the lady. I joined in the work, still softly singing. When the lady was washed and dressed, myself and the care worker left the room. Neither of us spoke. Before I left the room, I had whispered "au revoir" to the lady, and a quick "a demain", (until tomorrow).

Later that day, the care worker, came to me to tell me that she had never seen the lady like this before. The singing had somehow touched something inside of her and calmed her. The carer said: "she's peaceful as a sleeping baby even now, even though its hours since your visit". The care worker asked me if I would come back to see the lady another day. I said I would.

A few days later, as it was nearing Christmas time, the carers in that home had prepared a room with a very large Christmas tree, and a fireplace with Christmas stockings hanging on it, and were bringing the residents, in small groups down to this cosy room to sing carols and have mince pies and tea. I was asked to come to one of these gatherings in the hope of being able to give some company to this French lady.

Only one resident had turned up so far, so it looked like it was going to be a quiet gathering. I was sitting on the floor beside the fireplace wrapping small presents for the residents when Marie-Therese was wheeled into the room in her wheelchair.

As she came in, I just knew she had spotted me out of the corner of her eye. I was right, she did an about turn and looked straight at me. I know she recognised me. I continued to sit on the floor and wrap the presents, humming the same French medieval song that I had sung a few days earlier. Marie Therese stared at me. Slowly I got up and very cautiously moved nearer to Marie Therese and sat in the chair beside her. I passed her a drink and a small piece of mince pie.

She sipped the drink and I started to talk to her about Christmas. I wished her a "joyeux noel". It was a one-sided conversation for about 20 minutes. Then something remarkable happened. Marie-Therese spoke! She had never spoken before and everybody thought she couldn't speak. I didn't understand what she said to me but I knew it was French, so I replied in French. I kept talking about ordinary things, my name, where I came from, how I love Christmas, how I love snow, etc. She listened and then spoke again. I will never forget what she said. It was, "C'est horrible ce cafe." - "This coffee is horrible." Well, I did say she was French, and only the French know how to make good coffee!

So, we had a real breakthrough. I had one more visit with Marie Therese, after Christmas, and this time, I thought I'd go for a song she must know,- The Marseillaise, the French national anthem. I'll never forget the look on the carer's face when I broke into- "Allons enfants de la patrie, le jour de gloire est arrive..." completely out of the blue, but what I most remember is the sight of Maria-Therese's lips moving as she mouthed the words with me. I was too choked up to sing it to the end.

Unfortunately, I was unable to keep up my contact with Marie-Therese, but I will never forget her. She taught me a priceless lesson and that is: deep within our subconscious, in the area of procedural memory, we have stored vast amounts of treasures. These may be snippets of tunes we heard when we were kids, snippets of songs we sang when we were lovesick teenagers, snippets of lullabies we hummed as we paced the floor with a sleepless infant, and even snippets of our National Anthems which we learned with pride when we were young.

What Marie-Therese taught me is that these treasures are most likely not lost. They are locked in the recesses of the brain just waiting for someone to find the key or keys to release them. The power of song may well be one of the keys that does just that.

• **An un-named Lady: (Becoming a person again, - by the power of reading).**

In his wonderful book, Hiding the Stranger in the Mirror, Dr. Cameron Camp tells a very interesting story about reading and people with dementia. He tells how he was at an assisted living community for persons with dementia. He was about to provide some training to hands-on care staff when a resident with advanced dementia came into the room the staff were entering. The resident wore an apron with pockets, all stuffed with "collectables" she had gathered in her wanderings around the facility - eating utensils, knick-knacks, etc. He says the woman was completely silent as she walked up to a table and sat down in a chair next to a staff member. He says nobody paid any attention to the lady until he handed her a book about Gene Kelly, opened it to the first page, and said, "What does this say?" The woman proceeded to read the entire page out loud. He says he could not help but notice that the staff member sitting next to the lady appeared startled. He thanked the resident for helping read the story, and she then smiled and left the meeting. He asked the staff member nearby why she was startled when the resident read the page. The staff member said, "I didn't even know that she could talk."

Dr. Camp writes: "The point of these examples is that reading is a habit. We just do it, often without thinking about it. It is a habit, it is an ability that is seen in many persons with dementia, even in its advanced stages." p35

When people are elderly and they are living with dementia, we tend to become so focused on the things they can't do that we forget all about the things they can do. One of these things is the ability to read. People living with dementia should be given opportunities to read either on their own or with someone who could perhaps chat about the book or the magazine they are reading. It is remarkable that the ability to read is a strength that often remains intact even in persons living with advanced dementia. Reading a passage often leads to a follow-up conversation allowing the person living with dementia to communicate his/her feelings, memories or opinions. As such it is vital that we milk this remaining strength for all it's worth.

- **Cedric: (Re-living your history through the power of words).**

Cedric was in his eighties. He had late stage dementia and lived in a care home. He couldn't speak, as far as any one knew, and for the past few months, seemed to be really slipping way into an abyss of silence and immobility.

One afternoon, as he lay half asleep in an armchair in the communal room, a lively resident suddenly shouted out:

"we shall fight on the beaches,
we shall fight on the landing grounds,
we shall fight in the fields and in the streets,
we shall fight in the hills;
we shall never surrender....".

Before he got any further, Cedric had bolted up and was standing strong shouting:

> "we shall fight on the beaches,
> we shall fight on the landing grounds,
> we shall fight in the fields and in the streets,
> we shall fight in the hills,
> we shall never surrender....."

The only other staff member in the room besides me, was a young care-worker who I think was too young to appreciate the significance of these words. But even she was rendered speechless.

The incident was remarkable but it was over as quickly as it began. Cedric sat back down and went back to sleep in the armchair.

The words were from one of Winston Churchill's famous speeches to the nation of Great Britain during the second world war and they hold huge importance and emotional significance for any British person and rightly so.

No one in the care home knew whether Cedric had played an active role in the war. He may well have. Many British men of his age did. These words certainly meant something to him.

Sadly, Cedric passed away a few days after this incident.

Perhaps if someone had known a little more about him they could have read some of Winston Churchill's speeches to him and perhaps he would have joined in as he did on that day when he made that remarkable impromptu speech.

So, what we see in all of this is that an aged man could be "just a paltry thing", a "tattered coat upon a stick", UNLESS we help his soul to sing and "louder sing for every tatter in its mortal dress".

At this point in time, Montessori Based Programmes for people living with Dementia are being designed to do exactly this and we believe they point the way forward towards how we might successfully "help the human being in the later years".

Epilogue:

Maria Montessori started her life's work in the area of brain dysfunction. It was pathology she was working with, not health. Through her dogged persistence and painstaking hard work she managed to break through into the chaotic mind of the mentally retarded child. She broke through the walls of silence, the screaming, the crying, the erratic behaviours, the biting, the aggression, the grabbing onto others, the pacing up and down, the hand flapping, the head-banging, the constant attempts to "escape."

Through her genius she was able to transform the quality of the lives of thousands of so called "idiot" children. Most of these children were never completely "cured" but their lives were enhanced, given meaning, given purpose, and they were afforded an opportunity to make their contribution, in whatever way they could, to the world they found themselves in.

We believe that Montessori-based programming for people living with dementia has the potential to do exactly this. It may never "cure" dementia, but it has the potential to enhance, to give meaning, purpose and a sense of human dignity to the millions of people who are living with dementia. It has the power to uncover the human being behind the illness, even though for some, this may only be for a few fleeting moments in time.

Since this work builds on the genius of the woman named Maria Montessori, we think it is fitting to conclude this section with her words:

"I set to work feeling like a peasant woman who, having set aside a good store of seed-corn, has found a fertile field in which she may freely sow it. But I was wrong. I had hardly turned over the clods of my field, when I found gold instead of wheat; the clods, concealed a precious treasure. I was not the peasant I thought myself. Rather I was like Aladdin, who, without knowing it, had in his hand a key that would open hidden treasures."

(The Secret of Childhood) p121

We, the joint authors of this book, believe passionately, that Montessori based programming for people living with dementia is a "key" that can open "hidden treasures" in our ongoing battle to find solutions for the millions of people throughout this world who are living every day of their lives, with dementia.

PART EIGHT

PREVENTIVE MEDICINE

(Montessori for a New Generation)

57

CAN MONTESSORI EDUCATION PREVENT DEMENTIA?

(Re-organising the Brain to off-set the Symptoms of Dementia)

"This is not merely a new way of amusing children- it is
the beginning of a reorganisation of the human mind."

The New Children
Talks with Dr. Maria Montessori
Mrs. Sheila Jamieson Radice(1919)

A "re-organisation of the human mind," is this the key to staving off the debilitating effects of dementia? If we cannot, as yet, stop the disease from occurring, can we prevent its devastating effects by re-structuring the mind 'in advance' of the onset of the disease? (like soldiers facing battle who move to a safer position before the enemy strikes).

We, the authors of this book, believe the answer is yes. We believe that the revolutionary approach to education developed by Dr Maria Montessori, over a hundred years ago, which begins at conception and aids the development of the human being throughout childhood, adolescence and early adulthood, is the answer.

Let us explain.
Dementia primarily affects semantic and episodic memory, but initially it leaves procedural memory "spared". Therefore, the strategic thing to do is to direct education towards procedural memory rather than towards semantic memory which is the first area of memory to suffer attack. Why put all our soldiers out in the firing line, so to speak? Let's keep most of them behind the bunkers in the safe area of procedural memory.

Now, traditional educational systems are geared towards semantic memory and have always been that way since compulsory education began. This is where the biggest mistake in education is made. Montessori education, on the other hand, is geared towards procedural memory. Reading, writing, mathematics, geography, history, music and so on are all presented to the child in a manner which by-passes semantic memory and goes straight to procedural memory.

For example, writing is arrived at unconsciously as the child draws over and over with "insets" which incorporate every shape of the alphabet, so that when the child suddenly starts to write, he has no recollection of anyone ever teaching him this skill. It comes as an explosion of spontaneous activity.

Similarly, reading comes about as a result of several physical exercises such as training the tips of the fingers to discriminate "rough" and "smooth" surfaces using the "touch boards".

This is followed by training the tips of the fingers to feel the shapes of sandpaper letters while pronouncing their sounds. This activity fixes the letter shapes and their corresponding sounds into "muscle" or procedural memory.

Mathematics, an undeniably abstract subject is presented to the child in a concrete, tangible fashion. The child, through the use of the materials gains a muscular impression of length, width, height, quantity, etc. Even algebraic concepts are presented through concrete materials such as the binomial cube and the trinomial cube.

Geography is presented through concrete models of land forms and beautiful maps which are designed like special jig-saws to enable the child to physically gain an understanding of continents, countries, cities, oceans, rivers, mountains etc.

History is presented using long time lines which the child physically lays along the floor or along corridors if he needs to.

This concrete materialisation of abstract concepts continues in Montessori education for older children. The materials become even more imaginative. The pythagorean theory becomes a game with concrete pieces that the child lays out in a pattern demonstrating the theory.

Moving into adolescence, the young person manipulates concrete models in the study of chemistry, physics and biology. The materials for these areas of learning are endless, the student may even invent some himself during the course of his learning.

Montessori made many more suggestions about how to make further studies "procedural". This would involve adolescents in producing, directing and performing in dramas and pieces of literature.

It would involve adolescents in playing musical instruments alone or as part of a band or an orchestra.

It would involve adolescents in movement and dance both individually and as part of a group.

It would involve adolescents in a multitude of "hands-on" and not "head-only" learning.

The assistance of mentors, coaches and guides would be part of it, but exams and tests would play no part in it. The adolescent would move from one level of independence to the next revealing "the inner evolution of the individual".

Montessori's "vision of the future," of what learning could be is thrilling and exciting. It offers hope to the young human being. If traditional schools continue to ignore it then parents should run, not walk away from them before their children are robbed not only of their present but of their future.

Montessori education changes the physiology of the brain, in a good way. It builds up brain reserve, it creates new neural pathways.

It makes the child, adolescent and the young adult, see things differently, and consequently do things differently. Most importantly, it is geared towards the part of the brain that is "spared" in dementia i.e the procedural memory.

In view of this, isn't it incumbent on us to create more authentic Montessori schools which may give "cradle to grave" protection to the human being in the course of his development.

Some sceptics may pose the question, - what if we make all these changes to education and then we find that Montessori education doesn't actually prevent dementia?

Our reply is, what if we find that it does!

58

WHY WE SHOULD ALL BE KARATE KIDS.

(The Power of Indirect Learning To Keep Dementia At Bay)

According to a recent Alzheimer's International Report, the number of people worldwide currently living with dementia is estimated to be 35 million. The report further states that this figure is expected to double in 2030 to 70 million and more than triple by 2050 to 115 million. Research is constantly ongoing into dementia causes and possible treatments, but, as yet, there is no cure.

Human beings have a long history. We have faced many giants in the form of diseases, wars, climactic catastrophes and acts of God. But, the amazing thing about the human being is his ability to find creative solutions to problems. While dementia presents a massive problem to the world, we must be careful to focus on the positives that exist in the midst of the negatives surrounding dementia.

One very important positive is the fact that the procedural memory is usually "spared" in dementia. Because we know this, we need to take pre-emptive action in the upbringing of the next generation. They need to be "Karate Kids".

For those of you who have never seen the film The Karate Kid, here's a quick summary. Daniel, a teenage boy, and his widowed mother move from New Jersey to California when his mother is offered a new job there. While his mom makes a good transition, Daniel, a pleasant, mild-mannered boy is picked on by bullies. He tries to teach himself self-defence to protect himself. Then he discovers that the caretaker, Mr. Miyagi, at his apartment seems to be a former grand master in karate. Daniel asks Mr. Miyagi to teach him karate to protect him from the bullies. Mr. Miyagi agrees. So the teaching begins.

When Daniel arrives for his first "lesson", Mr. Miyagi hands him a sponge and tells him to wash and wax several cars. Mr. Miyagi's instructions are very specific. Daniel is to use the sponge and waxing cloths while moving his hands and arms in wide circles. He must "wax on / wax off". He must also breath deeply while doing this, in through his nose and out through his mouth. The next "lessons" involve sanding a walkway in Miyagi's garden, staining the fence that surrounds his property and painting his house. With all of these tasks, Miyagi gives Daniel very precise procedural instructions about how to move his hands and arms.

After some time at this, Daniel gets cheesed off feeling that Mr. Miyagi is just using him as free labour. So he confronts Miyagi complaining that he has had no lessons as promised. Miyagi orders Daniel to show him the movements he had been using to carry out the chores. Miyagi suddenly yells and throws several punches and kicks at Daniel. Daniel blocks them successfully automatically using the arm and body movements he had employed in the various chores, from washing and waxing cars to painting fences.

Daniel quickly realises that the movements he perfected in doing the chores are actually also karate defence moves. Without any conscious learning Daniel has learned Karate! For the next "lessons," Mr. Miyagi gets Daniel to work on his defensive techniques and perfect his physical balance skills by standing in a rowboat trying to stay upright in the ocean surf. (Reminds me of the things young children try to do until we stop them).

So, what really happened with Daniel? Well, it's simple really, "wax on, wax off" became part of Daniel's "muscle memory," but it didn't stop there. The key principle is that Daniel used this skill to do karate, an entirely different task. This is the principle of "indirect learning" which Montessori education is built on, and it is the principle that should be foremost in the planning of education for the next generation. It is stupid to close the door after the horse has bolted. We know that procedural memory is spared in dementia, so it is incumbent on us to develop ways of training the next generation how to use procedural memory in new ways to off-set the limitations imposed by the declarative memory dysfunction which is the hallmark of dementia.

We need to teach the next generation how to "wax on and wax off," and more importantly, how to transfer those skills to other tasks.

This is the challenge for those of us who want to prevent the next generation from being deprived of "living," while living with dementia.

59

WHY WE SHOULD ALL BE DANCING.

(The Power of Dance To Keep Dementia At Bay)

" What ye doin' on your back?
You should be dancin'....yeah
You should be dancin'....yeah"

So go the words of that wonderful song by the Bee-Gees and how prophetic it was!

In a longitudinal study (a 21 year study) of seniors, 75 years and older, led by the Albert Einstein College of Medicine in New York City, funded by the National Institute on Ageing, and published by the New England Journal of Medicine, (June 19 2003), it was found that:

"Dancing was the only physical activity associated with a lower risk of dementia."

We need to say that again.

"Dancing was the only physical activity associated with a lower risk of dementia."

Other physical activities, such as cycling, swimming or playing golf, while affording protection to overall physical health, especially cardiovascular health, were not shown to have a significant preventative effect against the development of dementia.

However, frequent dancing was indisputably shown to have a very protective effect against the development of dementia.

So, why does frequent dancing have a very significant protective effect against the development of dementia? The answer is straightforward: brain reserve.

Dancing creates more neural synapses, (connections), so if dementia attacks the brain of a dancer, it does not deplete it, because the person who dances has created new neural paths.

This means that the dancer's brain has more ways than one of connecting to the data-base of stored information,(i.e semantic memory) and the data-base of personal memories (i.e episodic memory).

So the dancer's brain has "reserve," it is not reliant on one set of stepping stones to get across the stream, it has several options. So if dementia starts to remove the stepping stones on one route to stored memories, it can just use another route.

With 35 million people currently living with dementia and that number set to triple by 2050, we need to ask the following questions:

- Why is dance not treated as the most important activity in every school day?

- Why are our children not being offered the protective benefits of dance as a matter of priority?

- Why are most people unaware of the importance of dance for their general health and well-being?

- Why is dance either totally ignored by curriculum planners or relegated to the lowest place on the list of "subjects"?

There is really no more for us to say on this matter except:

" You should be dancing, yeah".

60

WHY WE SHOULDN'T WAIT TILL HEAVEN TO PLAY THE HARP.

(The Power of Playing A Musical Instrument To Keep Dementia at Bay)

Most of us in the western world are familiar with the pictures of little chubby cherubs (angels) playing harps in heavenly places.

Well, we need to make sure we don't wait that long to start playing our harps because research now suggests that playing a musical instrument, as opposed to just listening to music, may protect our brains from the ravages of dementia.

Professor Dr. Christo Pantev, a neuroscientist involved in research at the Baycrest Centre for Geriatric Care in Toronto, noted that elderly persons who played a musical instrument appeared to be much more active and engaged in life in their senior years than those who had never played a musical instrument.

He saw this difference even in people who were in the early stages of dementia. As memory fades with dementia, the last thing to go, appears to be, the ability to remember music.

Why is this? Professor Pantev believes he knows the answer. Over the years, Professor Pantev's research into music and the brain, suggests that the study of music appears to change the way the human brain is actually wired, i.e it appears to change the actual physiology of the brain.

Now, the question Professor Pantev is interested in is this: could learning a musical skill such as playing the piano, violin, guitar, etc in childhood, physically change the brain and improve cognition and perceptive skills in children and, by altering the way the brain is wired actually stave off mental illnesses (such as dementia) in later life?

The answers to these questions are not conclusive as yet but Professor Pantev's "intuition" tells him that the answers to both questions are probably yes.

Another neuroscientist hoping to find that music playing does indeed stave off dementia is Professor Brenda Hanna-Pladdy, assistant professor of neurology at Emory University.

Her research is in the area of cognitive functioning among musicians.

Professor Hanna-Pladdy points out that "If you can delay the presentation of (dementia) by five years, then you add an extra five years of functioning to an individual at the end of the life span". "In terms of fiscal cost and everything, that's actually quite a lot".

In Sweden, a large study, involving twins has been examining, amongst other things the question of whether music playing can stave off the onset of dementia.

By using twins as the basis for their research, scientists have been looking for answers as to why one twin who shares almost the same set of genetics as his brother gets dementia and his brother doesn't, (fraternal twins share about 50% of genes, and identical twins share almost 100%).

Professor Margaret Gatz of the University of Southern California and director of the Study of Dementia in Swedish Twins, says: "To me, the most intriguing aspect is, in a pair, if one twin becomes demented and the other doesn't, what did one not do? or what did the one who did become demented do that might give you some clues about ways that other people can mitigate their risk?"

Professor Gatz agrees with the general twin data which shows that "a more engaged lifestyle is a good thing for the ageing brain." She points out that brain stimulation may work to counteract brain decline making it possible for a person to function for longer.

Professor Gatz also points out that "music playing" is something that people can continue to enjoy for a lot longer than strenuous physical activities.

Music playing also has the benefit of physical, cognitive and possibly social dimensions to it, so it engages several brain networks simultaneously.

Unfortunately, the twin study does not include brain imaging or autopsies, so the precise ways in which music may help to stave off dementia is not clear yet.

Other evidence that playing music could stave off dementia has to do with the concept of "brain reserve". Both Professor Gatz and Professor Hanna-Pladdy are in agreement on this area of thought. The argument is that we can delay the detrimental effects of ageing by creating "brain reserve" and music playing is one way to create "brain reserve". To put it simply, "brain reserve" means having more than one "pathway" to reach our data banks of memory.

Another way of explaining it would be to imagine a line of stepping stones reaching towards our data banks of memories. If we are hit by dementia, the stepping stones will randomly sink making it impossible for us to reach our data banks of memories, but if we create a "reserve" we will have other options when some stepping stones start to sink. We can simply take an alternative route to that data-base.

Professor Hanna-Pladdy's research shows that significant instrument training, (ie playing for 10 years or more) provides a cognitive benefit that can be life-long.

The research also shows that even if the participants did not continue to play music as they got older, they still showed significantly better performance on tasks that involved; naming objects, the demonstration of visuospatial memory skills and rapid mental processing, than people who had never played musical instruments at all.

So even if the natural ageing process prevents a person from continuing to play an instrument e.g. arthritic problems or failing eyesight, the protective benefit is not lost.

The research also showed that people who began their instrument playing before the age of nine had a better working memory i.e. short term memory, than those who started to play musical instruments later than nine years, or those who didn't play musical instruments at all.

Prof Hanna-Pladdy states: "continuing to play music in advanced age added a protective benefit to individuals with less education, which has previously been demonstrated (to be) one of the most robust ways to create cognitive reserve".

She adds: "Thus musical training appears to be a viable model for cognitive stimulation, and can be conceptualised as an alternative form of education".

For these reasons alone, surely we shouldn't wait till we get to heaven to play the harp!

61

WHY WE SHOULD ALL LIVE A "MONTESSORI" LIFE.

(The Power of a "Montessori" Life to Build "Whole" Human Beings)

In December 1919, Dr. Maria Montessori was invited to address the British psychological Association in London. She anticipated a hostile audience. She knew she would be addressing "some of her most inflexible opponents" in Britain. However, following her "remarkable lecture," which was followed by rapturous applause, it was clear that she had convinced everyone in the room of the truth of her arguments.

Mrs Sheila Radice, who was present at the lecture wrote :

"When Dr. Montessori gave her lecture (interpreted by Dr. Crichton Miller) before the medical section of the British Psychological Society, the keynote of that meeting was the question whether the work that she is doing will eventually make the work of the "nerve-specialist" superfluous. As Dr. Crichton Miller said to her and to me, when the Montessori system is established in all schools, almshouses will have to be set up for the psycho-analysts. For the troubles that psychoanalysis discovers and disperses are such as, if human growth followed its normal course, should not occur". p139.

> Mrs. Sheila Radice
> The New Children:
> Talks with Dr. Maria Montessori.
> (1919)

This is the key point, "if human growth followed its normal course," deviations in development, at any age, should not occur.

Dr. Montessori summed this up very concisely when she wrote:

> "What has to be defended is the construction of human normality.
> Have not all our efforts been aimed at removing obstacles from the
> child's path of development, and at keeping away the dangers and
> misunderstandings that everywhere threaten it."
>
> (The Absorbent Mind p17)

Since its inception people have misinterpreted what Montessori education is all about. Let us bring some clarification.

Montessori education is all about "the construction of human normality." It's about "how to build a human being." It's about allowing "human growth" to "follow its normal course". It's about not placing obstacles in front of the human being which impede his normal growth forcing him to detour off the main road of normality, and go down side roads which always lead to deviations in personality and behaviour.

Dr. Montessori looked at the human being from birth to adulthood and she saw clearly that nature has divided human life into four stages: infancy, childhood, adolescence and adulthood.

She saw that all of these stages naturally divide into two parts, early infancy, 0 to 3, late infancy, 3 to 6, early childhood, 6 to 9, late childhood, 9 to 12, early adolescence, 12 to 15, late adolescence, 15 to 18, early adulthood, 18 to 21 and adulthood, 18 to 24.

She saw that nature has ordained it that there is a purpose to fulfil, a goal to reach and an aim to achieve in each of these periods of development.

She saw that nature provides aids to the human being in the form of sensitivities to guide the human being towards the things he needs to focus on during each of these periods of development.

She saw that any obstacle standing in the way of the human being's efforts to follow the guidance of nature during this period will send the human being "off course" making him deviate down side roads which are always negative and damaging and may even cause his death.

She saw clearly that it is the role of true education to aid the human being to grow as nature intended, i.e. to work with nature rather than against it.

An education which is ignorant of nature's plan cannot help the human being because it is attempting to build without the blueprint, and consequently it will do harm.

Dr. Montessori's message is surely urgent, vital, timeless and of monumental importance. The human species is destroying itself from within. The canker sets in from the minute the infant is born.

There is only one way to alter this blind, hapless, procession towards our own destruction, and it is not complex. It is as simple as the transformation of the caterpillar into a cocoon and then into a butterfly.

We must allow the human being to live in environments that are suitable to his needs at each stage in his development.

If the caterpillar is deprived of a cocoon he will not become a butterfly, because when the laws of nature are breached, the results are negative not positive.

As we quoted already, Montessori wrote:

"Life is divided into well-defined periods. Each period develops properties the construction of which are guided by "laws of nature". If these laws are not respected, the construction of the individual may become abnormal, even monstrous. But if we take care of them, are interested in discovering them and cooperate with them, unknown and surprising character features which we never even suspected may result."

(The Formation of Man p91)

If all of us could have the benefit of a Montessori life, we would, in fact, be living a life as nature intended. We would be like the flower that blossoms in season, the fruit that falls to the ground when it is ripe. We would be people who have been built according to the BLUEPRINT, therefore we would be less likely to be abnormal, less likely to have the symptoms of aberration and deviation.

We would be built by nature, which, whether we like it or not, has as a superior knowledge than any of us has, about "how to build a human being".

ABOUT THE AUTHORS

Stephen and Bernadette Phillips have been involved in Montessori education and research for over 30 years.

Stephen is originally from Wiltshire, in England and Bernadette is from Dublin, Ireland.

They home-schooled their own children from childhood to adolescence using the Montessori approach while running Montessori schools for young children.

They have lectured on all aspects of Montessori education and in recent years have focused their research on Montessori Programmes for People Living With Dementia.

They passionately believe that even dedicated Montessori followers have only touched the tip of the ice-berg in Montessori pedagogy and that the true potential of what Dr. Montessori discovered about the human being is yet to be revealed.

It is their ambition to help to reveal as many of these discoveries as possible to the world at large in straightforward, easy to understand language. They hope that this book is a first step in that direction.

The authors now work as freelance Montessori Consultants and can be contacted in relation to all things "Montessori" at the e-mail addresses below.

The authors welcome any feedback, good or otherwise on this publication and can be contacted at -   bernadette_phillips@yahoo.co.uk

(or)   sendsteveane@yahoo.co.uk